MW00627482

The Myth of
the Revolution

The Myth of the Revolution

HERO CULTS AND THE INSTITUTIONALIZATION OF THE MEXICAN STATE, 1920–1940

Ilene V. O'Malley

CONTRIBUTIONS TO THE STUDY OF WORLD HISTORY, NUMBER 1

GREENWOOD PRESS
NEW YORK • WESTPORT, CONNECTICUT • LONDON

Library of Congress Cataloging-in-Publication Data

O'Malley, Ilene V.
  The myth of the revolution.

  (Contributions to the study of world history,
ISSN 0885-9159 ; no. 1)
    Bibliography: p.
    Includes index.
    1. Mexico—History—1910–1946. 2. Revolutionists—
Mexico. 3. Heroes—Mexico. 4. National characteristics,
Mexican. 5. Sexism—Mexico. I. Title. II. Series.
F1234.043 1986   972.08'2   85-30488
ISBN 0-313-25184-3 (lib. bdg. : alk. paper)

Copyright © 1986 by Ilene V. O'Malley

All rights reserved. No portion of this book may be
reproduced, by any process or technique, without the
express written consent of the publisher.

Library of Congress Catalog Card Number: 85-30488
ISBN: 0-313-25184-3
ISSN: 0885-9159

First published in 1986

Greenwood Press, Inc.
88 Post Road West, Westport, Connecticut 06881

Printed in the United States of America

The paper used in this book complies with the
Permanent Paper Standard issued by the National
Information Standards Organization (Z39.48-1984).

10 9 8 7 6 5 4 3 2 1

In memory of my father,
who lived a hard life.

Contents

Acknowledgments

This book has been long in the making and many people have helped me along the way.

I am most grateful to the late Dr. Charles Gibson, the finest of scholars and the kindest of human beings. His faith in me kept me going when I might have otherwise given up. I also thank my good friend Dr. John Broomfield for the guidance and help he has given me from the very beginning of this work.

A Fulbright-Hays Research Fellowship (1979–1980) allowed me to do research in Mexico City. I extend my gratitude to Fernando del Moral of the Cineteca Nacional for access to a number of films about the Mexican Revolution; the Cineteca has since been destroyed by fire—a terrible loss that increases my appreciation of the opportunity I had to use its excellent resources and facilities. Eugenia Meyer of the Instituto Nacional de Antropología e Historia granted me access to the interviews with revolutionary veterans and other notable Mexicans compiled by the Programa de Historia Oral. I especially thank the entire staff of the Hemeroteca Nacional whose consideration and friendliness eased the countless hours I spent there.

The comments of Dr. John Womack, Jr., whose book *Zapata and the Mexican Revolution* first inspired me to study Mexican history, have been extremely useful and much appreciated throughout my research and writing. Dr. Carlos Blanco Aguinaga, Dr. William Gamson, Dr. Norris Pope, Dr. Rebecca Scott, Dr. Enrique Semo and Dr. Frances Wyer have also made helpful comments on this work at various stages of its development.

Then there are the people who helped me with my work by helping me with my life: Ken Pittman, for all the beers and bus rides while chasing Zapata's ghost through Morelos; Heriberto Rodríguez and his family in Nezahualcoyotl, for their hospitality and decency; Mary Ann Pohl, for her intelligence and enduring friendship; Michael Polen, for typing and typing and typing and listening to me talk about Mexico for eight years; and Anna, for being her lovely self.

Chronology

November 1910	Madero's revolt breaks out.
June 1911	Triumphant maderistas sign Treaty of Juarez.
November 1911	Madero elected President; Zapata issues the *Plan de Ayala*, denouncing Madero.
February 1913	The *Decena Trágica*; Madero and Pino Suárez assassinated; Huerta assumes the presidency.
March 1913	Carranza issues the *Plan de Guadalupe*, launching the Constitutionalist movement.
April 1914	U.S. Marines occupy Veracruz.
July 1914	Constitutionalists defeat Huerta regime.
October 1914	The Convention of Aguascalientes begins.
December 1914	Villa and Zapata, heading the Convention's forces, occupy Mexico City.
January 1915	Carranza issues land reform decree.
March 1916	Villa raids Columbus, New Mexico; Pershing leads the Punitive Expedition into Mexico.
February 1917	New constitution promulgated; Car-

	ranza elected president shortly thereafter.
April 1919	Zapata assassinated by carrancistas.
April 1920	Obregón heads the Revolt of Agua Prieta.
May 1920	Carranza assassinated by obregonistas; Adolfo de la Huerta appointed interim president.
July 1920	Villa retires to Canutillo.
December 1920	Obregón inaugurated as president.
February 1921	Government sponsors Madero memorial events.
April 1921	Government sponsors Zapata memorial in Morelos.
July 1923	Villa assassinated.
December 1923	De la Huerta Revolt breaks out.
December 1924	Calles inaugurated as president.
Autumn 1926	Cristero Revolt breaks out.
October 1927	Serrano and Gómez revolt.
July 1928	President-elect Obregón assassinated; Portes Gil becomes interim president.
May 1929	PNR founded; Escobar Revolt breaks out.
1930	Zapata and Carranza officially honored in Mexico City memorials for the first time.
August 1931	Carranza's and Zapata's names inscribed on the walls of the Congressional chambers.
December 1934	Cárdenas inaugurated as president.
April 1936	Calles exiled.
March 1938	Cárdenas expropriates foreign oil companies; Cedillo revolt aborted.
December 1940	Ávila Camacho inaugurated as president.

The Myth of
the Revolution

CHAPTER 1

The Myth of the Revolution

The Mexican Revolution of 1910–1920 brought the overthrow of a dictator of thirty years, internecine war, and eventually changes in the governmental, legal, and economic systems. While there is substantial debate over the nature of these objective changes, most will agree that Mexico has undergone a tremendous subjective change of national consciousness. The revolution brought a surge of creativity to the arts unparalleled since the pre-Columbian era, provoked a mania for the "truly Mexican," and inspired countless ballads and stories which have become the modern Mexican folklore. This folklore has in turn been taken up as themes in movies, comic books, novels, and even in the decor of discotheques and restaurants with names like "Pancho Villa's Follies." Villa, a popular revolutionary leader, is probably the most famous Mexican in the world. He and the peasant leader Emiliano Zapata are the prototypes of the "revolutionary/macho," who, with cartridge belts across his chest, a huge sombrero, and a large mustache, has become one of the most prevalent symbols of the Mexican internationally and in Mexico as well.

As shall be seen in the next six chapters, the association of the revolutionary with the macho is neither accidental nor innocent, but for the present let us consider Mexico's self-conscious fascination with the 1910 Revolution.[1] It is necessary to understand that fascination in order to understand Mexican society today. The revolutionary motif that pervades it is no mere curiosity or fluke of style. The Revolution has a fundamental ideological role.

Even today the Mexican government claims that it is the contin-

uation of the revolution and that the ideals of the revolution inform
its programs. The Institutional Revolutionary Party (PRI—*Partido
Revolucionario Institucional*) is for all practical purposes synonymous
with the government, having been in power under three different
names since 1929. Such longevity surely merits the adjective "institutional," for the Mexican government is technically one of the
most stable in the world. But what of the adjective "revolutionary"?

The attempt to discern what is meant by "revolution" leads into
a labyrinth of reasoning within which it is possible to find one's
bearings by internal signposts of value and historical reference, but
out of which it is very difficult to emerge with a discrete definition
of "revolution." At times, the term "Revolution," with a capital *R*,
functions merely as a label for the government, and instead of definition there is tautology: "The Revolution is the Revolution." This
dictum has become a truism in Mexico. Often it is used to admon-
ish people whose faith in the Revolution is waning to keep their
faith when appearances seem not to merit it.[2] In effect, the admo-
nition is akin to the notion that God's ways are inscrutable and that
calamity should be suffered serenely in the faith that God's ways
are good, for were they not, God would not be God.

Many people reject the government's rhetoric. Some argue that
the term "institutional revolution" is an oxymoron; others, who may
even believe that the government is progressive, believe that change
has been too moderate to be called revolutionary, which usually
connotes more rapid, thorough, or violent change. Persons with
highly theoretical concepts of revolution often cannot fit the Mexican case into their categories and therefore deny that the present
government is revolutionary or that Mexico ever had a true revolution. Others simply wonder how one can speak of the Mexican
Revolution when so many Mexicans still suffer wretched poverty
and political repression. But from the bemused observer to the outraged dissident, the government's revolutionary posture occasions
remark and is widely regarded as the hallmark of Mexican political
style.[3]

This posturing is possible in large degree because the definition
of "the Revolution" has purposely been kept vague, even though
the 1910 Revolution remains the historical referent for the posturing. Mystification is central to the official ideology of the Mexican

regime as well as to the political culture which supports and is supported by it. My use of "mystification" is related to Roland Barthes' concept of myth as "a type of speech . . . not defined by the object of its message, but by the way it utters this message."[4] Mystification produces myth, which here is not the same as "story" or "fable," as in "there are many myths about Zapata's ghost riding in the hills"; nor does it mean a direct lie. Instead it is a confusion, not so much of facts as the way one thinks about facts. Barthes writes:

Myth does not deny things, on the contrary, its function is to talk about them; . . . it purifies them, it makes them innocent, it gives them a natural and eternal justification. . . . It abolishes the complexity of human acts, . . . it does away with all dialectics, . . . it establishes a blissful clarity: things appear to mean something by themselves.[5]

A myth's message is distinct from or even contradictory to the strict meaning of the words and images it employs. The seeming paradox—that messages should have two meanings at once—occurs because there are two coinciding languages: in Barthes' terminology, the primary language and the metalanguage. The metalanguage is constructed from the already constructed units (whole phrases, songs, pictures, rituals, etc.) of the primary language. While the primary language "means what it says," the metalanguage uses the primary language to mean something not said. When the myth is successful, the coincidence of languages goes undetected. Consider the following example.[6]

Typically, on the anniversary of the death of Emiliano Zapata, the great campesino revolutionary, the government conducts a memorial at the site of his assassination. Portraits of a heroically stylized, emphatically mestizo Zapata are strung in the streets. A crowd of campesinos, including veteran zapatistas, attends the ceremony, where speakers—perhaps the president himself—praise Zapata's personal integrity and declare the government's fidelity to his ideals.[7]

The myth conveyed here may be something like this: "The government is paying public tribute to this mestizo who fought for land for the campesinos and against the wealthy 'white' class which exploited and oppressed them. Therefore the government also champions campesinos' rights, which relieves the campesinos of the need to push for agrarian reform themselves. Because the government is their champion, it cannot be blamed for the socioeconomic problems that beset them as a class." In short, the myth uses the figure of Zapata to imbue the campesinos with a nonrevolutionary sentiment that Zapata himself did not have: dependence on and loyalty to the government.

If the myth is unsuccessful, the observer will see that the rhetoric does not fit the facts. Logically, official elegy is not necessarily an indication that official policies reflect the values of the elegized person, although that is part of the myth's intended meaning. It may also be seen that the government itself is largely responsible for the insufficiency and corrupt administration of the agrarian reform program. And while Zapata's humble Indian origins are praised for their "true Mexicanness," the living, truly Mexican, Indian campesinos at the ceremony have weathered faces, legs bowed by childhood protein deficiency, and a deferential manner. The old zapatistas are crippled, emaciated, and in rags. They stand in the hot sun and leave on suffocating, rickety, perilously overcrowded buses.

In contrast, the officials doing the praising are quite European in appearance, well-groomed, and expensively dressed; they sit under a shade and leave by limousine, private bus, or helicopter. A comparison of the two groups of people reveals socioeconomic inequalities incompatible with the myth of the ceremony, while the meaning of the primary language remains true: "Zapata was a simple campesino of Indian extraction. We pay our respects to him today."

The historical study of myth poses special problems because it is so difficult to pin down the phenomena to be studied. Myth is "a kind of nebula, the condensation more or less hazy, of a certain knowledge. Its elements are linked by associative relations."[8] An investigation of the association offers little of the certainty of what are usually called facts; one must delve instead into the realm of impression, connotation, and the emotional resonance of words and images. It is hard to catch myth red-handed, as it were, falsifying history, for myth slowly appropriates and transmutes the meaning of the primary language, which remains "not false."

I have nevertheless tried here to catch the myth by pinning down one of its most palpable aspects: the transformation of key revolutionary leaders—Francisco I. Madero, Emiliano Zapata, Venustiano Carranza, and Francisco Villa—into official national heroes. In life these men led conflicting factions of the revolutionary forces. All were assassinated (in 1913, 1919, 1920, and 1923 respectively) and all but Madero were felled by fellow revolutionaries. Yet in death their conflicts were purposely obscured by the new regime, which in the decades following the revolution fomented the public celebration of "hero cults" on the anniversaries of their assassinations. Periodicals reported the celebrations and further commemorated the heroes with special historical articles, commentaries, and elegies. All four heroes were eventually incorporated into the official hagiography of the regime, whose politics often conflicted with the ideals for which they had fought so ferociously.

The official character of the hero cults makes them quite documentable, but the documents (mostly newspaper articles) yield a distinctly elite or "top down" perspective on the mystification process. While hardly the only way to view the myth, it is an instructive one, for it refutes the common assumption that the myth is an apolitical, "natural" phenomenon that needs no explanation. This study will show that the mystification of the revolution was guided by the government, that it perpetuated the bourgeois character of the regime by utilizing deeper cultural constructs, and co-opted the revolutionary potential of the popular classes to the point that the Revolution became a counterrevolutionary myth.

Foremost among the constructs that facilitated the mystification of the revolution was patriarchy, one form of which is Mexico's famous machismo. There is nothing unique about Mexican machismo if one is referring only to an attitude of male superiority and patriarchal social forms, for these are evident to some degree in every country in the world; what gives Mexican machismo its peculiar quality is its self-consciousness, its "officialness," its openly proclaimed status as part of the national identity. Even the casual observer of Mexican society will notice that nationalism and machismo are somehow related—witness the Mexican braggart's frequent claim that Mexicans are more virile than gringos—and more serious study will confirm that first casual impression.

The two most influential essays on the character of the Mexican, for example, Samuel Ramos' *El Perfil del Hombre y la Cultura en*

México and Octavio Paz' *El Laberinto de la Soledad*,[9] describe, in somewhat different terminology, the macho as the quintessential Mexican. Both regard machismo as an attempt to make supposedly greater masculinity compensate for the inferiority complex that most Mexicans, by virtue of their racial and economic status as well as their heritage as a conquered, colonized people, suffer relative to richer, "whiter," and/or more Anglo-European people from the conquering, colonizing, more "developed" countries.

This is fine, as far as it goes. But it should be pointed out that being "more masculine" has compensatory potential (psychologically, for it changes the real socioeconomic basis of power not one jot) only because the superiority of men over women is presupposed, that is, because the society already has patriarchal values. Furthermore, the fact that societal sources of the Mexican males' inferiority complex aggravate the sexual doubt that is an attendant aspect of patriarchy (part of the rivalrous tension between father and son) helps explain why a reaction against socially based inferiority might take a sexual outlet rather than a political one.

While this study presumes the now standard theories of machismo first offered by Ramos and Paz, as well as the general psychological descriptions of the patriarchal mentality, it cannot undertake to explain them fully or to advance them in terms of the psychology of individuals. The study's approach is instead historical, focusing on machismo's political uses during the first two formative decades of the present Mexican regime. Machismo has long been a recognized behavior in Mexico, but its institutionalization seems to have more or less paralleled that of the Revolution.

The following chapters demonstrate how the values and psychology of patriarchy fostered and were fostered by the mystification of the revolution, and how that same process identified machismo as an expression of *lo mexicano*. The evidence threads through the narrative, which seeks to preserve the individual and chronological character of the hero cults as it examines them in light of the political machinations of the 1920s and 1930s. In the final chapter patriarchy's part in the co-optation of the Mexican Revolution will be addressed directly.

A simplified history of Mexico from 1910 to 1940 is given here as a background for the subsequent chapters and to distinguish among "revolution" as the events of 1910 to 1920, as a theoretical concept, and as the Mexican government. But there may still be confusion at times, for the ambiguity of the term "revolution" is an essential part of the myth of the Mexican Revolution.

A BRIEF HISTORY OF MEXICO, 1910–1940

Porfirio Díaz had ruled Mexico for some thirty years when the opposition gathered the strength to topple him from power.[10] The 1910 Revolution was a heterogeneous movement led by the wealthy Francisco I. Madero, who wanted to establish political democracy. His rallying cry, "effective suffrage, no reelection," became a basic tenet of the revolution. Francisco Villa, a minor campesino leader from the north, became one of the more celebrated members of Madero's army.

In November 1911, a half-year after the defeated Díaz left Mexico, Madero was elected president in what are commonly held to have been the freest elections the country has known. Despite the fact that he had been swept into office by a tremendous popular desire for reform, Madero filled his administration with the politicians of the Díaz regime and left the old army intact. Thus, Madero's government had little inclination to pursue even limited political reforms.

At the same time, the popular demand for reforms exceeded what Madero had called for. When reforms were not forthcoming, many of Madero's supporters grew disaffected and revolts against his new "revolutionary" government broke out around the country. The most troublesome revolt occurred just south of Mexico City in the small state of Morelos, where a peasant movement led by Emiliano Zapata called for the expropriation of the haciendas. The zapatistas had cooperated with the maderistas to overthrow Díaz but repudiated Madero when he would not begin agrarian reform immediately. A brutal government campaign to crush the zapatistas ensued, but they continued to fight for the demands articulated in their *Plan de Ayala*.

Conservatives were alarmed by the mass rebelliousness unleashed by Madero and by his inability to control it. In February 1913 during ten days of war in the capital (known as the Tragic Ten, the *Decena Trágica*), General Victoriano Huerta, with the support of the U.S. ambassador, led a coup against Madero.[11] Madero

and Vice-President José María Pino Suárez were assassinated, and
Huerta assumed control of the government for the purpose of restoring a Díaz-like regime. The "respectable" classes of Mexico City
lamented the assassinations but greeted the new counterrevolutionary government with relief.

Outside the capital, however, there was widespread opposition
to Huerta. Under the leadership of Coahuila's governor Venustiano
Carranza, many groups that had previously turned against Madero
united with still faithful maderistas to throw out "the usurper" and
to restore constitutional rule. Francisco Villa led the most powerful
unit of the so-called Constitutionalist army, the *División del Norte*.
The zapatistas also fought Huerta, and their demands for immediate agrarian reform stimulated similar demands among other revolutionaries, especially Villa and his followers.

Huerta lost the U.S. government's support when Woodrow Wilson became president. In early 1914 U.S. Marines invaded the port
of Veracruz, cutting off the trade, customs revenue, and arms needed
by Huerta, while arms sales to the constitucionalistas boomed across
the U.S.–Mexican border.[12] Huerta tried unsuccessfully to use the
anti-Yankee sentiment aroused by the invasion to unite the country
behind him. The Constitutionalists opposed both the U.S. occupation and Huerta's usurpation, and won. Huerta went into exile
in July, and several months later the Marines withdrew from Veracruz.

But even greater difficulties lay ahead. The rebel forces had barely
contained their differences while they had a common enemy. With
that enemy gone, they had to face each other and decide what to
do with the nation they now had in their hands.

It is difficult to distinguish precisely between the conservatives
and radicals within the revolutionary movement. The popular factions especially seldom stated their goals coherently, and even within
factions ideological consensus was often lacking. Nevertheless, there
were discernable tendencies.

Middle-class insurgents tended to be economic nationalists and
to want national political power. Díaz had granted many concessions to foreign capital, which shared economic domination of Mexico
with a small domestic elite. In the colonial tradition, the elite of
the *porfiriato* (the period of Díaz' rule) were culturally oriented toward
Europe, regarding things Mexican as inferior. The Mexican middle

class's economic growth was hampered by the hegemony of foreign business in their country, and their pride was offended by the snobbery of the foreign and Porfirian elite. Thus the middle-class revolutionaries wanted Mexicans to control the economy and had a patriotic preference for *lo mexicano*—within limits. Except for a few of the radical intelligentsia, who often joined more popular factions, they still believed in the sanctity of private property and the need to keep firm control of the masses, who might otherwise go "too far, too fast." Having wrested power from the old Porfirian oligarchy, they were not about to let it fall into the hands of the lower classes.

The chief leader of the middle-class revolutionaries was Venustiano Carranza. A mayor, senator, and governor of Coahuila during the Díaz regime, he represented the most conservative tendency in the revolution.

At the other end of the sociopolitical spectrum were the campesino movements. They were in a sense pre-ideological, guided by suspicion and distrust of the classes above them. "They are men who have slept on soft pillows," said Villa. "How are they going to be friends with people who have suffered all their lives?"[13] The campesinos did not develop their own plans for national political control, accepting instead the leadership of the more sophisticated and educated revolutionaries until that leadership behaved in a manner they believed to be contrary to their class interests. Zapata was the most articulate of the campesino leaders and the most radical in his demands for and implementation of agrarian reform.

The other major campesino leader, Francisco Villa, was less articulate and more cooperative with middle-class leaders during the early years of the revolution, when he had, in contrast to Zapata, supported Madero fully. Nevertheless, in comportment and sympathies, Villa was identified with the rural masses. From his days as a maderista officer, his military daring had made him famous throughout Mexico and in the United States as well. Villa's extreme popularity and formidable army gave him an immediate political clout that the zapatistas could not equal.

Personal tensions among the revolutionary leaders, Villa and Carranza especially, and divergent class interests came to the fore when the revolutionaries met at the Convention of Aguascalientes in 1914 to form a national government. The revolutionaries of the popular classes, and even many of the middle classes, threw their support to Villa and adopted the basic tenets of Zapata's *Plan de Ayala*. When Carranza refused to recognize the legitimacy of the Convention, the revolutionaries split between those loyal to Carranza (the bulk of the middle-class revolutionaries) and those who honored the Convention or preferred Villa.[14] War ensued.

The convencionista forces, headed by Zapata and Villa, soon held most of the country; in December 1914 they triumphantly entered Mexico City. Villa and Zapata, who had never met before, conferred but were unable to secure their territorial and political gains. The Convention gradually disintegrated, while the carrancistas recuperated their strength.

In 1915 the tides began to change in favor of Carranza, largely as a result of the political astuteness of General Álvaro Obregón, who had learned the importance of wooing the campesinos and lower classes. The proclamations of agrarian and labor reforms issued from Carranza's headquarters in Veracruz undermined popular support for Zapata and Villa, especially in Mexico City. Obregón gained many new recruits for his army and marched north to several stunning victories over the previously undefeated Villa, who disbanded the *División del Norte* by the end of 1915. The United States, which had informally supported Villa in part because he seemed bound to win, now gave official diplomatic recognition to Carranza, who benefitted politically and materially by the increased access to arms as Villa's access to arms from the United States decreased.[15]

Villa and Zapata continued to fight and even to win battles, but they were losing ground. Villa lived as a renegade despite the fact that his 1916 raid of Columbus, New Mexico, revived his popularity and made him a symbol of Mexican nationalism.[16] The carrancista army confined Zapata to an ever smaller area and interned, deported, or massacred the Morelos peasants suspected of sympathizing with the zapatista guerrillas.

At the end of 1916 Carranza assembled a purely carrancista constitutional convention. Nevertheless, social reform had become a sufficiently pressing need that the convention drew up one of the most progressive constitutions in the world at that time. The constitution of 1917 would ever after be Carranza's claim to fame. It was also his "proof" that he was revolutionary, even though he did not implement the mandated reforms. Instead, he suppressed the labor movement he had employed in the campaign against the convencionistas and disappointed even the mildest agrarian reformers, going so far as to return land confiscated during the revolution to the large landowners.[17] One of Carranza's most trusted generals, Pablo González, oversaw the plot that led to Zapata's assassination on April 10, 1919.

Fatally, Carranza also alienated the military elite by insisting upon a civilian government. Both General Pablo Gonzáles and General Álvaro Obregón hoped to succeed Carranza to the presidency in the scheduled 1920 elections. Carranza, however, chose as his own candidate the relatively obscure diplomat Ignacio Bonillas. Presidential support was tantamount to guaranteeing a candidate's success, and it was thought that Bonillas would simply be a proxy for Carranza. Carranza was widely criticized for violating the essence of the revolution's basic tenet, "effective suffrage, no reelection."

Accusing Carranza of betraying the revolution, Obregón rebelled in April 1920. Most of the army and key political figures, including the surviving zapatista leadership, seconded the so-called Revolt of Agua Prieta. Carranza fled Mexico City with a small entourage and much of the national treasury. On May 21, 1920, some of Obregón's supporters killed Carranza while he slept.

With the triumph of the aguaprietistas, General Adolfo de la Huerta became interim president until Obregón's inevitable election six months later. De la Huerta attempted to reconcile the badly divided revolutionary forces. He worked out a settlement with Villa, who had continued to fight the government, granting him a hacienda and the right to maintain an armed escort; Villa swore loyalty to the government and devoted himself to his land.

But reconciliation was not easy. When Obregón became president he was soon confronted with a revolt by the carrancista general Francisco Murguía, who was captured and executed. Political opposition in general met with intimidation and violence, while Obregón maintained the support of military leaders and other potential rivals by tolerating graft, favoritism, and corruption that produced an extremely wealthy "revolutionary" elite.[18] Such corruption also debilitated the country's postwar recovery and undermined the reforms Obregón nominally supported.

Nevertheless, Obregón was sufficiently more reformist than Carranza to cause the U.S. government—still alarmed by the Russian revolution—to fear he would lead Mexico into "bolshevikism." It refused to recognize his government. Obregón needed U.S. recognition to facilitate the acquisition of foreign loans and to function well in international affairs. In 1923 Obregón negotiated an unofficial agreement, the Treaty of Bucareli, which in return for the United States' diplomatic recognition exempted the United States from compliance with those articles of the 1917 constitution that impinged on its economic interests. U.S. oil companies were permitted to retain their Mexican holdings despite Article 27, which declared that the subsoil—including "petroleum and all gaseous, liquid, and solid hydrocarbons"—was the property of the Mexican nation.[19] Mexico also agreed to begin payment on its foreign debt.

Outrage over the Bucareli agreement, which had been arranged without the approval of the Mexican Congress and was regarded by many as a sell-out to Yankee imperialism, clouded Obregón's popularity. The July 1923 assassination of Villa cast more suspicion on Obregón and his right-hand man, Plutarco Elías Calles. When Obregón picked Calles as his presidential candidate for the 1924 elections (thereby thwarting the ambitions of de la Huerta, who probably would have enjoyed the valuable backing of Villa, had he lived), de la Huerta revolted. He accused Obregón of "imposing" the next president in violation of democratic principles. The revolt was quite extensive, but Obregón crushed it within several months with military aid from the United States, which now regarded him as a friend.

Calles became president in 1924 and adopted a more radical stance than had his predecessor. His preference for currying the favor of organized labor rather than that of the agrarian organizations, as Obregón had done,[20] created rivalry between the callistas and the obregonistas. Calles' attempt to enforce the anti-clerical clauses of the constitution, mostly ignored by Obregón, brought the regime into confrontation with the Catholic Church and precipitated the Cristero Rebellion in 1926. Some one hundred thousand people may have died in the war, which ended only in compromise in 1929.[21]

In late 1926 Obregón decided to run again for president in the 1928 elections—legally possible because of a new constitutional amendment, made for the occasion, that permitted a second nonconsecutive term in office. Obregón's candidacy eclipsed all others.

Generals Arnulfo Gómez and Francisco Serrano, who both had been considered for official candidacy, instead became opposition candidates. Later, they revolted against Calles and Obregón. Serrano and numerous supporters were murdered (the Huitzilac Massacre) after being arrested by federal troops, and Gómez was executed after being captured. Death was the standard penalty for treason, but many people regarded Serrano and Gómez as victims of Calles' and Obregón's suppression of electoral democracy.[22]

Obregón won the election but was killed in July 1928 by a Catholic fanatic before he took office.[23] That left Calles the de facto leader of Mexico. Suspicion that he had been involved in Obregón's assassination was so great that Calles promised to withdraw from public office.[24]

Calles did not, however, withdraw from public affairs. In late 1928 he called for a reassessment of the Revolution and set about organizing a political party that would provide an institutional means for arbitrating the differences among the former carrancistas. The resultant *Partido Nacional Revolucionario* (PNR) became the official party of the government. The PNR and the government stressed the importance of propaganda and patriotic festivities in the promotion of national unity and support for the regime. In May 1929, the PNR founded the newspaper *El Nacional Revolucionario*, which became one of the major dailies of Mexico City.

The increased emphasis on propaganda continued a trend begun in 1925, when the municipal government (*ayuntamiento*) of Mexico City, "desiring to put an end to the irregular propaganda . . . carried out by various groups in commemoration of the great and solemn anniversaries of the nation,"[25] formed an Official Committee of Patriotic Commemorations, comprised of citizens' groups and municipal and federal committees which worked together to create ideological "uniformity" in public ceremonies. When the *ayuntamiento* was made a branch of the federal government and named the Department of the Federal District (DDF), it retained control over propaganda and reflected the policies of the federal government even more closely. Together with the PNR, the DDF organized the public ceremonies that would help promote the official version of the Mexican Revolution.

In addition, the PNR conducted its own highly centralized campaign to inculcate national pride, civic responsibility, and support for the party and the government. In one of the pamphlets for its weekly program *Domingos Culturales* (Cultural Sundays),[26] President Emilio Portes Gil (1928–1930) suggested that party stability depended upon creating cultural and spiritual ties with the people, implicitly through propaganda:

Usually political parties are created casually and transitorily with exclusively electoral ends; . . . they revolve around individuals, . . . and for this same reason they have a precarious, casual, and transitory life also; nevertheless, if we imagine the party as the true teacher . . . to which all citizens may go to resolve their doubts . . . ; if we imagine the party as the originator of the people's social life; as the best agency where the primitive manifestations of the popular soul are perfected, then its existence will not be subject to the waxing and waning of militant politics, but will endure because it is founded upon the deep wellspring of the spirit.[27]

In the long run the construction of the single party system, with its elitist approach to defining and increasing mass involvement, was Calles' most significant contribution to the stabilization of the Mexican regime.

At the time of its founding, however, the PNR failed to appease the obregonistas, who still desired the power they had under Obregón. A callista, Portes Gil, was then interim president, and obregonistas hoped one of their own would be his successor. Calles disappointed them by choosing the manipulable Pascual Ortiz Rubio as the official presidential candidate. Rebellion and scandal rocked his campaign.

The Escobar Rebellion was staged largely by obregonistas who accused Calles of Obregón's murder and of betraying the principle of effective suffrage. Although thirty thousand men and a third of the officer corps supported it, President Portes Gil quelled the rebellion with the help of arms sales from the United States, and the obregonistas ceased to be a political force in the country.[28]

The greatest scandal of the campaign occurred when the bodies of some hundred supporters of opposition candidate José Vasconcelos were discovered at Topilejo, just outside of Mexico City. An obviously political crime of such magnitude could not have taken place without the knowledge of the callista leadership, and the Topilejo Massacre testified to the violent repression that helped forge the new party system.[29]

Mexico's relations with the United States improved when Calles turned to the right in the late 1920s. The Communist Party was outlawed, ties with the Soviet Union were broken, and leftists were persecuted,[30] while social reform took a backseat to economic development during Calles' unofficial rule, 1929–1934 (known as the *maximato* because Calles was called the *Jefe Máximo*, Maximum Chief).

The Great Depression renewed interest in social reform in the early 1930s, leading to the election of the progressive Lázaro Cárdenas to the presidency in 1934. He threw off the role of Calles' puppet that the three prior presidents had played. When Calles publicly complained about Cárdenas' aggressive reformism, Cárdenas peremptorily exiled him, definitively establishing the supremacy of the president in Mexican politics from that time forward.[31]

Cárdenas distributed more land to the campesinos than any previous president[32] and encouraged agrarian and labor organizations to work to improve their class welfare. In 1938 Cárdenas ordered the expropriation of foreign oil companies that refused to comply with Mexican law, nullifying the Bucareli agreements in the most dramatic "anti-imperialist" move made by any Mexican president.[33]

While such moves made Cárdenas extremely popular among a large part of the population, they also antagonized conservatives. Oil companies and some government officials in the United States talked of invading Mexico. As the domestic situation polarized, Cárdenas moved to prevent a right-wing backlash by halting the leftward drift of the popular organizations that he had previously encouraged. Because those organizations had been incorporated into the *Partido Revolucionario Mexicano* (PRM, a more centralized version of the PNR, which was reorganized in 1938), they could not resist Cárdenas' new policies. Cárdenas bypassed the likely leftist candidate for the next presidency, choosing instead the moderate Manuel Ávila Camacho.[34] When Ávila Camacho assumed the presidency in 1940, the Mexican government had basically acquired its present form. It rejected social reform as its primary concern in favor of capitalist development, even as it continued to call itself the Revolution.

CHAPTER 2

The Public Image of
Francisco I. Madero

From the early days of his campaign against Porfirio Díaz, the conservative press reviled Madero. It called him crazy, nicknaming him "the Deluded" and "the Invisible," and charged him with cowardice when he failed to fight during the early, halting start of the revolution. Because Madero came from a very wealthy landowning family in Coahuila, he was accused of being ungrateful to the regime in which his family had prospered, and there was a great deal of cynicism about the sincerity of his reformism.[1]

Conservatives exploited class and racial prejudices to further discredit Madero, pointing out that his supporters came from the lowest classes, the rabble and the "individuals without prestige," while Díaz' supporters were "decent people" and "persons of social significance."[2] Conservatives feared too that Madero's appeal to the popular classes and his acceptance of "bandits" like Zapata and Villa into his movement would arouse a revolution that sought not only the popular suffrage and free elections that Madero called for but greater social reforms as well.[3]

The conservatives' fears would ultimately prove correct, although they did not materialize immediately upon the revolutionaries' defeat of the Porfirian army after only six months of war. Madero failed to consolidate his victory over Díaz. Instead he negotiated the Treaty of Ciudad Juarez (site of the decisive battle), in which many concessions were made to the old regime. Díaz himself was exiled to France, but Madero allowed the Porfirian bureaucracy and the army to be incorporated into the new regime. He also let a porfirista, Leon de la Barra, serve as interim president.

Between the "triumph" of the revolution in June 1911 and the November election of Madero as president and José María Pino Suárez as vice-president, Mexico was ruled by a government that wanted to limit reform and to disband the rebel forces.

For many of the lower-class maderistas, social and particularly land reforms—however vaguely understood—had been the goal of the revolution. They felt betrayed when neither the interim government nor Madero's government implemented such reforms. Madero began to lose the support of campesinos, who in numerous instances carried out their own attacks on the local landowners.

In Mexico City, too, Madero began to lose support. Madero permitted an unprecedented freedom of the press, which allowed the conservative newspapers to criticize him as they had all along. Many of Madero's erstwhile supporters—angry because they thought him too conservative or too reformist or simply too inept to govern amid the demands from the left and right—joined in mocking him.[4]

It was all the easier to ridicule Madero because he had already disappointed popular expectations about his person and personality. While he was advancing victoriously toward Mexico City, the *capitalinos* awaited a conquering hero who fulfilled their macho concept of a leader of men. What they got was a mild-mannered vegetarian who practiced spiritualism and lacked flair in public—in their eyes, a weak fool. According to John Rutherford:

His slight build, together with his inoffensive gentleness . . . should not be underestimated as elements contributing towards his . . . rapid loss of popularity after June 1911. They meant that he was at the great disadvantage of not being able to claim any degree of machismo for himself.[5]

But if ridicule of Madero focused on his lack of "machismo," it nevertheless reflected the mounting alarm with which many people viewed the situation in Mexico. The capital's press railed against the rebellions that continued throughout the country and demanded that Madero quell them. It was most troubled by the zapatista movement, which was turning hacienda land over to the campesinos. Many people regarded the zapatistas' attack on private property as an attack on civilization itself, and their proximity to Mexico City heightened their distress. When zapatistas struck at the outskirts of Mexico City, newspapers inflamed public fears by insinuating that rape and carnage would occur should they actually enter the capital.

Madero attempted to come to an agreement with Zapata, but he believed too strongly in the right of private property to accede to Zapata's demand for immediate land reform. As a result, Zapata revolted against Madero. Yet conservatives felt that Madero had been too reluctant in going to war against Zapata, whose strength grew rapidly in 1912. As they saw it, their world was endangered and Madero was doing nothing to save it.[6]

When Madero and Pino Suárez were assassinated in the coup of February 1913, the conservative press was quick to applaud the end of his government, although some newspapers criticized the methods employed and the destruction of the city during the *Decena Trágica*. Most of the "respectable" people were complacent toward or relieved by the coup, which they believed would restore law and order to the country.[7]

Many people, however, were horrified. In the capital, loyal maderistas attacked the offices of newspapers they believed to be morally complicit in the murders of Madero and Pino Suárez; the poor people set up a humble memorial at the place where the murders occurred.[8] Outside the capital, especially in the northern states where maderismo had its origins, the coup triggered widespread opposition. Many people who had not previously been involved in the revolution, or who had even come to oppose Madero, joined with loyal maderistas to oust the "jackal" Huerta. Reaction against the coup raised Madero's reputation from the depths to which it had sunk. Forgotten were the complaints about his government and personal fecklessness—in the aftermath of his death Madero acquired heroic dimensions he had not had while president.[9]

The revolutionary forces that fought against Huerta's reactionary regime included the zapatistas in the south and, in the north, the constitucionalistas, headed by Carranza. The most important Constitutionalist generals were Álvaro Obregón, Pablo González, and Francisco Villa, the last of whom was the only campesino and the only one to have been active in the early days of the Madero revolt.

In the course of the war, the revolutionary forces became more differentiated politically; after victory, they entered even longer, bloodier struggles among themselves. The growing class consciousness of the masses, who provided the backbone of all the factions, pushed the revolutionary movement leftward, although they never fully outgrew the tutelage of the middle-class revolutionary leaders. Given that the revolutionaries had moved to the left in very different degrees, political democracy—symbolized by Madero's formula "effective suffrage, no reelection"—remained one of their few common goals, even though it would be honored only in the breach in the years to come.

The factional warfare that began in 1914 was beset by corruption, greed, personal ambition, and treachery which often obscured or superceded the political principles at stake. Growing cynicism about the revolution, or at least its post-1914 stage, intensified the idealization of Madero that had begun when he was assassinated.[10] The more progressive insurgents—including the zapatistas, who bore no illusions about the extent of Madero's concern for the poor— understood the inadequacy of electoral reform as a solution to the inequalities of Mexican society. But others remembered the maderista phase of the revolution as a time of unity and noble aspirations. When President Carranza violated the spirit of "effective suffrage, no reelection" by attempting to "impose" his own successor in 1920, many saw it as proof that the revolution had been betrayed.

In Mexico City old guard maderistas formed a club, the *Agrupación Pro-Madero*, to revive the revolution's original ideals, especially anti-reelectionist sentiment. They organized a public commemoration of the "sacrifice" of the "apostles" Madero and Pino Suárez on February 22, 1920, the seventh anniversary of their assassination. Amid great fanfare they removed the body of Pino Suárez from its humble tomb to a more fitting place of repose near Madero in the *Panteón Francés*. The director of *El Heraldo de México*, Vito Alessio Robles (a prominent maderista and constitucionalista), gave the key address in praise of the "martyrs."[11]

The following year's commemorative ceremony took on a more official air, with the new president Álvaro Obregón and other high government officers in attendance. The chief speaker was one of Madero's earliest supporters, Antonio Villarreal, who had been in exile under Carranza but now served as Obregón's minister of agriculture and development. Villarreal urged that they, "the victorious men of the revolution," overcome the "envy," "appetites," and "passions" that corrupted the Revolution and seek to acquire the goodness that had made Madero such a pure revolutionary.[12]

Villarreal's exhortation to unity stopped short of including the carrancistas. Unlike Carranza, he said, Obregón recognized Madero's true merit—Obregón had first rescued Madero's memory from Carranza's "dry and cold indifference" by visiting his tomb when the constitucionalistas entered Mexico City in 1914. Villarreal likened Carranza to Huerta, claiming that Carranza had only pretended to be outraged by Madero's death in order to deceive the public. He accused the carrancistas of hypocritically speaking of liberty even as they "established the cruelest of tyrannies" and "sated all their churlish appetites." In contrast, Obregón would restore Madero's "decency and forgivingness" to the government and "moralize" the Revolution.[13]

At another civic ceremony in 1921 the speaker Federico González Garza, also an early maderista, pursued the same theme. He described the "movement of 1913" as having "avenged" Madero's death, but then Madero's "virtues remained . . . forgotten" and his noble principles were replaced by the "insincerity, immorality, and despotism" rooted in Carranza himself. To raise the Revolution from the corrupt depths to which it had fallen, it was necessary to emulate Madero, the "prototype of the patriot," whose dedication to his cause evinced a strength of character that González Garza attributed to a "virility of a past era, now lost among us."[14]

Such speeches strengthened Obregón's revolutionary credentials. They claimed that he would fulfill the original promise of the revolution and that he therefore was a true maderista, even though Carranza had actually fought with Madero against Díaz and Obregón had not. In this light Obregón's rebellion against Carranza appeared as a restoration of the revolution, which alone gave one the authority to govern, rather than as an attack on a legal government.

In the next two years the Madero memorials grew with the help of the government. Street cars were provided to transport government employees to the ceremony at the *Panteón Francés*, which was attended by a panoply of delegates from political organizations within the city and from several states as well. There was a parade and elegant *veladas*[15] were held in the major theaters that evening. Public schools suspended classes in order for the children to attend lectures about the two "martyrs."[16]

Obregón, his entire cabinet, and representatives from all the states attended the memorial in 1923. Alfonso Cravioto, speaking for the Freemasons, called Madero "this new Christ who fell with his breast pierced by treason's bullets." In true macho fashion, he also attributed a genital deficiency to his opponents when he compared Madero's critics to "castrated men who condemn all audacity because they cannot attempt it without being ridiculous."[17] Cravioto (an old anti-Díaz satirist, and Senate president in 1921)[18] referred to Madero as one of the Revolution's "precursors," a term that was picked up and repeated by the news reports of the February 22 ceremony.

The description of Madero as a precursor was significant. It marked the beginning of a major transformation in the official version of the revolution, for it implied that the maderista era was pre-revolutionary and, therefore, that the "real" revolution occurred at some later date. The official Revolution was being shifted forward in time toward the program of the government itself. While Madero and the maderistas, precursors all, apparently assumed a more hallowed place in official history, they were being subtly retired from the realm of the contemporary political struggles.

There were few naysayers to the public adulation of Madero. In 1921 an editorial in *Universal* had condemned radical agrarianists who used Madero's good name to justify their attacks on private property, when Madero had in fact supported the inviolability of private property.[19] But that was not a criticism of Madero, only of some of those who waved his banner. It was also an example of an increasingly common practice: conservatives attacked progressives in the name of the "true" Revolution rather than in the name of openly acknowledged conservative principles.

One of the few outright criticisms of Madero came from Mexico City's most conservative paper, *Excelsior*. On the anniversary of his assassination in 1923, the editorial proclaimed that "there is no need to give Madero proportions of a martyr." Carranza's crime, it said, was that he had inspired hatred that led to the devastation of the nation, while Madero's crime was that he had ever assumed the presidency at all, for he was "one of the Mexicans with the least capacity for such a high position."[20] For this criticism, which resurrected the old image of an ineffectual Madero, *El Mundo*, directed by maderista Martín Luis Guzmán, nastily rebuked *Excelsior*, "our distinguished anti-labor and anti-democratic colleague."[21]

Such bickering, however, was insignificant compared to the dissension created in the highest ranks of the obregonistas by the Bucareli agreement and Obregón's choice of Plutarco Elías Calles as the candidate for the upcoming presidential election.

Adolfo de la Huerta, interim president between Carranza's death and Obregón's election, was disappointed that Obregón did not select him as his candidate. De la Huerta and other top obregonistas denounced Obregón for "imposing" what they deemed Calles' unpopular candidacy in violation of democratic principles and revolted in December 1923. Some forty to sixty percent of the army joined the De la Huerta Revolt, as did such political notables as Antonio Villarreal, Vito Alessio Robles, and Martín Luis Guzmán. Among those loyal to the president were army officers Francisco Serrano, Arnulfo Gómez, José Gonzalo Escobar, and Saturnino Cedillo (all of whom would subsequently lead unsuccessful revolts of their own) and Emilio Portes Gil, Lázaro Cárdenas, and Manuel Ávila Camacho (all future presidents). The insurrection lasted into the spring of 1924, with the loss of an estimated seven thousand lives.[22]

At the height of the rebellion in February 1924 the federal government did not conduct a memorial for Madero and Pino Suárez. Perhaps officials regarded such an activity as inappropriate in a time of civil strife, or perhaps they wanted to avoid providing a forum for critics who accused the government of "reelectionism." The *Agrupación Pro-Madero* proceeded on its own, but its small memorial had no speeches and received little notice in the press.[23]

In 1925, with the rebellion over, the official contribution to the Madero *homenajes* was renewed and expanded when the Mexico City municipal government adopted a new policy of coordinating and promoting patriotic festivities. A choir of two thousand children sang patriotic songs at the Madero memorials, which were attended by dignitaries of every sort. Their names were carefully listed in the newspapers: it was politically necessary to pay public respect to the "apostles." The press also reported who made floral donations, the bands that played, and other strictly ceremonial details, while frequently failing to describe the history or politics of maderismo. Only its leaders' "tragic" deaths were mentioned regularly.

Ritual prevailed over content, and Madero was, in a manner of speaking, promoted "above politics" to sainthood. The memorials were said to be "sacred" affairs where "politics should not be discussed."[24] In one instance a speaker who did dare to discuss poli-

tics (apparently criticizing the government) was admonished that
the ceremony was a "solemn act to which political passions should
not be brought" and where one should not engage in "partisan expostulations."[25]

In practice, accusations of "partisan expostulations" were only
made against members of the opposition, and Madero was put "above
politics" to prevent his memory from being used to make unflattering comparisons with the government. The pretense of apolitical
memorials was itself a political ruse to help the government preserve Madero for its own purposes and to give it a freer hand in
using the memorials to secure its hegemony over rivals.

In the 1920s, the government's most powerful rival was the
Catholic Church. Under Obregón, anti-clericalism, which tended
to be more vehement among government supporters, had led to an
attack on the archbishop, a bombing of the altar at the shrine of
the Virgin of Guadalupe, and armed clashes between the Catholic
Association of Mexican Youth and the labor union CROM (*Confed-
eración Regional Obrera Mexicana*), even though Obregón had in effect ignored the anti-clerical provisions of the 1917 constitution.
The situation deteriorated still more when President Calles tried to
implement them: Article 3 prohibited church-run primary schools;
Article 4 closed monasteries and seminaries; Article 24 restricted
the performance of religious rites to church buildings designated
by the government; Article 27 gave the nation possession of church
buildings.[26]

When Calles began to close down churches that failed to comply
with the newly enforced laws, the Catholic Church's opposition to
the Revolution's "godless socialism" deepened.[27] The faithful were
further outraged by the founding of the schismatic church by an
ex-priest, José Joaquín Pérez, and other Catholics discontented with
the Roman church. On the night of February 22, 1925, Pérez and
another ex-priest seized a church. They were attacked the next day
by angry Catholics; a riot ensued. The government gave the schis-
matics a church for their own use, and under the name of the Mexican National Church, they acquired a minor following. The schis-
matics never seriously threatened the Roman Catholic Church, but
strengthened Catholics' belief that Calles was trying to destroy their
religion.[28]

In this volatile political climate CROM conducted its first Madero memorial in 1925. The memorial took place where none had taken place before—the Villa de Guadalupe, site of the shrine of the Virgin of Guadalupe and for Catholics the holiest place in Mexico.[29] CROM was the most powerful union in the country, largely as a result of its corrupt leadership's close cooperation with Calles. The head of CROM, Luis Morones (notorious for his diamonds and debaucheries) even served as Calles' minister of industry, commerce, and labor.[30] A CROM-sponsored ceremony in the Villa de Guadalupe was tantamount to an invasion of traditional church territory by the strongest agents of the "anti-Christ" Calles. Regardless of the ceremony's content, by virtue of having occurred at all it constituted part of the administration's campaign against the Catholic Church.

Accompanying what could be called the government's attempt to secularize religion was a tendency to treat the Revolution more religiously. Spiritual language abounded in the memorials held by the *Agrupación Pro-Madero* in 1925 and 1926. Speaking for the group, the influential journalist Juan Sánchez Azcona expanded on the often-made comparison of Madero to Christ by likening the members of the *Agrupación* to the Disciples. The representative from the Department of Internal Security (*Gobernación*) said that the "miraculous intuition" of the "enormous soul of the people" had caused them to respond to the "holy and salvational" nature of Madero's struggle.[31]

The profoundly Catholicized nature of Mexican society partially accounted for the frequent use of religious teminology and concepts, which were readily understood by virtually everyone, Catholic or not. Yet the religious imagery in patriotic rhetoric also helped to create for the state a symbolism with deep cultural resonance. At a time when many people felt that the government was taking away their traditional source of spiritual comfort and that the government's materialism made it insensitive to the "higher" aspects of human nature, government propagandists imbued the regime, nationality (as distinct from regional loyalties), and the Revolution with spiritual meaning.

The use of religious imagery to promote the Revolution reinforced a counterrevolutionary worldview which regards people as "the acted upon," the passive objects of some extra-human force, not as historical actors. The memorial speaker who said that the "revolution passed through the destructive period; it has led us to the constructive era" inverted the cause-effect relation between the Mexican people and the course of the revolution. The inversion implicitly belittled human activity. Another speaker went so far as to claim that the revolution had been won by an idea, that Madero was capable of "victory without the support of the armed masses and sustained only by the justice of his ideal"[32]—a false claim that mystified the revolution. Similarly, to attribute Madero's popularity to the "miraculous intuition" of the popular soul instead of to people seizing the opportunity to improve their lives was to portray the masses as irrational followers.

The stress placed on the supposedly Christ-like qualities of Madero elevated him above the common human and tended to diminish people's appreciation of human and, therefore, their own capacity for political action. The sanctification of the hero carried the message that people should wait for a savior instead of saving themselves. As befitted the religious approach, the secretary of public education suggested at the time of the 1926 memorial that children should not be given holidays on the "great anniversaries of the *patria*"; instead they should be encouraged to "work with more diligence" and to "meditate on the debt of gratitude that we have."[33] It was not said that the children should be taught to fight (as Madero did) for their political beliefs.

Indeed it did not behoove the government to encourage political militancy in general, unless it could also control people's beliefs—which, despite all its efforts, it could not. Already Catholics' dislike of the administration's policies had erupted into the Cristero Rebellion, the longest and bloodiest civil war of the post-revolutionary period. In addition, in 1927 the government faced growing opposition to Obregón's still unofficial candidacy for a second term as president.

The opposition was led by an anti-reelectionist group formed by prominent maderistas, such as Juan Sánchez Azcona and Enrique Bordes Mangel, who occasioned a flurry of political excitement about the anniversary of Madero's death by conducting their own memorial in the main streets of Mexico City. "Anathemas against reelection" were heard, and the speakers denounced the government for betraying Madero's principles.[34] Bordes Mangel called for the defense of those principles and declared:

Of the virtues that characterize the martyr and that we disciples should imitate, . . . his infinite piety, his benevolence are not what we need now; . . . let us ask . . . for his virility, his energy, his high sense of justice as weapons . . . against those who destroy his work. . . . The dolorous path we travel is seeded with cadavers. If destiny needs to devour more lives, let us offer them. . . . [35]

There were apparently no immediate reprisals against the organizers of this opposition event, but there was less tolerance for the dissent within the officer corps. Generals Francisco Serrano and Arnulfo Gómez were killed when they revolted in late 1927. In 1928, with Obregón's now unopposed campaign under way, the administration avoided the possibility that the anti-reelectionists might again use a Madero memorial to protest its policies by conducting no official memorial at all and prohibiting all speeches at Madero's tomb on the anniversary of his death.[36]

The assassination of President-elect Obregón in July 1928 dissolved the unity with which the callista-obregonista camp had countered the anti-reelectionist threat. Some obregonistas suspected that Calles had been involved in Obregón's murder, which left him the de facto leader of Mexico just when they had been about to resume power. To assuage tension, Calles chose Emilio Portes Gil—acceptable to callistas as well as obregonistas—to serve as president until a special election could be held. However, Calles' choice of Pascual Ortiz Rubio, thought to be his yes-man, as his candidate for that election provoked a new wave of opposition. The obregonistas were disgruntled at being excluded again from the inner sanctum of power, and anti-reelectionists regarded the choice as a violation of the spirit, if not the letter, of "effective suffrage, no reelection."

In March 1929 obregonista military leaders revolted, taking about a fourth of the army with them. The rebels had their own presidential candidate, General José Gonzalo Escobar, but were joined by two other opposition candidates, Gilberto Valenzuela and Antonio Villarreal. The Escobar Rebellion, as it was called, was strengthened because the government still had to contend with sporadic *cristero* attacks and with yet another opposition candidate for the presidency, José Vasconcelos.

Generals Lázaro Cárdenas, Juan Andreu Almazán, Saturnino

Cedillo, and Joaquín Amaro remained loyal to the government. The campaign to put down the revolt continued through May 1929; it was the last full-scale military revolt in Mexico. The excellent relations that had developed between the astute U.S. ambassador Dwight Morrow and the increasingly conservative Calles stood the Mexican government in good stead. Mexico was able to buy war materiel from the United States, and the escobaristas were crushed.[37]

Ortiz Rubio officially won the election of 1929, although Vasconcelos protested that he had received the most votes. Vasconcelos had not supported the Escobar Rebellion, which he termed a contest between obregonista and callista army officers. But as the architect of the public education system, a promoter of the arts, and outspoken critic of the government's criminal and anti-democratic acts, Vasconcelos had been a very popular candidate. His supporters had been harassed throughout the campaign, and several weeks after a Vasconcelos sympathizer tried to assassinate Ortiz Rubio at his inauguration on February 5, 1930, the strangled bodies of over one hundred vasconcelistas were found buried at Topilejo. The assassination attempt also served as a pretext to jail numerous leftists and to deport those who were not Mexican.[38]

The tumult of 1928 to 1930 resulted, as did most of the conflicts since 1917, from power struggles among the upper echelon of the middle-class factions. It also coincided with the formation of the PNR. Through the government's continual repression of political activity outside its aegis, the PNR emerged as the official party of what was essentially a single party system.

Against this background of coercion, the PNR adopted a conciliatory view that all the factions, past and present, were part of a unified revolutionary movement, with differences that were only to be seen as different facets of the Revolution rather than as real conflicts. The PNR stressed cultural and civic activities as a way to enhance popular support for the government. In 1929 the Department of the Federal District (DDF) began opening numerous civic centers in Mexico City where, in cooperation with the PNR, patriotic educational programs and festivities were conducted. The year marked a significant expansion of the government's use of propaganda.

In 1929 the government resumed its commemoration of the anniversary of the deaths of Madero and Pino Suárez. Its efforts to build factional unity noticeably improved the way the propagandists treated Carranza at the ceremonies that year and the next. The carrancista Luis Manuel Rojas, a major author of the 1917 constitution, praised the usually maligned Carranza for having "raised the banner of the legalist revolution in order to avenge" the murders of Madero and Pino Suárez.[39] His praise drew the *Primer Jefe* back into the maderista heritage of the "true" Revolution and undoubtedly pleased the old carrancistas who had been a political outgroup since the Revolt of Agua Prieta. Similarly, in 1930 the official speaker José L. Cosío praised Carranza, Obregón, and Calles together for having furthered the revolution begun by Madero,[40] despite the Agua Prieta revolt and despite the rivalry that developed between Obregón and Calles in the last years of the latter's presidency.

Speakers in 1929 and 1930 also emphasized the importance of institutionalizing the Revolution. At a time when the government sorely needed to reinforce its rule, Rojas' use of the term "legalist revolution" implied that the revolution had been fought for the purpose of restoring law and legal institutions. Another speaker used his criticism of Huerta to make a broader attack on "the unworthy military man who uses his arms to overthrow institutions, rather than to defend and respect them."[41] Instead of the usual condemnation of Madero's assassination on the ground that he was an admirable person, the speaker implied that the military owed allegiance to national institutions per se—a step toward the professionalization of the army and away from the *personalismo* that had long been a destabilizing force in Mexican politics.

After 1930 the PNR regime did become more stable. When President Ortiz Rubio resigned in 1932, internal party politicking rather than violence was used to select General Abelardo Rodríguez to finish out the term. As the 1934 elections approached, opposition candidates reported numerous incidents of harassment, but the level of repression did not reach the extremes of the 1929 presidential campaign. Repression was also less necessary, for the opposition was not as strong as it had been in the past, and the PNR candidate, Lázaro Cárdenas, enjoyed greater popularity than had the three previous presidents.

When Cárdenas became president in December 1934 he faced a nation stirred by renewed political currents that would polarize it before he completed his term in office. The government's drift to the right during the *maximato*, the appearance of fascist groups in Mexico, and the worsening economic conditions that came with the worldwide depression stimulated leftist groups and revived demands for agrarian reform, which had never been effectively carried out and which had been all but halted by Calles during Ortiz Rubio's administration.[42] Vicente Lombardo Toledano, far to the left of Luis Morones, had begun to eclipse Morones in the early 1930s as the foremost labor leader in the country.[43] Cárdenas himself represented the left wing of the PNR.

In addition to Cárdenas' more radical conception of the Revolution, he was more determined than his two predecessors to be fully in charge of his administration. His relations with Calles became strained as he insisted on policies—such as encouraging the new militancy of the labor and agrarian movements—that *el Jefe Máximo* did not like. As a confrontation seemed to be building, federal and state political leaders began to choose sides. At first a majority favored Calles, whom past experience had shown to be the safe choice, but Cárdenas worked to secure his position.

The tensions between Calles and Cárdenas, as well as the related polarization of Mexican politics, produced the only interesting aspects of the Madero memorials of the 1930s.

With neither Calles nor Cárdenas in attendance (although both sent floral wreaths), the 1935 commemoration of the assassination of Madero and Pino Suárez was an innocuous affair that attracted routine notice from the press. One speaker, Colonel Rubén García, praised the "absolute purity" of Madero's election and claimed that his program anticipated the progressive changes mandated in the 1917 constitution. Madero, he said, wanted "to Mexicanize Mexico."[44] García's attempt to make Madero seem more up-to-date politically also placed the state within the tradition of maderismo, thereby promoting an image of a unified, continuous Revolution.

The participation of the "fascist-like" *Acción Revolucionaria Mexicanista* (ARM) in the homage to Madero, however, showed how little unity existed among those who regarded themselves as the true heirs of the revolution. ARM members, known as *camisas doradas* (Gold Shirts) and led by the former villista general Nícolas Rodríguez, would attack the Communist Party offices only two weeks later, but no incidents were reported at the February 22 memorial.[45]

Less dramatic than the appearance of militaristic squads of ultra-rightists, yet still a sign of the times, were the biographical sketches of Madero and Pino Suárez printed that day in the PNR's *El Nacional*. Predictably, they praised the "martyrs" and Cárdenas for carrying out the martyrs' ideals, but Carranza received atypically warm praise for erasing the stain of the martyrs' murders from Mexico's history: ". . . strong spirit, man of masculine mettle, he convoked the masses with the Plan of Guadalupe [the proclamation of the Constitutionalists against Huerta]. . . . "[46]

Such praise countered the negative image of Carranza as a man indifferent to the welfare of the people and drew him into the supposedly unified revolutionary heritage. It had as well a more immediate utility for Cárdenas, who in his effort to secure political control needed the support of Carranza's son-in-law Cándido Aguilar, the political boss of the important state of Veracruz and an influential senator.

Later in the year, Calles issued a strong criticism of what he termed the treasonous disorders created by Lombardo Toledano and the militant labor movement. In effect he condemned Cárdenas' labor policy without directly criticizing Cárdenas, who responded by replacing the entire cabinet, which had supported Calles' criticism, with his own supporters. Factional tension in Congress erupted in a shoot-out within the Chamber, which led to the expulsion of a number of callista congressmen. Cándido Aguilar became the new president of the Senate, a position with broad power.[47]

Thereafter, Calles became persona non grata, the object of ridicule and criticism. Arguing that their presence in Mexico encouraged anti-government conspiracies, Cárdenas exiled Calles, Morones, and Luis Leon, one of Calles' strongest supporters. On April 10, 1936, they were abruptly placed on an airplane and flown to the United States. The fact that Calles had been reading Hitler's *Mein Kampf* when he was taken into custody was seen by many as indicative of how far to the right he had moved.[48]

The triumph of cardenismo ended not only Calles' political life but also Obregón's high official status. (Since his death, Obregón had been the most lionized public figure in Mexico.) As Cárdenas' nationalistic policies drew the country toward a confrontation with foreign oil interests, both Calles and Obregón were denounced for the concessions they had made to those interests. This trend, combined with Carranza's new respectability, produced a new anti-Obregón and anti-Calles sentiment that was evident at the 1937 memorial in the attendance of "numerous exiles who . . . recently returned to the country."[49] Pancho Villa's widow, Luz Corral, was a guest of honor, marking the first time Villa was so acknowledged at a Madero *homenaje*.[50] Even though he had been devoted to Madero and had been crucial to the Constitutionalist victory, Obregón's and Calles' hostility toward Villa was apparently so severe that such recognition had not previously been extended to him.

In 1938 there were more obvious signs of anti-Calles and anti-Obregón feelings. Various senators sought to erect a monument to Madero more imposing than the one already built in honor of Obregón. They argued that Obregón should not be allowed to overshadow the memories of Madero and Carranza.[51] The now dishonored former presidents came under more direct attack at the memorial, as key speaker Antonio Villarreal criticized Obregón because he was "at first democratic, but . . . later it occurred to him to impose Calles and to put an end to democracy, which was killed anew with the Treaty of Bucareli." Villarreal called Calles and the PNR the "gravediggers" of democracy, and further described the party as the "incestuous child of the Bucareli conventions and of . . . Calles."[52]

Up to that time foreign oil companies had been allowed by the Bucareli agreements to operate normally despite Article 27 of the constitution, which made oil the property of the nation. When some companies refused to obey Mexican labor laws in long-standing labor disputes, Cárdenas expropriated them on March 18, 1938, invoking the constitution and revoking the Bucareli agreements. Many critics had always regarded the agreements as Obregón's betrayal of national honor, as a surrender to Yankee imperialism. Although several English companies were also affected, Mexicans were most gleeful about the expropriation of the American-owned companies.[53] The nationalization of the petroleum industry marked the apogee of Cárdenas' leftist policies and his popularity. Shortly thereafter, Cárdenas restructured the PNR to more fully incorporate popular labor and agrarian organizations and renamed it the *Partido Revolucionario Mexicano* (PRM).[54]

Within the United States, reaction to the expropriation varied. When Franklin Roosevelt became president in 1933 he began a "good neighbor" policy to improve relations with Latin America, which had reached a low point in the late 1920s when U.S. Marines occupied Nicaragua. When the petroleum expropriation occurred, Roosevelt hesitated to jeopardize the improved inter-American relations or to risk losing the Mexican oil trade altogether should he take a hard stance against Cárdenas. Nevertheless, Secretary of State Cordell Hull, who opposed cooperating with Cárdenas, was able to influence government policy toward the expropriation.[55]

The U.S. government and oil companies refused to negotiate for the conditional indemnities offered by the Mexican government and used their international clout to practically halt the purchase of Mexican oil and silver, two of the country's most important exports.

To weather the ensuing economic crisis, Cárdenas asked the labor movement to forego the pursuit of narrow class interests for the good of the nation in its difficult moment. For the most part, labor complied because it supported the nationalization of the petroleum industry and because it believed Cárdenas would continue to support it as he had in the past.[56] But as the economy deteriorated, many people, including many who approved of the nationalization, grew disenchanted with cardenismo and joined ranks with the conservative opposition. Anti-communist groups grew.

Some of the strongest criticism of Cárdenas came not from avowed conservatives, but from old revolutionaries like Antonio Díaz Soto y Gama, Saturnino Cedillo, and Juan Andreu Almazán, who believed that Cárdenas had betrayed the "true" Revolution by leading it toward communism. Díaz Soto y Gama's criticism was relatively unimportant, for he had been at odds with every administration since Obregón's. Cedillo's dissatisfaction was more worrisome because he, like Almazán, had been a powerful ally of Cárdenas for years.[57]

Cedillo, a large landowner, had already resigned his cabinet post in protest against Cárdenas' agrarian reform policies. In March 1938 he rebelled against the government. The president defused the insurrection before it got off the ground, although Cedillo himself was killed in a skirmish many months later. Nevertheless, Cedillo's rapid defeat did not stop the mounting conservative hostility toward the government.[58]

Apparently fearing a severe right-wing backlash, Cárdenas began to moderate his policies. Rather than confronting the right, as he had earlier, Cárdenas tried to antagonize it less. In the process of building and integrating popular-based organizations into the political system, Cárdenas had pressured them to eliminate the more extreme leftists or independents who did not believe that class interests could be served by, or should be subordinated to, those of the state. Thus, when Cárdenas began to pursue a more centrist course in 1938, and the difficult moment became a way of life for labor, the major popular political groups and labor organizations could do nothing about it.

As the situation grew more volatile, Cárdenas sought to preserve a political center. In 1939 three men in the PRM were potential candidates for the 1940 presidential election: General Juan Andreu Almazán, who enjoyed substantial support from the army and the upper classes; Manuel Ávila Camacho, who had the support of many governors and congressmen; and General Francisco Múgica, whose politics most resembled Cárdenas' and who was his personal friend. Cárdenas selected the moderate Ávila Camacho to be the PRM candidate. The U.S. government also favored Ávila Camacho, for it disapproved of the leftist Múgica and, with the outbreak of World War II, was disinclined to tolerate the incipient fascism that might have accompanied Almazán's election.[59]

Ávila Camacho announced his candidacy on the day of the 1939 *homenaje* to Madero and Pino Suárez. One of the main speakers at the *homenaje* was General Múgica, who represented the Society of Revolutionary Precursors (as veterans of the maderista phase of the revolution were now known).[60] The fact that Múgica participated in the ceremony and that he did not rebel as so many other disappointed presidential hopefuls had done demonstrated the success of the Revolution's institutionalization. But it was perhaps even more indicative of how dependent the left had become, for the right showed more determination to have its way.

General Almazán did not accept political disappointment as quietly as Múgica. He resigned from the army and the PRM to form the *Partido Revolucionario de Unificación Nacional* (PRUN), whose program called for the replacement of the "communistic" *ejido* system of communally held land with small, privately owned land parcels. Some PRUN adherents were openly fascist and anti-Semitic, although some leftists also joined as a way to oppose the all-powerful PRM/government political machine and its peculiar brand of socialism.[61]

A parade of athletes to an obelisk that was unveiled at the site where Madero and Pino Suárez were assassinated provided a bit of novelty to the uneventful 1940 memorial events. *El Nacional* and Lombardo Toledano's newspaper, *El Popular*, contained articles that argued that Madero had been a victim of his own unwillingness to definitively defeat the counterrevolutionaries[62]—an argument obviously meant to encourage a hard line against the right wing in 1940. But as in 1939, the memorial ceremony was nevertheless designed to calm the opponents of the Revolution rather than to antagonize them. Speakers emphasized the importance of patriotism, and there were inklings of a new conciliatory attitude toward the Catholic Church.

Despite the compromise settlement of the Cristero Rebellion in 1929, church-state relations had been tense throughout the 1930s but began to improve when the new archbishop (appointed in 1937) lent his support to the government during the oil crisis. In itself the selection of Ávila Camacho presaged a moderation of the government's anti-clericalism, for he was the first official presidential candidate to acknowledge his Catholicism in public. Religion was no longer to be regarded as a yoke for humankind, but as an inspiration. In praising Madero at the 1940 memorial, Ricardo de la Barrera proclaimed that the *mártir* had

loved his country, . . . this dear Mexico as those who are predestined to become heroes know how to love. . . . [It] is impossible to conceive of anyone who excites and inspires men . . . without bearing ideals of great excellence; like those of religion, like those of the nation.[63]

The Mexican government survived the crisis of 1938–1940 and entered a new era of stability. Almazán's threats of rebellion came to naught, and despite violence and accusations of fraud at election time, Ávila Camacho's assumption of the presidency was the smoothest transition of power the post-revolutionary government had yet achieved. The official party's presidential candidates would never again face any serious electoral challenges. The institutionalization of the Revolution was for all practical purposes complete.

The cult of Madero fared poorly in the new phase of the Revolution. Prior to 1940 Madero had had obvious propaganda value for the government. He had been the first to galvanize people into revolt against the old regime, and his principle of "effective suffrage, no reelection" was one of the few ideals shared by all factions of the new regime. Unlike Zapata, Carranza, and Villa, Madero had been murdered by avowed counterrevolutionaries, not other revolutionaries, in a period when the greatest danger to the revolution still came from "the reaction" rather than internal factionalism. And although his social background and moderate politics made it easier for the relatively conservative supporters of the revolution to identify with him, Madero was held in affectionate esteem by much of the population. More than the other three heroes considered here, Madero could be utilized by the government as a symbol of revolutionary unity.

In the 1920s and 1930s, however, various opposition groups also claimed Madero as their symbol. They argued that the government represented the betrayal of maderismo because the elections were not truly free and democratic, and/or because it pursued reforms never envisioned by Madero himself. Complaints about the lack of democracy were widespread, while the complaint that the government was going too far with its reforms was more typical of middle-class conservatives. (Others complained that the government had not carried its reform policies far enough.) The activities of the maderista opposition helped preserve Madero as a revolutionary symbol, which may have in effect necessitated the official Madero cult, for the government tried to appropriate all such symbols in order to be identified with and as the Revolution.

But after 1940 the maderista opposition itself faded from view. Twenty years of political defeat and repression dwindled the ranks of those who had militated under the anti-reelectionist banner. Additionally, as the regime abandoned its populist policies and pursued policies favoring capitalist development, middle-class and conservative satisfaction increased. This meant that the maderista opposition lost much of its traditional base and that the government no longer needed to rely so heavily upon propaganda to woo that segment of the population.

Much of the more progressive segment of the population had long regarded maderista politics as irrelevant to the continuing problems of poverty and social injustice. And while propagandists largely succeeded in changing Madero's earlier pusillanimous image to one of saintly benevolence that commanded perfunctory respect, they failed to give that image enough manly appeal to invite popular identification or excite fantasies. The official cult of Madero became a superfluous and ineffective form of propaganda.

CHAPTER 3

The Public Image of Emiliano Zapata

In 1909 Emiliano Zapata was elected head of the small village of
Anenecuilco in the sugar-producing region of Morelos. He continued his predecessors' struggle to halt the encroachment of the haciendas, which had taken so much land that Anenecuilco—a village
for some seven hundred years—was in danger of disintegrating.
Discouraged by fruitless dealings with government bureaucracy and
city lawyers, Zapata and eighty other armed villagers invaded the
fields of a local hacienda, fields traditionally theirs, and began to
farm them in the summer of 1910.[1]

Many communities in Mexico, particularly in the south-central
region, faced difficulties similar to those of Anenecuilco. The liberal constitution of 1857, designed to break the economically stul-
tifying grip of the traditional landed elite (which included the Catholic Church), also disincorporated indigenous communities whose
land and water rights had been protected under the Spanish Crown.[2]
Under Porfirio Díaz, a new entrepreneurial class soon constituted
a new landed elite neither socially nor legally bound to respect the
traditional rights of indigenous or other poor communities. When
the zapatistas proclaimed that they would defend with gun in hand
their right to work their own land, many campesinos were ready
to follow suit.[3]

The growing peasant insurrection in the south coincided with
the growing maderista movement in the north. In late 1910 Madero
called for the overthrow of Díaz and the establishment of a democracy. The *sureños* (southerners) soon joined the revolution.

Zapata was a barely literate campesino. Because his family had some livestock and a small piece of land, Zapata did not consider himself poor, yet it was only in relation to the extreme poverty of most campesinos that anyone else would have considered him anything but poor. Zapata distinguished himself as a horseman and liked to dress as a *charro* (Mexican horseman). When drunk he could be sexually aggressive, and he demonstrated no special concern for the children of his numerous extra-marital unions.[4] Even after Zapata became nationally important, "he and his aides relaxed in the plaza, drinking, arguing about cocks and fast and frisky horses, discussing the rains and prices with farmers who joined them for a beer." The "normally taciturn" Zapata was a respected member of his community, someone the local people trusted because he was one of their own.[5]

The same qualities that made the campesinos trust Zapata made the upper classes despise him. Their anger when zapatistas attacked property on the southern edge of Mexico City expressed, beyond disapproval of the specific acts, a less specific fear of a class of people they regarded as inferior.[6] The pro-Díaz newspaper *El Imparcial* described Indian soldiers as having "the white teeth of the wolf cub"; it ridiculed the *huaraches* (leather thong sandals) and straw hats of the zapatistas as well as Zapata's "barbaric" handwriting.[7] The capital's press referred to them as "hordes" and "bandits" and dubbed Zapata *el Atila del Sur* (the Attila of the South).[8] Even after Díaz' defeat, it by and large continued to excoriate Zapata and to exhibit contempt for the lower class. "In these days of disequilibrium," said one magazine article about Zapata, "there have appeared in various caves . . . some types of legendary rebels, despotic, irreducible, sediments of agitation that are chemically precipitated from the lowest social depths. . . ."[9]

Although he doubted Madero's wisdom in demobilizing his troops while the Porfirian army remained intact and counterrevolutionaries occupied chief positions in the Morelos state government, Zapata attempted to cooperate with Madero but soon came to an impasse with the interim government when it refused to distribute land to persons who could not prove legal title to it. The zapatistas refused to disarm until land distribution was underway. The government sent some one thousand troops to crush the intransigent peasants.[10]

Madero tried to reduce friction between the two camps, but once elected president, his respect for private property won out. He took virtually the same stance toward Zapata as the interim government had, demanding his full disarmament in order to be pardoned for his rebellion.[11] The zapatistas denounced Madero as a traitor to the revolution in the *Plan de Ayala*, signed November 25, 1911.[12] The plan spelled out a program of land distribution, the conditions of indemnity, made provisions for assistance for widows and orphans of revolutionaries, and recognized the paramount right of the people to conduct their own affairs and to rule their own communities. In contrast to other land reform programs which obliged the peasants to prove their right to obtain land, the *Plan de Ayala* obliged the *hacendados* to prove their right to keep land.[13]

Thus, Madero's government came to wage war on the zapatistas, just as had the two previous governments and as the subsequent governments of Huerta and Carranza would also do. But the tenacious zapatistas would neither surrender nor cooperate with any government that would not recognize their immediate right to land. Within their own territory they were able to implement much of the *Plan de Ayala*, but by the end of the decade defeat was at hand.

On April 10, 1919, federal troops killed Zapata in Chinameca, Morelos. Jesús M. Guajardo, who contrived the artful assassination with the help of General González, received a military promotion and a large sum of money for the deed. Carranza praised González for the great service he had rendered the nation;[14] editorials congratulated Carranza for the same reason and reported popular jubilation.[15]

Despite their gleeful reaction to Zapata's death, newspapers did not hesitate to capitalize on the romantic aspects of his life. In addition to reporting minute details of the fatal ambush as they filtered in and reviewing the history of Zapata's insurrection, they featured sentimental tales such as "The Last Love of Zapata,"[16] and the story (which was to be repeated for years) of the mysterious woman who warned Zapata of Guajardo's treachery, along with lurid accounts of his "bestial" appetites. ("Many mothers remember that their innocent daughters had been dragged from their homes and sacrificed at the alters of the sensuality of Emiliano.")[17]

Zapata's death stunned the peasants of Morelos. Although his bloated cadaver was displayed in Cuautla, rumors circulated among the campesinos that the body was not that of Emiliano, who had a

small mole here or a scar there that the dead man on display did
not. Some said that they saw Zapata riding in the hills, some that
he had gone to Argentina, or that he was in hiding. Fifty years
later Zapata's son Nícolas still maintained that the man killed was
not Zapata, but "some jerk [*pendejo*] from Tepoztlán."[18]

Contrary to González' expectations, the elimination of Zapata
did not destroy the zapatistas, who regrouped under their *jefe*'s right-
hand man, Gildardo Magaña, to continue their struggle for "land
and liberty."[19] But they were weakened, and a year later they made
an alliance with Obregón when he led the Revolt of Agua Prieta
against Carranza. This alliance was mutually advantageous. The
peasant rebels had already demonstrated that they were too difficult to defeat, and their proximity to Mexico City made them impossible to ignore. No government could truly control the region
just south of the capital without the zapatistas' cooperation, even
though the zapatistas were now incapable of mounting an offensive
against the government by themselves. Zapatista support was useful to Obregón not only in overthrowing Carranza, but afterwards
as well to prevent his own rivals (such as Manuel Peláez and Félix
Díaz, both of whom had sought zapatista support) from making an
alliance with them that might threaten Obregón's newly established political primacy.[20] And because the zapatistas had the
strongest peasant base and were the most radical advocates of agrarian reform, their support lent further credibility to Obregón's reformist image and helped dissociate him from Carranza.

In return for their support, Obregón gave the zapatistas the government of Morelos, and placed many leading zapatistas in federal
and military posts throughout Mexico. Although rank-and-file zapatistas would later charge that some of those leaders had prosti-
tuted their principles, Morelos enjoyed more agrarian reform than
most states and would not be the trouble spot for Obregón and his
successors that it had been for his predecessors.[21] The new prestige
of zapatismo, the presence of zapatistas in the government, and the
need to convince the campesinos that the government was fighting
for their cause soon led to the promotion of a new, positive public
image of Zapata himself.

The first anniversary of Zapata's death had passed unnoticed
during the Revolt of Agua Prieta. On the second anniversary, the
major metropolitan newspapers recapitulated the events surround-

ing his assassination and embellished romantic stories. The harbin-
ger of the shift in Zapata's image appeared in *El Heraldo de México*,
which published an interview with Gildardo Magaña, who had become a general in the federal army. The newspaper prefaced the
interview with the explanation that it wished to uncover the truth
about this "enigmatic figure hidden beneath a legend of crime".

As time passes and the serenity of the spirits yesterday excited by the
effervescence of political passions permits a serene analysis . . . of the past
ten years, the personality of Emiliano Zapata acquires a stature that makes
him stand above the vulgar mediocrity in which until recently [his detrac-
tors] sought to envelop him.[22]

El Demócrata's editorial elegized Zapata as a "modest Indian
farmer," a "defender of Democracy," a man of "healthy patriotism"
who had fought for the "future greatness of the Nation" rather than
for personal aggrandizement, and as a nationalist who had never
solicited nor received foreign aid. His followers, ridiculed before as
highwaymen and ragtag country bumpkins, were now described as
"admirably organized campesino soldiers."[23]

One purpose of Obregón's zapatismo was to convince people that
the government was the friend of the masses and that they would
get their land, but at the same time he wanted to assure other countries, especially the United States, that Mexico was a safe place for
investment. An article that had first appeared in the North American periodical *The Nation* quoted zapatista Rafael Cal y Mayor,
who worked for the government, as saying: "When Carranza fell,
our cause triumphed. The War has ended." It also quoted Secretary of Agriculture Antonio Villarreal as saying that so much land
had been distributed that within a year "all danger of revolution
. . . will have ceased to exist, because the agrarian problem will
be resolved," and that "businessmen and capitalists will be well
received."[24]

A similarly double message was expressed at the Zapata memorial organized in Cuautla, Morelos, by Governor José G. Parrés
and the National Agrarian Party (PNA). The chief speakers were
Antonio Díaz Soto y Gama (a middle-class zapatista and PNA co-
founder) and Villarreal.[25] The latter lambasted "land barons and
reactionaries" opposed to agrarian reform, but said the "reckless

radicals who want to get rid of all the defects of our social system
at once" and thereby "endanger our national sovereignty" were even
worse for the country.[26] The speakers glorified the "martyred" Zapata for his uncompromising struggle for land—for his refusal to
be patient, to reduce his demands, or to be deterred by fear of
retaliation. Yet they admonished their audience that they "must
conform" to and be "content" with the existing reform program
instead of "risking ruin" by attempting reforms that might antagonize other nations,[27] implicitly the United States, which feared
Mexico was becoming "Bolshevist."

In 1922 the homage to Zapata had a more consistently "radical"
tone. A message of condolence for Zapata's death was sent by the
Soviet Union and read at the ceremony, which featured an array
of leftist speakers, including the notable Deputy Rafael Ramos
Pedrueza and General Francisco Múgica.[28]

Mingling traditional and Marxist rhetoric, the speakers predictably reviled Carranza for having "turned into a tyrant when he tried
to impose a presidential successor" but also called him "the reactionary element within the revolutionary ranks." Zapata, a man
"oppressed by capitalism," symbolized "the redemption of the rural
proletariat." Zapata had "felt his flesh bleed beneath the lash of the
foreign overseer" and had witnessed "innumerable times" the dis-
honoring of the "wives, daughters, and sisters of the plantation's
semi-slaves" before engaging in a "virile rebellion" against "bourgeois tyranny."[29] On a lighter note, Zapata was described as "frank,
simple, and very accessible to the poor the same as the rich," an
affable fellow who "loved the bullfights, but in the style of the
[Mexican] *ranchos*, without all the paraphernalia of the Spanish
style."[30]

Despite their references to class, the speakers apparently did not
think, or did not think the public would think, class oppression per
se justified Zapata's revolt. On the one hand, they presented Zapata as an agent of class struggle; on the other, they appealed to
Christian values, nationalist sentiment, and the code of machismo
to make him acceptable. They cast him as a patient, self-sacrificing,
Christ-like man who had long endured physical abuse and insult to
his manly honor before taking up arms. The remark about Zapata's
openness to rich and poor softened the notion that he disliked individuals of the upper classes, while the remarks about the foreign

overseer (as opposed to a Mexican one) and his Mexican ways showed Zapata as a man with whom all Mexicans who appreciated the "national culture" and resented foreign domination had something in common.

The propagandists needed to make Zapata seem admirable and likeable "as a person" in order to overcome the prevailing negative image of him. Only in Morelos and adjacent areas did Zapata have a strong following and real popularity, although even there the "better" classes had fled. Conservatives everywhere opposed zapatismo, and many ordinary people, especially in Mexico City, disliked Zapata because of the vicious, frightening tales printed about him prior to Obregón's presidency and occasionally thereafter. To extend Zapata's popularity beyond his native turf, the propagandists had to dispel the notion that he was a monstrous barbarian.

The most vigorous defenders of Zapata declared all criticism of him to be false. One attributed the falsehood to the "turbulent sea of our political passions . . . this last decade," which had supposedly blinded people to the truth; others blamed the malice of the vaguely defined "reaction" that had "tried in vain to cover the head of this sincere selfless fighter with the repellant crown of infamy: he was the rabble-rouser, the bandit, the destroyer of villages, the hyena thirsting for human blood, the exterminating angel of the Apocalypse."[31] To all of that, the author replied "Lies!"—a rhetorical device that showed him to be one who understood what others had not, and emphasized the injustice of the opprobrium that Zapata had endured. The popular notion that Zapata was misunderstood reinforced his Christ-like, martyred image.

Zapata's more temperate defenders admitted that some of his bad reputation was justified but explained his faults as sociological, not pathological, in origin. Martín Luis Guzmán, for example, wrote that Zapata was "bloody and barbarous . . . , sunk up to his neck in the horrible atmosphere in which he was raised, but identified in the end with a great truth."[32] Another article acknowledged that Zapata was ignorant but argued that "he was uncultured because when he was a child, culture was a privilege of opulent men of fortune or shameless bootlickers."[33]

Zapata's apologists, however, were not universally successful. Conservatives staunchly opposed his glorification, a trend one described as "the new psychic epidemic" produced by the "menin-

gitic delirium of feverous Indian-lovers."[34] General González, calling
Zapata a "troglodyte, illiterate, and congenital criminal," charged
that Obregón's zapatismo had pushed the government into "Bolshevism."[35]

Apart from the controversy about Zapata himself, the administration's pretense of zapatismo and/or "Bolshevism" came under
question from both the right and the left. The die-hard *porfirista*
Francisco Bulnes pointed to the historical inconsistency of the government's position:

The bourgeois "grandees" of the 1910 Revolution, the state governors, were
Zapata's enemies, and lent themselves to his destruction, as did the majority of the military leaders. . . . Only a year ago Zapata was declared a
bandit, persecuted by carrancismo and assassinated in a plot rewarded by
the Fatherland with honors, wealth, and congratulations. . . . The Revolution changed its personnel and . . . its criteria and now . . . we are
obliged to put our consciences into reverse . . . for the Caudillo of the
South.[36]

The professed radicalism of the administration seemed hypocritical to many. Social programs proceeded slowly and often provided
more opportunity for political favoritism than public service. In
contrast to many "revolutionary" politicians' propensity for corruption and luxury, Zapata was praised for being "immune to palatial
splendor" and because "after having handled great fortunes," he
and his family remained poor—"proof of his immense honesty."[37]
According to J. M. Puig Casauranc: "[Zapata] never said, because
he didn't know there was such a word, that he was a bolshevist;
but he didn't pretend to be one while getting millions in rents, and
by changing his peasant jacket for a dinner jacket; nor by spitting
out threats against the bourgeoisie [while riding in] big fat . . .
cars."

Nor, said Puig, did Zapata "become a hacienda-owner overnight;
. . . [nor] cover his mistresses' necks with stolen jewels; he did not
besmirch his preaching for the betterment of the people with fab-
ulous foreign bank accounts."[38]

Such concern for the hypocrisy of the people in power was indicative of growing dissatisfaction with Obregón's administration,
which was tolerant of corruption in exchange for loyalty and intol-

erant of rival power or opposition. The resultant political tension surfaced at the commemoration of Zapata's assassination in April 1923.

For example, for several years General Pablo González had been a favorite of the conservative "revolutionaries" and a critic of Obregón, but the government had seemed unconcerned with his opposition. The propagandists had passed up the opportunity to defame González at the April 10 memorials, which because of his responsibility for Zapata's death offered a convenient theater for doing so, and had instead blamed Carranza and Guajardo for his death. In 1923, however, the attacks focused on González,[39] which suggests that the administration felt more insecure than it had in the past.

But the more serious threat was the dissension within the heart of the obregonista camp itself—the *Partido Nacional Agrarista* (PNA). Some PNA members, including Gildardo Magaña, were leaning toward the rival Cooperatist Party, and a memorial banquet in April almost degenerated into a brawl or gunfight as loyal PNA members and Cooperatist sympathizers impugned one another's revolutionary sincerity. Díaz Soto y Gama calmed things down by urging the men not to succumb to those who tried to provoke divisions among them (as the Cooperatists were accused of doing) and to focus on the memory of Zapata instead.[40] Violence was averted for the moment, but later that year many agraristas defected to the Cooperatist Party and joined the De la Huerta Revolt. With the revolt's defeat the Cooperatist Party disappeared, but the PNA survived as the major obregonista organization in the power struggles of the next half decade.

Newspapers reported the 1923 Zapata memorial at length and printed numerous related articles, one of which said that:

zapatismo, which from . . . 1910 was burning . . . in order to sustain the revolution begun by . . . Madero, was a continual headache for the successive governments from the fall of . . . Díaz until the definitive triumph of obregonismo, which . . . attracted . . . all the factions opposed to the carrancista regime, which had been impotent to consummate the great work of union that was so needed among the great Mexican family.[41]

This version of the revolution juxtaposed Obregón's zapatismo with Carranza's indifference to social reform and cast Obregón as

the heir of Madero and Zapata—common devices in the administration's propaganda. The novelty lay in the implication that Zapata was also Madero's heir. Except in a chronological sense, it was
not true that Zapata "sustained" Madero's revolution, for he was
far more radical than Madero and had been at war against him.
This historical distortion was convenient for Obregón, for the implied unity between Madero and Zapata radicalized the bourgeois
image of the former, lent respectability to the dangerous image of
the latter, and hid the contradiction in Obregón's claim to be the
heir of both men. The unidentified author also clearly shared the
patriarchal attitude that equates political and male sexual power;
implicitly, "potent" obregonismo had consummated the union and
Obregón was the father of the "great Mexican family."

In general the pro-Zapata propaganda of 1923 reiterated earlier
themes of his supposedly enigmatic personality, his humble ways,
his Catholic and patriotic virtues. In a speech at the Cuautla ceremony, Crisófero Ibáñez, whose rhetoric indicated that he was not
a campesino, combined these themes in a way which quite lifted
Zapata out of the realm of the human political leader and into the
superhuman:

[Zapata] is simple and coarse, like a campesino; penetrating and divining,
as a wise man; he has the indomitable fury of a warrior and the loving
. . . holy flame of the worldly saint, with appetites and yet nobly disin-
terested. . . . [This] human side brings him close to the humble, who feel
they are his equals and the divine side . . . illuminates them. Zapata is a
warrior, with all his sins, who had the high moral force to pronounce
among those who suffered, the sermon on the mount. . . . [42]

Ibáñez compared those opposed to agrarian reform to the descend-
ants "by blood or spirit" of the Spanish conquerors. He used anti-
Spanish sentiment to anathematize the opposition and sanctified
Zapata while still promoting his virile image. This appealed to nationalism, Christianity, and machismo all at once: something for
every taste.

Ibáñez also participated in the Cuautla memorial ceremony of
1924, where he blamed capitalism for everything the people suffered. Other speakers included the feminist-socialist María del Re-
fugio García and an Indian who addressed his Indian audience in

its native Nahuatl tongue as a "salute to the Aztec race and the races that compose the State of Morelos."[43]

The leftward shift reflected the more radical reputation of Plutarco Elías Calles, Obregón's choice in the upcoming presidential election. Although a protégé of Obregón, Calles had cultivated an independent power base among labor organizations, which therefore shared the Cuautla platform with the obregonista agrarian groups that had officiated at the previous Zapata memorials. The callistas at the ceremony showed considerable diplomacy in dealing with the agraristas' apprehension about the impending change of government. The speaker for CROM stated that "the men of the South" (the zapatistas and by extension the obregonistas) had provided the more revolutionary example for "the men of the North" (implicitly the callista camp) to follow:

Those from the North have to recognize that the most important social reform accomplished in Mexico came from the South, and even when in the North they fought for the anti-reelectionist principles, the desire of the revolution was not this, it was the economic betterment of the worker, which is being accomplished now.[44]

The speaker implied that social reform, not electoral democracy, was the true object of the revolution (personified as capable of its own desire) and made room for worker and peasant alike under the conveniently broadened banner of Zapata. He flattered the regional pride of the southern men and the political preferences of the agrarianists. But Calles himself made the greatest gesture to the obregonista-agrarista camp when he declared that he too was a zapatista:

A few days ago one of the mouthpieces of the reaction . . . said . . . that I was coming here to ratify the revolutionary program of Zapata. What they said mockingly, is true. It is correct. . . . [It] is necessary that the Mexican reaction and the foreign reaction know that I will always be with the most advanced principles of humanity. . . . the revolutionary program of Zapata, that agrarian program is mine.[45]

"Zapata's Program Is Mine" blazed across the newspapers on April 11, and editorials began tackling the question of exactly what Calles had meant. *El Universal* gravely warned that the government—for

Calles was sure to be president—must not adopt a program so radical that it violated the constitution. Days later in a radio broadcast
Calles quieted such alarm by explaining that "we have not sought
. . . , we who desire social renovation, to convert property and
wealth into ruin," and that his concept of agrarian reform included
"the creation and development of small property."[46] *El Universal*
noted:

The candidate had said, "The agrarian program of Zapata is mine." But
this, to judge by his later words, should not be understood in its broadest
sense. To the contrary, we should reduce it to its minimal expression. . . . Zapata's program and the program of the . . . candidate do
not coincide except on one point: sympathy for the poor. And in this
sympathy . . . we are all agreed.[47]

That so much revolutionary talk could be reduced to an expression of sympathy for the poor was symptomatic of the dilemma the
government created by identifying itself as the Revolution. The
distance between the "man of the people" image politicians cultivated and their elite position was becoming more obvious with the
continuous scandals about coercion, illicit riches, and moral dissipation. Even their attempts to show fraternity with "our" campesinos revealed their patronizing attitudes and social unfamiliarity
with them. So-called zapatista orators were usually professional
politicians, and the ex-zapatistas with important official positions
usually had middle-class backgrounds. They often shared the
grandstand at the Cuautla festivities with other luminaries, while
the campesino veterans of Zapata's "Liberation Army of the South"
were "honored" by being permitted to march in review and by
being awarded medals. Although the middle-class zapatistas had
once been dedicated to the campesino movement, their class distance from the peasants reasserted itself when Obregón made
agrarismo a central part of his political appeal.

For example, as part of the 1924 Zapata memorial in Cuautla, a
banquet was held for agrarianists from Mexico City and the local
campesinos. The reporter observed that "the latter . . . found
themselves seated at the same table as the former," and that both
groups were served the same food, which consisted of "national
dishes only."[48] It would seem, then, that eating together was a rare

ceremonial event for the campesinos and the *políticos* who supposedly championed their interests. The remark about the food—an example of petty nationalism—also assured the reader that the politicians still ate what the common folk ate and were not putting on culinary airs.

But Calles' proclaimed zapatismo was only a ploy for the support of an important political faction during his election campaign. As president, Calles ceased to court the agrarian sector, and public commemoration of Zapata's death subsided accordingly. Indeed, during Calles' administration, newspapers on April 10 often gave as much or more attention to the Easter holiday and especially to Mother's Day, which *Excelsior* had invented in 1925 to combat the "socialist threat" (legalized divorce, civil marriage, and so on) to traditional family values, even though Mother's Day fell a full month later, on May 10.

Declining interest in Zapata as a political hero was accompanied by some increased interest in him as a romantic hero. In 1925 *El Demócrata* printed an article by Leonor Célis Gil, who might well have used the popular film star Rudolf Valentino as a model for her elegy to Zapata:

That youth who inspired love by disdaining, who on his charger . . . crossed ridges and valleys like lightning, was of the brown race, of burnished bronze, of that profound, intelligent, melancholic gaze that is called Mexican! Of that race . . . destined to be great, if it enlightens itself and works to achieve its liberties. He who kissed and burned with his lips, was he who sought out danger and reveled in it; the restless and fiery one with the intelligent and melancholic gaze was Emiliano Zapata.[49]

This melodramatic homage was noteworthy because the few references which might be construed as political—"he sought out danger," for example—were transformed into signs of his virility. The author praised Zapata's masculinity, not his revolutionary role, and in rather racy terms for the times. She furthermore described his Mexicanness as racial characteristics that enhanced his sex appeal. In short, she transformed the "revolutionary" into a new version of the hot-blooded Latin lover, the Mexican macho, who has since become one of the country's predominant stereotypes.

The appeal of the macho image notwithstanding, Zapata's name was still bandied about by the politicians wishing to play down or play up their agrarian policies. In 1925, in a reversal of his declared zapatismo of the year before, Calles assured a northern audience that his administration was not agrarista,[50] while only a few days later Aurelio Manrique, the staunch obregonista governor of San Luis Potosi, praised Calles for carrying on Obregón's zapatismo.[51]

These contradictory claims resulted from more than the tendency of politicians to tell every audience what it wanted to hear; they also reflected the growing struggle between the PNA and CROM, which was part of the greater struggle between obregonistas and callistas for national power. Although in 1925 the PNA speaker at the Cuautla ceremonies assured the audience that there was no split between the two groups,[52] the falseness of his assurance was quite apparent in 1927. By that time the PNA, which had organized the Zapata memorials since their inception, had been squeezed out by CROM. For several years CROM had been organizing the Worker and Peasant Regional Councils (*Consejos Regionales de Obreros y Campesinos*) in Morelos, usurping thereby the PNA's political and geographical territory. These councils began to conduct the Zapata memorials in Cuautla and in lesser towns of the state.[53] They advertised the ceremonies to an unusual degree, but the change in organization took its toll on the festivities. According to *Excelsior*, "the absence of the agraristas, who had been accustomed to come . . . every year to render homage, was marked," and the events did not have "the splendor they used to have."[54] *Excelsior* buried the story in the back pages, and *El Universal* did not report the ceremony at all.

The tension between obregonistas and callistas came into full view with Obregón's second presidential campaign and put the anniversary of Zapata's death in the front-page news again when the obregonistas organized a memorial not in Morelos but in Mexico City itself, where apparently none had been held before. The press all but ignored events in Cuautla in favor of the Mexico City ceremony, whose newsworthiness derived from its status as a "first" and because it was part of the broader political contest. The obregonistas capitalized on Obregón's agrarianist reputation by holding the memorial in the *Casa del Estudiante Indígena*, an agricultural boarding school for Indian boys. Speakers Aurelio Manrique and Antonio Díaz Soto y Gama, leaders in the reelection campaign, lectured the students on the meaning of zapatismo and declared that Obregón would continue Zapata's work. Díaz Soto y Gama assured them that "the Mexican Revolution is holy, although it may have its violent characteristics, because it pursues justice and equality for all Mexicans. Carry a clean conscience back to your homes."[55]

Obregón did indeed "win" the election, but only to be assassinated before taking office. Suspicion about Calles' possible role in the murder pressured him into appointing an interim president acceptable to the obregonistas as a demonstration that he was not trying to prolong his own influence. Calles also began organizing the PNR to reduce the deadly factionalism that divided the "Revolutionary Family."

In the short run, these acts failed to placate the obregonistas or to break Calles' power. Many obregonistas joined the Escobar Rebellion in 1929, but with its defeat they lost the political clout they had had for almost a decade. This left the callistas the unquestionably dominant faction. Calles' control of the PNR was so complete that critics sometimes charged that he had created it for the very purpose of retaining his power.

In the long run, nevertheless, the founding of the PNR marked a turning point in Mexican politics toward the triumph of institutional over personal power. Although coercive violence would never be fully abandoned, the government and the PNR increasingly relied on propaganda and cooptation to maintain control.

This new trend could be seen in the very fact that in 1929 the government commemorated April 10 with new vigor—balm for the wounded pride of defeated obregonismo. After 1924 (the year of Calles' "I am a zapatista" speech), the memory of Zapata was "submerged for some years,"[56] but in 1929 the major capital newspapers—including, for once, *Excelsior*—dedicated an unusual portion of their front page and photographs to the ceremony in Cuautla. The ceremony itself was more elaborate than it had been since 1924, and, apparently for the first time, several members of Zapata's family attended as guests of honor.[57]

Speeches that day included typical remarks about Zapata being the ideal of the campesinos and time erasing the calumnies that had been heaped upon him, but in addition they altered zapatismo to fit the regime's new policies of cultural advancement. One speaker

tied the theme of the death of the *caudillo* of agrarianism in with the cultural program developed by the Revolution in favor of the campesino classes, which now by educational means will complete the conquest of their independence, which since 1910 they had been gaining through armed force.[58]

The speaker equated the government with the Revolution and implied that its new cultural programs superceded and would finally accomplish what the previous "armed phase" had not: independence. The speaker's emphasis on education and his subsequent admonitions to the campesinos about the evils of alcohol suggested that independence was a matter of personal betterment, of campesinos pulling themselves up by their bootstraps. The caption under a newspaper photo of Zapata echoed the same tone—it read, "Chief of the armies [huestes] of campesinos who fought for their moral redemption."[59]

The idea that personal success could be achieved by education and the avoidance of vice expressed the individualism of the middle class. It ignored the social basis of the problems of the rural poor and so implicitly denied the need to restructure the class system which benefitted the bourgeoisie. This updated zapatismo, a government-run self-improvement campaign, was a far cry from that of the peasants who had challenged the class system by physically and ideologically assaulting the haciendas during the previous decade.

Indeed, the updated Zapata was himself a far cry from what he had been a decade before. The change was not simply from a negative to a positive image, for even though a negative image had predominated, a positive one had always existed; it also entailed a substantive change in his positive image. Prior to Obregón's adoption of Zapata as a government symbol, favorable tales about Zapata had been generated almost exclusively by the common people of Morelos. Their corridos (ballads) stressed political issues such as Zapata's dedicated struggle for land and his break from Madero and Carranza, not on Zapata as a glamorous or personally likeable character. But as the number of official, urban, and/or middle-class defenders of Zapata increased, the romantic aspects of his life (real or fabricated) became a greater part of his image.[60]

The preference for romantic personal anecdotes about Zapata was illustrated by a series of stories published by Octavio Paz (Senior) in El Universal in 1929. Paz lingered over descriptions of Zapata's fine horse and horsemanship, his elaborate charro dress, his popularity among the campesinos. He gave Zapata a sexual aura by spicing up the stories with references to his handsomeness, his manliness, and comely peasant girls:

> a dark beauty, with very black eyes and long, lush lashes, with a bounteous bosom . . . , with robust and well-shaped calves . . . approached the victorious Emiliano and gave him a bouquet of beautiful flowers. . . . [61]

Paz' anecdotes also manipulated Zapata's image to fortify government policies. During the first half of 1929 the government had finally settled the Cristero Rebellion by relenting in its enforcement of the anti-clerical clauses of the constitution in exchange for church loyalty.[62] In the summer of 1929, one of Paz' stories in *El Universal* depicted Zapata as tolerant of others' Catholicism, or "fanaticism," as the government and anti-clerics termed it. In that story, Zapata explained why he permitted people in his territory to practice their faith:

> I do not do this because of fanaticism, I do have liberal ideas . . . , but I do not want to be intransigent with the people, nor offend them in their religion; and I think the best way to get rid of fanaticism is to establish schools and leave them at liberty; I remember when I was a kid whatever they stopped me from doing was what I wanted to do most.[63]

Here religious tolerance did not indicate a lack of revolutionary zeal, but rather an enlightened understanding of human psychology and sympathetic respect for the common people. With this view government supporters could moderate their anti-clericalism and still be good Revolutionaries. (It is interesting to note that Paz included Zapata personally in the liberal camp, though there is no indication that the zapatistas were more, or less, anti-clerical than most campesinos, with whom they shared the sometimes unorthodox Catholicism of the countryside. Polemicists on all sides of the religious question pointed to Zapata's supposed faith or lack thereof to bolster their own causes.)

Despite the increased fanfare at the 1929 memorials, the annual ceremonies were still essentially local affairs—organized in the heart of zapatista territory by ex-zapatista politicians, attended primarily by zapatista peasants. The one commemoration held at the *Casa del Estudiante Indígena* in 1928 had been related to Obregón's presidential campaign but was not, strictly speaking, government-sponsored.

Only in 1930 did the government finally see fit to organize a full-scale memorial to Zapata in Mexico City—a symbolic advance in Zapata's evolution as an official national hero. Among the memorial events were the placement of a plaque on the house where Zapata had stayed during the 1914 occupation of the capital and a *velada* at the DDF's Álvaro Obregón Civic Center.[64] One newspaper reported that "persons from all our social classes" attended, yet the style of the *velada* suggested how distant it was from the man and the movement it nominally honored. The *velada*'s program included "three minutes of silence. Next followed a musical composition. Next the señora Josefina de Moreno recited a poem by Vereo Guzmán titled "Brother Campesino," and was soundly applauded for her emotive style."[65]

With the usual exception of *Excelsior*, which denounced "the socialist concept of the family" and conducted its "Most Prolific Mother" contest instead,[66] Mexico City's major dailies devoted extensive space to articles about Zapata and the numerous events commemorating his death. The articles and ceremonial speeches, in keeping with the government's push to consolidate its control, downplayed armed struggle as a means for social change. Speaker Cal y Mayor, president of the League of Agrarian Communities, claimed that "the southern revolution was able to sustain itself more by the strength of [Zapata's] ideals than by the strength of arms," and stressed the "spiritual rebellion" of Zapata, who planted in "the dark spirits [of the peasants] the feeling of rebellion" and "awakened in them the idea of armed struggle."[67]

Other official voices stressed the importance of law and the government in affecting change. One columnist in *El Nacional Revolucionario* wrote that Zapata—"the Great Sacrificed One," the "Apostle of Agrarianism," the "Martyr of Chinameca"—had the "virtue" of awakening the "legitimate ambition of the people who had lost the right to ask [the government] for the restitution of . . . the land." He said that the "rural proletariat owed one of the most beautiful conquests that the Revolution crystalized" to Zapata, who deserved the "glory of having been the precursor of Agrarian-ism."[68] Another writer declared that the campesinos had been changed into revolutionaries because they suffered from a "lack of help from a Government which only attended to capitalism."[69]

Such reformist rhetoric cast Zapata into a "precursor" position, which implicitly identified the contemporary government with the "real" revolution, and once again portrayed the revolution as an emotion or attitude rather than action. Furthermore, "revolution" was defined as an attack on a government that failed to "help" the poor, rather than on the class system. In these terms, the acquisi-tion of the legal right to ask (*pedir*) for land rather than the actual appropriation of land—by force if necessary, as Zapata had done—could be equated with revolutionary victory. In these terms, a gov-ernment that gave the peasants the right to ask for land, that as-sumed a benevolent posture toward them, could claim to be revo-lutionary regardless of how much land the peasants actually received or whether it also tended to the needs of the capitalist class.

In 1931 efforts to formally recognize Zapata continued to esca-late. The street of the house where Zapata had stayed during the 1914 occupation of Mexico City was renamed for him; children at the Francisco I. Madero School uncovered a plaque which com-memorated "the fact that there the first bust of the *caudillo* was erected by working-class children."[70] The school ceremony, which received the most newspaper coverage, did not honor Zapata di-rectly, but honored a previous generation of children for having honored Zapata. Although the ceremony ostensibly taught the chil-dren about Zapata, it also taught them that venerating the nation's heroes was in itself a virtue, thereby reinforcing patriarchy's wor-shipful attitude toward "great men."

The year 1931 also brought the "transcendental" culmination of the trend to honor Zapata. The people of Xochimilco (site of the 1914 conference between Zapata and Villa) petitioned the Mexican Congress to add Zapata's name to the list of national heroes.[71] Sev-eral months later a similar request was made with respect to Car-ranza, and Congress considered the two petitions together.[72] Speakers argued that such honors were appropriate at a time when national "harmony [seemed] to be growing stronger."[73] According to one *diputado*:

History has judged already and magnanimously pardoned the minor errors
[of] . . . the venerable icons of the great revolutionaries who have made
Mexico the nation most advanced in its legislation, in its ideology, and in
its democratic procedures. . . . [It] is up to us to reward and thank [them]
disregarding the ephemeral partisanry and fleeting creeds which . . . now
have been united under the *Partido Nacional Revolucionario*.[74]

On August 25, 1931, the Mexican Congress voted to declare both
men national heroes and to have their names inscribed in gold on
the wall of the congressional chambers. Thus Zapata was officially
incorporated into the hagiography of the Revolution.[75]

The incorporation, however, did not render Zapata's image static;
the government continued to remold him in its image, not itself in
his. The transformation was at times only a matter of tone or style,
as a description of Zapata as "the prestigious agrarianist" subtly
illustrated.[76] More imposing illustration came with the 1932 Cuautla *homenaje*, when Zapata's remains were transferred to a crypt in
one of the main plazas. Atop the crypt stood a granite Zapata on
horseback, looking down to and placing a hand on the shoulder of
a simple campesino, who looked up to him in admiration. One
newspaper described the statue as "capturing the commanding posture [*actitud arrogante*] of the apostle of agrarianism, a cavalier on a
spirited mount."[77] Where was the humble Zapata of yesteryear?

The relationship between the horseman and the campesino in the
statue was not fraternal, nor one of class solidarity—it was one of
superior to inferior, father to child. Rather than the camaraderie
and social equality that characterized the relationship between Zapata and his supporters, it showed a superior man who helps the
humble people, who depend on him, not on themselves, for care
and guidance.

The statue, then, symbolized a patriarchal concept of a hero as
well as the government's concept of its relationship to the people.
Through its pronouncements and conspicuous adulation of revolutionary leaders, the government strove to maintain a revolutionary
image, yet its relationship to the people was authoritarian—at times
benevolently so—but that did not alter the imbalance of power in
any fundamental way. The government would lead, the people were
to follow.

In the promotion of an authoritarian political culture, the patriarchal ideal of the son complemented that of the father. In one of the most apocryphal, oft-told stories about Zapata, his father was reduced to despair by the loss of family land to greedy *hacendados*, and the boy Emiliano, distressed by his father's misery, cries out, "Father, when I am a man I will make them give back our land!"[78] Besides its prophetic appeal, the story elicited sympathy for the injustice suffered by a family and for a child's anguish. And it implied that manhood was the fulfillment of filial love, of one's promises to one's father. Whereas stories taking a child's perspective are often used to question the wisdom of authority over the weak, this tale glorified the patriarchal structure by portraying Zapata as the filial ideal.

Given the patriarchal character of Christianity, father and son images easily blended with images of the Holy Trinity. In the early 1920s a simple comparison had been made between Zapata and Christ; in the early 1930s the regime's propaganda had fully adapted Christian, especially Roman Catholic, psychology and morality to the regime's need for unity and loyalty. The "religion" of the Revolution emphasized obedience, hierarchical authority, self-denial, and the glory of martyrdom. Zapata was praised because he "knew first to dominate himself serenely in order to tolerate the humiliation he and his people suffered."[79] Overlooking his acts of rebellion, praise went instead to his fabricated personality: he was a "pure man, without stain," with "great character, great simplicity, [and an] irreproachable private life."[80]

A pamphlet distributed by the PNR's new "Friends of the Campesino" Brotherhood in 1934 provided the most extravagant example of religious analogy, picturing Zapata as the Father, Son, and Holy Ghost, all incarnate in a PNR organization:

The disappearance of the father . . . of the campesinos left a vacuum . . . in the struggle . . . for the redemption of the slaves of the land.

. . . many refuse to believe in the death of their redeemer and await the new coming of Him.

And not without reason. The spirit of Zapata . . . has been reincarnated in the P.N.R. Brotherhood, "Friends of the Campesino."

Brother campesino: Be confident. A new day is born. Now you can have someone to look out for you in place of the great disappeared one, and defend your rights, as He did.

The thoughts of Zapata have been reborn, . . . and are once again in action, with greater faith and vigor, under the . . . "Friends of the Campesino."[81]

But while the religious analogies developed, so also did the theme of Zapata's manliness. As before, there were remarks about his handsomeness, his "markedly virile face," his "typically Mexican mustache," his reputation as a womanizer ("they say he had a fair number of women").[82] Writers and orators commented about the deprivation he suffered during the revolution and about how he managed to have a love life even during the revolution. According to Baltasar Dromundo: "He loved among serenades, among the magnificent . . . orchards, . . . the warm . . . nights of the southern towns whose . . . romantic quality he never ceased to enjoy despite the demands of the Revolution." Dromundo falsely claimed that Zapata had been responsible for the children of any woman he had "had even once," and that Zapata symbolized "the most ancient indigenous nobility in the fulfillment of family duty and in the romantic and sentimental aspects of his life as a man."[83]

Whether as father, son, saint, or man of flesh and blood who "shared his class's pleasure in women,"[84] the propagandists usually depicted Zapata as fulfilling the patriarchal values appropriate for the various roles. This placed Zapata in a positive light because patriarchal values were important in Mexican culture. Yet the reverse was also true: by showing Zapata, one of the most radical and uncompromising of the revolutionary leaders, as living up to patriarchal ideals, the propagandists conveyed the message that those ideals were appropriate for revolutionaries. The perpetuation of patriarchal values reinforced traditional familial relations in themselves and as the prototype for all social organizations, in which every "superior" commanded from all "inferiors" the obedience due a father.

One of the political ramifications of the patriarchal mentality was a tendency toward personalism, or *caudillismo*, in which men acquired a personal following that gave them power (especially military power) independent of the government. The numerous revolts of the 1920s were to a great extent engendered by the personalist nature of the political factions. With the founding of the PNR, the Mexican government focused on the reduction of personalism and the promotion of popular allegiance to government institutions and office holders per se. The Zapata-related propaganda of 1932 reflected this trend. One speaker, for example, instead of claiming that a particular president was the true successor to Zapata, stated that his heirs "are all of our presidents . . . who . . . all, without egotistical exceptions, live and will always live in the memory and heart of the proletariat."[85] It was said too that the men in government were the ones "who actualized fully, beginning in 1920," Zapata's ideals because they had "better tools and more refined talents as statesmen."[86] In other words, presidents and politicians were the "real" revolutionaries, and statesmanship, not armed struggle, was the best way to achieve revolutionary goals.

As Mexican politics became more institutionalized, Zapata also became an increasingly "institutional" hero, with ever greater state rituals conducted in his honor. Nevertheless, the government's concerted campaign to make Zapata a national hero coincided with a decline in its commitment to agrarian reform. By late 1929 Calles already believed that land reform was a failure; in March 1930 he told President Ortiz Rubio and the Cabinet that the partition of land into small parcels was unproductive and damaging to the economy and should be stopped.[87] Land distribution did not come to a complete halt, but it was neglected just as the pauperizing effects of the Great Depression were beginning to be felt in Mexico's dependent agricultural economy. The increased official attention to Zapata served as a smoke screen for the government's inattention to the plight of the campesinos.

In response to their difficult situation, campesinos formed the Confederation of Mexican Peasants (CCM) as part of, but more progressive than, the PNR's mainstream. Opposed to Calles' orientation, the CCM successfully pushed for a presidential candidate for the upcoming 1934 elections who was the most agrarianist of all the leading callista contenders: Lázaro Cárdenas.[88] The especially elaborate commemoration in 1934 of Zapata's death reflected the revival of agrarianism and anticipated the political shift that Cárdenas would bring to the government when he assumed the presidency.

Once in office, Cárdenas pursued agrarian reform with unprece-

dented vigor,[89] and Zapata became the supreme symbol of the Revolution. The practice of commemorating his death spread beyond
Morelos and the *Distrito Federal* into the north (home of Carranza,
Madero, and Villa), which had been relatively indifferent to Zapata. When Pablo González returned to Mexico in 1937 after many
years abroad, some political groups attempted, unsuccessfully, to
bring him to trial for the murder of Zapata;[90] in 1938 the *Comité
Reivindicador Pro-Zapata* and the *Unión de Revolucionarios Agraristas
del Sur* organized a public celebration of the twenty-seventh anniversary of the proclamation of the *Plan de Ayala.*[91]

In Mexico City, participants in the April 10 memorials seemed
as concerned to publicize the institutionalization of Zapata's heroic
status and other indications of his popularity as they were to honor
Zapata directly. Baltasar Dromundo said that Zapata's name "is on
the streets, villages, towns, unions, libraries, and schools." He described Zapata as "one of the most popular figures . . . in all of
Hispanic America," which he said was "an enormous prestige for
the people who have immortalized him in songs, *corridos*, and leg-
ends."[92] Rafael Ramos Pedrueza proclaimed that

> there are now a legion of writers of different nationalities, like Carleton
> Beals, Luis Araquistain, . . . Ramón del Valle Inclán, . . . José Inge-
> nieros, William Gates, . . . Henri Barbusse, . . . Upton Sinclair, J.H.
> Retinger, A. Goldschmidt, Scott Nering and many other profound con-
> temporary thinkers who . . . do [Zapata] full justice.[93]

Yet despite—or because of—the multiplication and expansion of
official ceremonies (now often broadcast over radio), the memorial
affairs seemed self-consciously contrived to impress the populace
with the government's popular sympathies. If the ceremonies did
in fact represent sincere zapatista or agrarianist politics, that quality was lost in the news reports. Press coverage concentrated on
the strictly ceremonial aspects of the memorials, which seemed *pro
forma* and repetitive. The Madero ceremonies were given an occa-
sional spark of political vitality by opposition groups protesting that
they, not the government, represented the true spirit of maderismo, but the government seemed to have monopolized Zapata and
the routinized annual *homenajes* generated little excitement during
Cárdenas' term in office.

The 1936 commemoration of Zapata's assassination was an exception, albeit a qualified exception in that the excitement stemmed not from the ceremonies themselves but from the fact that they coincided with Cárdenas' expulsion of Calles from Mexico. Overnight Calles became the national villain, denounced at the Zapata memorials throughout the country. In Mexico City the CCM called for the expropriation of Calles' various haciendas. Some of Cárdenas' supporters, anxious to dissociate him from his discredited former *jefe*, claimed that Cárdenas had never been Calles' "lackey."[94]

Cárdenas was also praised for renewing the Revolution. His forceful promotion of land distribution and labor rights won him tremendous support among the rural and urban working people, which in turn made it possible for him to pursue other progressive programs. Although April 10 was declared a national day of mourning in late 1937,[95] the Zapata memorial ceremonies were overshadowed that year and the next by controversy over Cárdenas' "leftist" actions: the granting of exile status to Leon Trotsky in 1937 and the expropriation of the foreign oil companies in 1938.

The expropriation and subsequent nationalization of the petroleum industry produced an immediate political and economic crisis that deepened during the remaining years of Cárdenas' term in office but had little impact on the Zapata *homenajes*. In 1939 the ceremonies were larger and more fully reported, probably because it was the twentieth anniversary of his death. (The fifth, tenth, and fifteenth anniversaries also had larger than normal celebrations.) The only thing unusual in the 1940 commemorative events was the exhibition in Cuautla of the blood-stained clothes that Zapata had been wearing when killed.[96] The press duly reported the physical details of the *homenajes*—the decorations, who donated flowers, and so on—while the memorial speakers recited the litany of Zapata's virtues.

The commemorative speeches gave some indication of the difficult situation. With politics becoming increasingly polarized, Vicente Lombardo Toledano (Mexico's chief labor leader) reaffirmed the "unity of the . . . men of the revolution of yesterday and the present directors, who, under . . . Cárdenas, actualize the most profoundly revolutionary program of our times."[97] Perhaps as part of the attempt to ease polarization, the party newspaper, *El Nacional*, ceded its role as the most vocal champion of the administration to Lombardo Toledano's newly founded *El Popular*. *El Popular* made the strongest attack on Cárdenas' conservative opponents ("little groups of reactionary agitators and stale old rebels"), including Díaz Soto y Gama ("ex-anarchist, intellectualoid traitor, sometime Christian, and finally, counterrevolutionary conspirator and fascist").[98]

In addition to attacking the right, Lombardo Toledano defended Cárdenas against leftist charges that his moderation and choice of Manuel Ávila Camacho would undermine the advances made by the Revolution. "It is a lie that the Revolution of yesterday and today can be diverted!" he said. "The Revolution is one, permanent, and indivisible."[99]

Exhortations to defend the Revolution against reactionaries had been heard since the days of Madero, but in 1940 they had new meaning because the right-wing presidential candidate, Almazán, was extremely popular. Although *El Nacional* toned down its attention to the anniversary of Zapata's death, leaving *El Popular* to be the chief glorifier of the fallen hero, it nevertheless chose the occasion to print an imaginary dialogue about the political situation:

You, the revolutionaries, always attacked each other because of brutal personalisms. . . .

You're right, . . . there were many heated personal struggles. . . . But the *caudillos* back then . . . were absolutely all revolutionaries and had, at bottom, the same intentions. They did not argue about programs: they fought for power.

. . . And it has continued like that for many years: Obregón against Bonillas; Calles against de la Huerta; Vasconcelos against Ortiz Rubio; Villarreal against Cárdenas. . . . And they were called reactionaries or impositionists. And there was blood many times. . . .

. . . In none of those cases . . . was the revolution in danger: all the candidates . . . were revolutionaries. One . . . or the other winning, the Revolution would have continued on its march. . . .

And now?

Now things have changed drastically. The battle is shaping up and the old revolutionaries of all kinds are joining. . . .

. . . the same as before: revolutionaries against revolutionaries. . . .

That's not true. . . . Now, more than ever, the old truism . . . "The Revolution is the Revolution" is realized. . . . Now, for the first time since 1913, the reaction confronts the Revolution.[100]

Rather than clearly defining the politics that made the government and its candidate, Ávila Camacho, worthy of support, this propagandist took the traditional way out—appealing to nationalism and invoking the Revolution, which had to be preserved not only from counterrevolutionary Mexicans but from foreign countries as well. Continued American opposition to the expropriation of the oil companies and rumblings about an invasion of Mexico provided a perfect cause for rallying support for Cárdenas.

The nationalization of the petroleum industry also permitted Cárdenas to be praised as a radical at the same time that serious questions about his "revolutionary" policies were smothered by patriotic rhetoric. At Cuautla, where Cárdenas' seizure of the oil industry was likened to Zapata's seizure of hacienda land, Lombardo Toledano declared the unionists' full support of the expropriation:

Now . . . a foreign government threatens us, . . . for that reason this homage acquires the proportions of a protest against that threat. . . . Because we had achieved part of our ideal . . . the ideal of Zapata . . . I have come to proclaim that before permitting what Mexico has already accomplished to be taken away, . . . the workers of the CTM will die. . . . [101]

Miguel Alemán, representing Ávila Camacho (and himself a future president), echoed similar sentiments:

[We] call on all Mexicans so that, united by the legitimate position of our government and the patriotic attitude of President Cárdenas, we will be able to defend Mexico . . . against any foreign incursion. [102]

The militancy of the speeches, however, belied the actual relations between the United States and Mexico at the time. The growing war in Europe, which reduced the flow of oil from the Middle East, encouraged President Roosevelt to seek friendlier relations with Mexico in order to concentrate on the war effort and to make sure that Mexico would not sell oil to the Axis powers. The U.S. government acquiesced to the expropriation of the oil companies. This constituted a victory for Cárdenas, but a compromised one, for the selection of Ávila Camacho was already a concession to North American and domestic fears of his socialist bent. The Mexican government could therefore count on the United States' support against the opposition movement.[103]

Cárdenas, then, preserved the Revolution by making it less revolutionary. It should be remembered that despite his popular sympathies, Cárdenas had been a carrancista, not a villista or zapatista, during the revolution, and despite his progressive vision of the role of the state, he had been a faithful PNR man since 1929. In short, Cárdenas believed firmly in strong government and the institutional Revolution. The limitations of the institutional Revolution were demonstrated by Cárdenas' management of the crisis of the late 1930s, when the institutional stability and the reformist policies of the government became dangerously incompatible. Perceiving a need to choose one or the other, Cárdenas chose to protect the government. This, his administration argued, was the best way to secure the gains already made.

Not everyone agreed. Many felt that concessions to the conservative opposition did not secure the Revolution, but only rendered it moribund. The government was not saving the life of the Revolution, it was merely preserving its corpse.

Still the Mexican government adamantly maintained that it was revolutionary. It accused critics of its conservative direction of being unpatriotic because they had "exotic" definitions of what a revolution should be. The notion of the inherent correctness of *lo mexicano* was used to justify the government's claim that it was revolutionary. At the 1940 Zapata memorial, Alemán proclaimed that "the Mexican Revolution should be proud of itself because rather than resorting to an imitation of foreign examples in its doctrine and method, with full consciousness of its reality and its destiny, it travels toward the future, procuring the happiness of all the nation."[104]

Since 1940, the Mexican government has continued to identify itself as the Revolution even though there is little revolutionary about it. Yet Zapata, rather than the more appropriate Madero or Carranza, has become the major official revolutionary hero today.

The contrast between the rise of Zapata's hero status and the decline of Madero's reveals limitations of the official hero cults and the way in which they functioned as a form of co-optation.

In the case of Madero, the government merely capitalized on his widespread popularity, although in the 1920s and 1930s it also struggled against maderista opposition groups for sole "possession" of Madero as a political symbol. Quite the opposite occurred with Zapata, whose popularity barely extended beyond his home territory or beyond his class. There were few middle-class zapatistas, and the government had absorbed a goodly number of them. The campesinos did not have ready means to challenge the government's appropriation of Zapata had they wished to do so. As a result, the government had almost exclusive domain over the propagation of Zapata's heroic image.

However, the lack of middle-class competitors for the mantle of Zapata did not assure the success of the official hero cult, for it also indicated how little the middle classes supported or cared about zapatismo. Between 1915 and 1940 maderismo was the subject of numerous novels, as was Villa, who also figured in both Mexican and North American movies. Yet Zapata or zapatismo was the main topic of only two novels during that period, although for the sake of argument the supporting role in the 1933 movie *El Compadre Mendoza* could be construed as a Zapata-like character.[105] The official cult may have improved Zapata's image and certainly increased his fame, but it apparently did not arouse the imagination of the general population. Zapata remained very much the hero of the campesino class.

It seems probable that the class identity accounts for the continued growth of the Zapata cult after 1940. It was suggested in the previous chapter that the Madero cult faded after 1940 because the greater satisfaction of the middle class lessened the need for propaganda aimed at that segment of the population. But the policies that satisfied the middle class did not equally benefit the lower classes, least of all the rural poor. By the 1960s the campesinos were carrying out various forms of protest against government policies and what they regarded as socioeconomic injustices. Rural poverty has worsened as the development of agribusiness has forced more peasants off the land. Zapata's motto, "The land belongs to those who work it," remained meaningful to campesinos, who often invoke Zapata's name in their protests.

The continued relevance of zapatismo has made it necessary for the government to continually try to coopt it. The struggle to "possess" Zapata as a symbol is most evident in the government's efforts to move Zapata's grave from Cuautla to Mexico City to be officially entombed near Madero, Carranza, and Villa. But one of Zapata's sons has refused to permit this final confirmation of his father's status as a symbol of a government that still has not fulfilled the goals of zapatismo. Despite the long effort to make Zapata a part of the official hagiography, he is still a vital and unfixed political symbol. It remains to be seen whether he will finally be a symbol of the Revolution or of revolution.

CHAPTER 4

The Public Image of Venustiano Carranza

Venustiano Carranza was a prominent, moderately wealthy citizen of the northern state of Coahuila. During the *porfiriato* he had served as mayor of his hometown, Cuatro Cienagas, as deputy and senator to the national congress, and as state governor. At the age of fifty he joined Madero's revolt, and after the maderista triumph he again became governor of Coahuila.[1] When Madero and Pino Suárez were assassinated, Carranza repudiated Huerta's illegal government and, in the *Plan de Guadalupe* of March 26, 1913, announced the formation of a Constitutionalist army that would fight to reestablish a democracy. Carranza himself was to be the *Primer Jefe* (First Chief) of the army and, upon Huerta's defeat, was to serve as president of Mexico until popular elections could be held.[2]

The Constitutionalist Army grew rapidly, winning successive victories over government forces as it advanced from the north toward Mexico City. Although the zapatistas did not recognize Carranza as their leader, their war against Huerta in the south helped the constitucionalistas, as did the countless small groups which took up arms against local huertista authorities. In July 1914 these combined revolutionary forces succeeded in overthrowing Huerta.

By then, however, Carranza was losing power. From the outset, Carranza's national prominence had been mostly a function of his role as the avenger of Madero's death—a reflection of Huerta's unpopularity rather than his own popularity. Carranza inspired little admiration as the commander of the Constitutionalist Army, whose true military leaders were Obregón and Villa. And many revolutionaries were alienated by Carranza's upper-class demeanor and

his punctilious insistence on his own authority. Villa, who claimed
he had at first respected Carranza as the leader of the war against
Huerta, changed his mind when he met him:

I then believed I had in front of me . . . an owner of an hacienda, not an
interpreter of the hopes of the laboring people; and if Madero impressed
me as a rich man capable of giving the shirt off his back to help a poor
man, [Carranza] struck me as a greedy man capable of leaving a poor man
shirtless.[3]

Carranza was in fact more conservative than many insurrectionists. By simply seizing hacienda lands, campesinos throughout
Mexico demonstrated that agrarian reform was a major purpose of
the revolution, but Carranza was not convinced. In some cases where
his officers had turned confiscated land over to campesinos, Carranza returned the land to the *hacendados*,[4] although he had fewer
objections to expropriating foreign companies and landowners.[5]
Carranza's critics believed that he at times jeopardized the revolution in order to subordinate Villa and to gain personal advantage.
Carranza had, for example, promoted Obregón and González, giving their troops the official status of "armies," while keeping Villa's
more important army at the official status of "division." On several
occasions Carranza had ordered Villa to halt his southward advance
and to divert his troops to less important objectives, and had denied supplies to Villa's army. There was no military advantage in
these moves, but there was political advantage, for if Obregón
reached Mexico City first, the glory of "winning" the revolution
would go to him and he would be able to set up a political situation
favorable to Carranza.[6]
Such criticisms did not bother many people who believed that
Villa and men like Villa—crude, uneducated, deeply resentful of
the upper classes—would be unable to govern Mexico according to
modern civilized norms and would lead the country into anarchy
and economic ruin. Carranza also gained support as a nationalist
because of his vociferous protests against the North American invasion of Veracruz in 1914. He declared that the protection of
Mexico's sovereignty should take precedence over factional struggles and rejected all U.S. government efforts to mediate a settlement of the revolution as an intolerable interference in Mexico's

internal affairs. Carranza assumed the role of the nation's spokesman and demonstrated his ability to perform well in international diplomacy. Carrancista apologists pointed to Villa's and Zapata's weak protests against the occupation of Veracruz as evidence of their provincialism and impugned their patriotism by arguing that they were concerned only with their factional struggles and not with the good of the nation.[7]

With Huerta gone, Carranza expected to assume the interim presidency according to the provisions of the *Plan de Guadalupe*. He attempted to convene the revolutionaries (minus the zapatistas, who still did not acknowledge his leadership) to formulate policies for the new government. But the reformist trend had grown too strong, and too many Constitutionalists had grown disaffected with Carranza. When Carranza proposed that the Convention take place in Mexico City, where he had the greatest influence, and Villa insisted that it take place in Aguascalientes, a city close to his stronghold, it was Villa who had his way.

In Aguascalientes the Convention delegates declared themselves the sovereign revolutionary assembly, no longer subordinate to the *Plan de Guadalupe* or the *Primer Jefe*. They invited the zapatistas to attend and formulated a program that incorporated the essence of the *Plan de Ayala*. Carranza found the program unacceptably radical and was outraged by what he regarded as the Convention's rebellious proceedings.

The Constitutionalists split between those who still supported Carranza and those who supported the Convention, which in effect meant Villa.[8] The carrancistas were generally more middle-class and conservative, although some reformists went with Carranza because they doubted Villa's capacity to govern. Those supporting the Convention tended to have humbler origins and a greater desire for reform, although some middle-class insurrectionists sided with Villa because they felt Carranza to be too autocratic. In the autumn of 1914, the two sides went to war—Villa and Zapata heading the Convention's forces and Obregón heading the carrancista army.

At first the convencionistas made rapid strides against the carrancistas, but Villa and Zapata failed to press their advantage or establish a viable government, which seemed to substantiate charges that they were unfit to govern the country. It also gave the carrancistas time to develop a political plan of attack.

Fortunately for Carranza, some of his advisors understood that the Convention's success was due largely to its promise of reform and that he would have to make concessions to the masses to regain a significant following. General Obregón pressured Carranza to decree various labor and agrarian reforms. The most famous of these, the Law of January 6th (1915), restored the communal land, water, and woods that villages had lost during the *porfiriato*; it also gave villages that had no claims to land the right to acquire it from adjacent areas and empowered the government to expropriate land in order to donate it to a needy village.[9]

Obregón continued to work to persuade the popular classes that carrancismo served their interests. When his army occupied Mexico City, Obregón took strong measures to remedy the food shortages there, feeding people and punishing merchants who hoarded or speculated with food or other basic commodities. He also forced the clergy to contribute to the war effort, conscripting those who would not—a move that helped win over the frequently anti-clerical urban radicals and organized labor.[10]

Obregón's policies gave him a personal following which he would later use against Carranza, but in the short run they won support for Carranza. More men joined the carrancista army, and in mid-1915 at Celaya Obregón led his troops to victory over Pancho Villa. In Mexico City, Carranza established a provisional government, which the United States recognized in October 1915. In late 1916 Carranza convened revolutionary leaders to formulate a new constitution, and this time there were no villistas or zapatistas among the delegates.

Nevertheless, a split between conservatives (those closer to Carranza) and reformists (those closer to Obregón) occurred once again, and once again the reformists prevailed.[11] On February 5, 1917, in the city of Queretaro (date and place of the promulgation of the 1857 constitution), the convention passed what at the time was one of the most progressive national constitutions in the world.[12]

On that same date, the last U.S. soldiers of the so-called Punitive Expedition were withdrawn from Mexican soil, thereby closing a very tense episode in U.S.—Mexican relations. The Punitive Expedition had entered Mexico some eleven months earlier in response to Pancho Villa's raid on Columbus, New Mexico. Although Carranza's critics charged that his defense of Mexico's sovereignty had not been as swift and adamant as it should have been, Carranza did protest the presence of Yankee troops in Mexico. And whereas both Obregón and diplomat Luis Cabrera, fearing a full confrontation with the United States, had on separate occasions negotiated settlements that restricted but did not end the operations of the expedition, Carranza refused to approve those agreements and insisted on the complete withdrawal of the expedition. President Wilson finally backed down, and Carranza improved his stature as an able, nationalist statesman.[13]

Carranza became the constitutional president of Mexico in May 1917. Neither Villa nor Zapata recognized his presidency, but they were fighting a losing battle. It was the high point of Carranza's career.

Yet Carranza soon sowed the seeds of his own destruction. In effect, he rescinded the concessions he had made to win support for his campaign against the convencionistas. Although he would ever after reap glory as "the Father of the Constitution," Carranza did not implement the reforms it mandated. On the contrary, he permitted many *hacendados* to retain or reacquire land while villages went wanting; federal officers sometimes served the local landowners' interests or became *hacendados* themselves.[14] Carranza persecuted the labor movement and revived an old law that made strikes illegal and punishable by death.[15] The masses of people were unable to discern what they had gained from the revolution.

In contrast, the carrancistas benefitted immensely. Their highest echelon mingled with what remained of the traditional elite, accumulated fortunes, and publicly paraded its new wealth and status. The lower echelons, including the troops, acquired such a reputation for pillaging villages and molesting civilians that a new vocabulary resulted: *carrancear* (to act like Carranza) meant "to steal"; *carranclán* (a play on the Spanish word for hurricane) referred to the damage caused by an encounter with carrancistas; and the nickname *conlasuñaslistas* (with the claws ready) ridiculed the carrancistas as avaricious, predatory animals.[16]

The ill repute of his supporters weakened Carranza's popularity, which had been tepid from the start. The popular ballads of the day suggest that popular attitudes toward Carranza degenerated from indifference to outright hostility during his presidency.[17]

But Carranza's most serious problem stemmed from his alienation of the military. Although he tolerated their corruption, Carranza was reluctant to share political power with the numerous generals produced by the years of war. Many generals, however, believed that political power was their due for having fought the revolution and that the military should have a place in government. They, along with those who objected to other aspects of Carranza's rule, expected things to change with the next presidential election. Conservatives hoped that Carranza would back the candidacy of his favorite, General Pablo González, while others thought he would lend support to the popular General Obregón.

Carranza disappointed them all by choosing Ignacio Bonillas as his presidential candidate. Carrancistas defended the selection on the grounds that the First Chief wished to assure that Mexico would have a civilian government because military leaders tended toward dictatorial rule. His critics, however, claimed that Carranza had chosen a weak candidate in order to prolong his influence after his presidency ended. The election of Bonillas, they said, would be tantamount to the reelection of Carranza, who therefore violated the spirit (if not the letter) of the maderista tenet "effective suffrage, no reelection."[18]

When, in April 1920, Obregón and other military leaders denounced Carranza as a traitor to the revolution, the Revolt of Agua Prieta was quickly joined by most military and political leaders in Mexico. Carranza fled Mexico City with his small coterie of remaining supporters and a good part of the national treasury, bound for Veracruz where presumably he would have sailed into exile as Huerta and Díaz had done before him. But his train was attacked by rebels, and he and his party took to the hills. They were intercepted by a squad of men led by Rodolfo Herrero, who, though a supporter of Obregón, identified himself as a carrancista and led them to a "safe" camp in the tiny village of Tlaxcalantongo. Early in the morning of May 21, Carranza was shot to death when Herrero and his men made a surprise attack on the camp.[19]

Carranza's death created a sensation in Mexico City. Herrero reportedly had at first told Calles that Carranza committed suicide when he realized he was about to be captured; newspapers in Mexico City reported that Carranza died in combat with Herrero's troops, then that he had been shot in his sleep.[20]

Had Carranza been killed in outright battle, his death probably

would not have caused much scandal. That it occurred in a treach-
erous sneak attack, and that none of Carranza's party seemed to
have made much effort to protect him but instead immediately declared their loyalty to Obregón, apparently offended the public's
sense of fairplay and further reminded them that violence was still
used to resolve factional differences. Suspicions that Herrero had
acted on orders from a higher authority would persist (and be
strengthened when Herrero was recommissioned as an army officer
after only a few years in prison), but Obregón's immediate reaction
was to disavow all responsibility for Carranza's death. Obregón
publicly repudiated the allegiance proffered by the men who had
been with Carranza at Tlaxcalantongo, stating that the fact that
none of them had been wounded in the attack suggested that they
had not even tried to defend their *jefe*. They were, he said, disloyal
cowards whose support would be as worthless to him as it had
been to Carranza.[21]

Such a scathing denunciation of those men's alleged disloyalty
would seem hypocritical coming from the man who only weeks
before had himself rebelled against Carranza. Obregón ignored his
vital role in creating the conditions that led to Carranza's assassination, blaming instead the men who accompanied the First Chief:
" . . . all the Nation knows," he wrote, "that you are necessarily
the ones most responsible for the unfortunate events that have so
disturbed the Republic during these last weeks."[22] In this way
Obregón implied that he put principles above all else and thereby
presented the Agua Prieta revolt as one of patriotic, revolutionary
ideals rather than of personal ambition. Obregón's scornful reaction
also involved a degree of macho posturing, for loyalty to one's *jefe*
was one of machismo's most dearly held values; "real" men's respect for other "real" men and their disdain for those who violated
the manly code of honor were supposed to transcend "mere" political differences.

Nevertheless, the widespread enmity toward Carranza outlived
the indignation caused by his assassination. The means used to re-
move him from power appalled some, but few were sorry that he
had been removed. Whereas the deaths of Madero, Zapata, and
Villa produced a spate of *corridos* that sang their praise, Carranza's
death produced a spate of *corridos* that condemned him,[23] and during the next two decades the novelists who referred to him did so

"with unanimous hostility and bitterness," regardless of whether they were "radical or conservative."[24]

Not surprisingly, no official honors were extended to Carranza when the aguaprietistas took power. He was buried in a humble grave without the pomp of a presidential funeral.[25] There were no official commemorations of the anniversary of Carranza's death during the rest of the decade, while the anniversaries of Madero's and Zapata's deaths served as occasions to revile the erstwhile *Primer Jefe*.

There were of course some loyal carrancistas, of whom only General Francisco Murguía had opposed Obregón's takeover militarily, only to be killed for his effort. Many carrancistas felt compelled to leave Mexico, and those who stayed tended to keep a low profile; very few participated in the private graveside memorials held by the Carranza family every year.

In 1925 the memorials began to grow larger, more public, and attracted more press coverage, probably because Obregón was no longer president. But while the press generally refrained from criticizing Carranza on these occasions, dislike for the carrancistas was still evident. Echoing the earlier charge that Carranza's friends were disloyal to him, *Excelsior* wrote: "It is curious to note that the majority of persons that attended this ceremony belonged to the popular classes and that many of those who enjoyed favors during the carrancista regime were most conspicuous in their absence. *Sic transit gloria mundi.*"[26]

The memorials attracted the greatest attention when the controversial intellectual and government critic Luis Cabrera gave the key address, which he did with some frequency. Over the years Cabrera had praised Carranza as a "strong man in every sense of the word," a man of "tranquil strength" and "natural nobility," whose image "grows every day, as the majesty of the volcanoes grows when we are more distant from them."[27] But it was Cabrera's criticism of Obregón's bid for reelection that made the memorial front-page news in 1927.

In his "Discourse of Political Transcendence," Cabrera compared Obregón's actions to Carranza's attempt to "impose" Bonillas in 1920—a comparison which could make Obregón look worse or Carranza better, but in either case lessened the distance that Obregón tried to keep between himself and his former *jefe*. Carranza fell, said Cabrera, because he underestimated the opposition to re-election (even if by proxy) and because of the "impatience of the militarists" who interpreted his desire for a civilian government as a desire to perpetuate his own power. Cabrera implied that people should reject Obregón and the ruling "militarists" and look for a new man "whose soul is not yet infected with the intrigue of the meeting." If they lacked the strength to do that, said Cabrera, directing a barb at the audience's machismo, they should "bravely accept the sterility of your mothers . . . ; cry like women for the liberty you did not know how to defend like men."[28]

Nevertheless, Obregón was reelected. But in the wake of his assassination, conflict between obregonistas and callistas became so severe that Calles orchestrated the reorganization of Mexico's political system to counteract the factionalism that had destabilized it for a decade. Complementing the structural changes was a propaganda campaign for unity which brought Carranza out of the cold and into the bosom of the Revolutionary family.

The first official commemoration of Carranza's death occurred in 1930, with ceremonies throughout the capital, including one (in the new spirit of forgive and forget) at the Álvaro Obregón Civic Center.[29] The usual graveside ceremony was attended by 150 people—a small number compared to the thousands who attended the Zapata and Madero memorials, but a large number for a Carranza memorial.[30] They heard "the Man from Cuatro Cienagas" praised as the "soul of the Revolution against General Victoriano Huerta, usurper of Public Power." *El Nacional* reported the ceremony on its front page, and the accompanying photograph was captioned "The Revolution has done full justice to the initiator of social reform in Mexico, recognizing despite all his errors, his indisputable glory."[31]

The next year the Mexican Congress formally incorporated Carranza into the pantheon of national heroes, striking a symbolic blow against factionalism by incorporating Zapata at the same time. But the incorporation of Carranza (or any hero) was more than a way of honoring him. It was also a way of encouraging a worshipful attitude toward "leaders" and of institutionalizing this somewhat authoritarian aspect of patriarchy as part of the state's cultural apparatus, thereby making obeisance to state symbols an essential part of "true" manliness. Speaking of Carranza, one *diputado* declared:

Veneration of the heroes, the consecration of the great men . . . in your
history, is a duty for everyone; . . . because the least that can be asked of
a man is that in order to be a man, he must know how to be grateful. . . .
Carranza acquires the contours of greatness as time passes. . . .
        . . . I remember [the] figure of [this] upright man, . . . the penetrating
look . . . prudent and wise, respectful and strong."[32]

The congressman went on to laud Don Venustiano for his unswerving opposition to the Yankee occupation of Veracruz and for
the social reforms decreed when he later held the same city, "where
the clear spring of nationalism shone, and the Carranza doctrine,
beyond covering the country's territory, seemed to extend over the
entire continent, an augury of better days."[33]

Despite the fanfare of 1930, in the next several years the government exhibited little determination to glorify Carranza. The official
ceremonies in his honor did not have the grandiose proportions that
other memorials had, nor were federal employees sent to them or
campesinos brought in for the occasion, as was the case with the
Madero and Zapata memorials. But even though Carranza's public
stature did not approach that of other revolutionary heroes, his place
in the official hagiography improved slowly.

Increased complaints about public indifference to Carranza sig-
naled this improvement. In an effusive article in *El Universal* on
May 20, 1932, José Guadalupe Mainero declared, "It is time to
prepare ourselves for . . . the rude debate that must be sustained
in order to take Carranza out of . . . the oblivion in which many
hold him or from the execration in which his enemies try to keep
him." History would know how to judge Carranza, but Mainero
considered it "lamentable that the cult of our heroes has been constantly debilitated or suspended for fleeting considerations." Those
fleeting considerations were undoubtedly political ones, reflecting
the notion that "politics" were less important than individual leaders. The same patriarchal spirit that moved the *diputado* who said
that veneration of heroes is everyone's duty also moved Mainero to
warn that "people that do not keep the fire of Vesta burning for
those who are worthy of it, also do not succeed in being inspired
by the example of superior lives. That loyalty to the eminent dead
is a fruitful value."

At the time of the 1933 memorial, "a movement to do justice" to

Carranza was said to have "commenced as political passions disappear[ed],"[34] and at the 1934 memorial Luis Cabrera alluded to this
change, declaring that "now . . . history . . . seems perplexed by
the prattle . . . that overturns whole libraries in search of words
with which to condemn him. . . . " The duty of Carranza's "friends
and admirers" was to show "history his patriotic works [that are]
the cornerstone over which it will have to erect a monument to his
immortality."[35] (As usual, Cabrera aroused special interest in the
Carranza memorial. Two anti-reelectionist parties had considered
running him against the PNR in the 1934 election, but Cabrera
rejected the PNR and the opposition parties as two faces of the
obregonismo that had overthrown Carranza. He called the entire
electoral process a farce and said he would refuse any party nomi-
nation offered to him.)[36]

Unlike Madero, Carranza did not suffer from an effeminate or
pusillanimous image (although he was satirized as Sir [*don*] Venus)
but neither did he possess the macho appeal of Zapata and Villa.
From the early years of the Constitutionalist movement, Carranza's
apologists had tried to give him a manly image based on the other
model of patriarchal manhood, the macho's austere and responsible
alter ego, the father figure. They played upon the fact that he was
the eldest and only full-bearded revolutionary leader to give him
the image of a heroic patriarch,[37] and reinterpreted his reputation
for stubbornness and egotism as single-minded, unswerving dedication to his revolutionary vision. An article by Fernando Cuen in
El Universal on May 21, 1934, provides one of the most hyperbolic
examples of this image of Carranza:

Of tranquil and majestic features. . . . [By] the constant and extreme tension in his nerve cords his soul's profound and concentrated work is perceived. . . . He has the lofty commanding quality of Michelangelo's "Moses"
. . . the rectitude of the *caudillo*, in whose spirit resonates the imperious
forces that triumphs and subjugates. . . . His public life is severe and
august. His attitude always dignified, noble. . . . All his ideas, concise,
luminous, and exact, exude loftiness and greatness. His private life is ex-
emplary, of spartan simplicity.

In addition to giving Carranza's dour figure a Mosaic or Olym-
pian aura, Cuen portrayed him as a fiery, indefatigable warrior.

Although this manly image was more suited to popular tastes, it was a far-fetched characterization of Carranza and more appropriate for Villa, whose macho glamor Cuen may have been trying to steal when he claimed that Don Venustiano

inspires and personifies . . . the insurrectional movement. At . . . his voice, armies spring forth from the earth. He is the numen of the revolution. . . . overwhelming the enemy with fearlessness, audacity and energy, he gallops across the plains of the North, . . . with impressive courage he crosses over the fields.

Reminding the reader that Carranza was "virile, made of iron," Cuen lengthily praised his patriotic stance during the invasion of Veracruz and compared him to Christ ("denied by his disciples . . . , betrayed and sold by one of the many Judases that people our history"). Cuen closed with the standard remarks about Carranza's anti-militarism and about his true glory being recognized as "time purified" the "passions."

Carranza, the most conservative revolutionary leader, finally achieved the recognition his devotees had long awaited during the administration of the most progressive post-revolutionary president, Lázaro Cárdenas. This counterintuitive turn of events resulted from the alliances that Cárdenas made to secure his power and to break the *Jefe Maximo*'s decisive political influence.

One of those alliances was with Carranza's son-in-law General Cándido Aguilar, who had left Mexico because of his part in the failed De la Huerta Revolt and returned a decade later to become the senator of Veracruz. As a stalwart carrancista, Aguilar might have been expected to support Cárdenas' conservative opponents. However, many of those opponents (Calles himself and Díaz Soto y Gama, among others) apparently had been too involved in the revolt against Carranza to be acceptable to Aguilar, who instead worked with the leftist camp of the government. In late 1935 he assumed the powerful position of president of the Senate, which, combined with his influence among some conservatives, made him a desirable ally for Cárdenas.[38] The improvement in Carranza's official image may have been part of Cárdenas' efforts to win Aguilar's support, or it may have been a direct result of Aguilar's own increased power.

Carranza's image also benefitted from the campaign to discredit Calles and Obregón after the exile of the former in 1936. Obregón was condemned for the Bucareli agreement, Calles for his reputed susceptibility to the conservatism of U.S. Ambassador Dwight Morrow, and both for their general cooperativeness with U.S. business.[39] Although their reasons were different, the cardenistas and the loyal carrancistas disliked the two men who had dominated Mexico since 1920. As the images of Calles and especially Obregón, Carranza's enemies, were tarnished with a barrage of criticism, Carranza's image shone comparatively brighter.

In an atmosphere so propitious for airing suspicions, rumors, and long-kept secrets about Calles and Obregón, the press revived discussion of the Huitzilac Massacre and the possibility of high-level obregonistas' responsibility for Carranza's assassination. There was also new interest in punishing Rodolfo Herrero, who led the attack in which Carranza died, and railroad workers in Veracruz petitioned to reopen the investigation of the assassination.[40] Aguilar and his wife (Carranza's daughter) presided over the 1937 Carranza memorial, which was called "especially interesting" because the speakers felt freer than before to "expound their ideas without going in circles or mincing words." A visit was made to the grave of General Francisco Murguía, who had been killed opposing the Revolt of Agua Prieta.[41]

From 1937 to 1939 *El Nacional* gave extensive coverage to the Carranza memorials, organized by the *Asociación Venustiano Carranza* and the Department of the Federal District's *Acción Cívica* with all the trappings of a state ritual. Police bands played, choirs sang, and speakers elegized the *Varón de Cuatro Ciénagas* (Man from Cuatro Ciénagas) in extravagant terms. "Mexican mothers are sad," said one, "because they know they cannot give the *Patria* more men like Carranza."[42]

The Carranza of the elegies differed from the one mockingly dubbed Don Venus some twenty-five years earlier. His deeds and personality were reinterpreted to make him a suitable cardenista hero. Deputy José María de la Garza portrayed him as a true agrarian reformer and even as the true precursor of socialism in Mexico.[43] At the 1939 *homenaje* a campesino gave thanks for the land his community (Ixtapalapa) received under Carranza, and Cárdenas' secretary, Luis Rodríguez, called Carranza "the purest man of the Revolution."[44]

Such unprecedented acclaim provoked some skepticism. One newspaper noted that "if Venustiano Carranza had had so many followers before, he could have confronted and beaten the supporters of the Agua Prieta [revolt]."[45]

In 1939 the carrancistas Francisco Coss and Leon Ossorio, of the ultra-right National Party of Public Salvation, disrupted the Carranza memorial, presumably because they objected to the government's representation of their former First Chief. After some commotion, Ossorio managed to speak. "It seems it has been systematically attempted to prevent free men from talking to the people on this anniversary," he said, "rudely" attacking the *Acción Cívica* organizers as "budget-eaters" (*presupuestivores*) and belittling their manhood by calling them "babes at the breast who do not know about these things." The newspaper did not say what those things were, but a good guess would be that Ossorio referred to the "truth" about Carranza and the revolution.[46]

One of the organizers "recommended that they respect the ceremony and refrain from expressing political ideas . . . that were not suitable for a ceremony of mourning, especially one in which an illustrious citizen and pure Mexican like Don Venustiano Carranza was honored."[47] The "agitators" Coss and Ossorio, described as agents of imperialist countries,[48] did of course express political ideas, "spouting calumnies against the Mexican people and their government." Nevertheless, their anxiousness to deny their political purpose ("I am a man," said Ossorio, "and I make politics from the balcony of the *Partido Nacional de Salvación Pública*. . . . ")[49] suggested that they shared with the organizers the common notion that such events should be above politics, which were implicitly seen as incompatible with "higher" feelings and rational judgement. This notion lay behind the headline "The Tomb of Venustiano Carranza Profaned" and behind the statements that the ceremony had come close to "degenerating into a political meeting" and that "as passions dilute, Carranza stands out more vigorously and provokes more admiration."[50]

The government was in fact "making politics" as much as Coss and Ossorio were, but its purposes were best served by appearing to be apolitical. By making Carranza and the memorial sacrosanct, social pressures concerning proper reverential behavior could be utilized to silence attempts to submit the government to an embarrassing historical or ideological scrutiny. Carranza's official heroization fended off the harsh criticisms leveled at him in years past, but it also reduced the possibility of criticizing the government by co-opting carrancismo, which could therefore no longer stand as a political alternative to the status quo.

Popular resignation to the suppression of criticism related to the belief that politics were inexplicable. One 1938 commemorative article rhetorically asked

Who provoked the Revolution? Madero!—answer the intellectuals of the past.—Porfirio Díaz!—answer the intellectuals of the left.—But intellectuality has been bankrupt for a long time. . . . The causes of revolutions are as obscure as those of earthquakes. A revolution erupts as do the rocks and springs after a geological process of millions of years.[51]

On the surface, this apolitical, anti-intellectual fatalism contradicted the "leftist" ideology of the Cárdenas administration, but it also facilitated the task of getting the population to conform with government policies, whatever they might be. As the political situation polarized, the government propagandists stressed the patriotic correctness of respecting the law and the country's institutions. It was perhaps inevitable under such circumstances that Carranza, "the Father of the 1917 Constitution," would develop as a symbol of law—the "paladin of constitutional rights" and the "paladin of legality." Carranza, said one speaker, "personified morality and the law and was the teacher of civic-mindedness."[52] In 1940 the *Asociación Venustiano Carranza* awarded medals to old carrancistas who were "faithful to Carranza and therefore to legality."[53]

Such stress on lawfulness in turn continued the inflation of Carranza's image as a god ordering the universe or as a Moses-like figure who was

erect physically and morally; who never knew discouragement nor excesses, nor greed, nor envy; . . . cold and implacable, but also clement; master of his nerves, master of his will; lord of himself and lord of lords! It is the Father of the Revolution!. . . .

He ordered the Mexican chaos as did the father of the gods in ancient mythologies. By his will, light was made and in all the latitudes . . . arose a society very different from previous ones, humanized and just.[54]

This hyperbolic praise ignored Carranza's dislike of the progressive measures expedience forced him to support, and so bolstered the illusion of a unified Revolution. It also bolstered the notion that exceptional leaders, not the masses, change society—all in keeping with the authoritarian tendencies of the government and of the culture as a whole.

There is a certain irony in the fact that the greatest advance in Carranza's slow rise to official heroization related to Cárdenas' effort to hold the government together against pressures from the right, while the nominal basis for Carranza's heroization was the reforms he had decreed in 1915–1917 in an effort to hold his nascent government together against pressures from the left. The government did hold together, and it entered the 1940s institutionally sound and with a presidency more exclusively powerful than it had been since the *porfiriato*.

These changes, along with the government's new conservatism, made a hospitable climate for the continuation of the Carranza cult into the 1940s and, as "the Father of the Constitution" and the first president of the Constitutional government, Carranza would ever after have a place of honor in the official hagiography of the Revolution.

Nevertheless, Carranza's popularity was insufficient to bring any real liveliness to his public image. He was too narrowly a middle-class hero and completely lacked the reservoir of popular affection that buoyed up Madero's image even after maderismo became politically irrelevant. As the regime's conservatism and increased prosperity made it less necessary to woo middle-class support with propaganda, Carranza became a superfluous political symbol and subsided back into the oblivion from which the government had rescued him in the 1930s. In death as in life, Carranza would be eclipsed by Francisco Villa.

CHAPTER 5

The Public Image of Francisco Villa

When Francisco Villa joined the maderistas in 1910, he already had a reputation as a cattle thief in the northern state of Chihuahua—a reputation that earned him the dislike of wealthy ranchers but not that of the Chihuahuan campesinos.[1] Journalists reporting on the revolution picked up the tales told about him—his cruelty, his appetite for women, his erratic temperament, his audacity in battle—and when Madero became president, Villa increasingly captured the public eye as the defender of the new regime. After Madero's assassination Villa joined the Constitutionalist Army. At the head of the *División del Norte*, he became spectacularly popular as the invincible champion of the war against Huerta. "Spectacularly popular" because the press indeed treated Villa as a spectacle: less than human, more than human, a "force," "the Centaur of the North," but never just a man.

Many villistas believed that Villa was a friend of the poor and a true revolutionary. In general, however, Villa was not popular because people thought he was good or bad or politically correct or incorrect, but because he fascinated them. Tales of explosive cruelty back-to-back with tales of teary-eyed compassion titillated and thrilled the public imagination. Rutherford writes:

Villa provides an example of another . . . legend-creation process, in which there is not that alternation between [positive and negative images] found in the cases of Madero and Zapata, but a continuous coexistence of the two, and to a certain extent an overlapping of them. The revolutionary legend of Villa was never really concerned to deny the two principal elements of the black legend—Villa's rude ways with women and his wanton and arbitrary destruction of life—but rather to glamorize them and incorporate them into the picture it presents of a he-man hero in the Mexican tradition of machismo, overpowering, dominant and larger than life.[2]

The attention given Villa during the revolution resulted partly from circumstantial factors. His proximity to the United States automatically sparked more Yankee interest in him than in other revolutionary leaders. American reporters and even moviemakers flocked across the border to get the "scoop" on the bandit-revolutionary.[3]

The grand and "picturesque" way Villa waged war also attracted attention. Neither Madero nor Carranza could, properly speaking, be called fighters or soldiers. And Zapata fought a small-scale, cat-and-mouse guerrilla war which was, in any case, far from the eyes of the curious gringo onlookers.[4] Villa led massive cavalry charges across awesome expanses of desert; he moved trains, artillery, troops. Eventually, so too did Obregón, but his middle-class background lent no romance, no intrigue to his fame as a military genius.

In contrast, Villa was surrounded with mystery. Little was known about his past, except that he was born Doroteo Arango to an extremely poor family. It was said that at the age of seventeen he murdered his sister's rapist, a local landowner's son. He then went into hiding, became a bandit, and assumed the name the world would come to know him by.[5] And Villa's class-related traits—such as "quaint" speech, "rustic" mannerisms, a mode of thinking foreign to Yankees and middle-class Mexicans alike—helped make him an object of curiosity and bemused condescension to people from "better" social backgrounds. Villa's image, says Carlos Monsiváis, was that of a "Prehistoric Man in a Cartridge Belt": "The Hollywood attraction for Villa . . . would perhaps be explained in terms of the self-complacent hypnosis that the "primitive" provokes in the "civilized"; in terms of the fascination that, from the metropolis, Tarzan or King Kong awaken."[6]

The "metropolis," Mexico City, regarded both Villa and Zapata as primitives, yet found Zapata repugnant, not fascinating. The difference was due to Zapata's greater intractability. Whereas Villa had been called Madero's faithful dog, Zapata had disavowed Madero and continued his war against the haciendas. Also, Villa operated hundreds of miles from Mexico City, Zapata on its very doorstep. Tales of Villa's brutality and military exploits thrilled readers in the nation's capital, but marauding zapatistas only a few miles away threatened their lives, or so they imagined. Villa was the stuff of fantasy, Zapata of nightmares.

In sum, many circumstantial factors assured growing publicity for Villa. Publicity engendered interest which created an audience for more publicity which became "proof" of his popularity, and so on, in a spiral of what today is called "media hype."

Nevertheless, many high-ranking Constitutionalists regarded Villa as a semi-savage who could be used against Huerta but who should be denied political power.[7] Villa's military might, however, derived in part from his large and zealous personal following, which meant, *ipso facto*, that he did have political power.

Villa, who well knew his own importance, disliked Carranza and did not behave as his subordinate, which he nominally was. Carranza's attempts to force that subordination precipitated a rupture between the two men in the spring of 1914.[8] A group of officers who believed the rupture endangered the revolution arranged an uneasy reconciliation. In the Pact of Torreon of July 8, 1914,[9] Carranza agreed to meet Villa's requests for supplies for the *División del Norte*; Villa recognized Carranza as the *Primer Jefe* of the revolution but stipulated that upon victory delegates from the various revolutionary armies would convene to arrange a democratic presidential election and to set up a new government that would procure the well-being of workers and the economic emancipation of the campesinos through an equitable distribution of land.[10] These stipulations led to the Aguascalientes Convention several months later and opened the door to greater reform than Carranza wished to see in the Constitutionalist movement.

A week after the Pact of Torreon was signed, Huerta admitted defeat, but peace would prove elusive. Disagreement over the organization of the Aguascalientes Convention provoked the final split between Villa and Carranza.

The convencionistas soon controlled most of the country; Villa was at the height of his power when he met with Zapata in Mexico City in December 1914. Villa kept his army well supplied by selling cattle (taken from expropriated haciendas) in the United States, maintaining good relations with the United States' government and border business community in order to protect that trade. The expropriations freed Villa from the need to extract revenues from properties owned by U.S. citizens. Carranza, in contrast, attempted to protect Mexican landowners while forcing U.S. owners of Mexican land to make payments to him. Not surprisingly, the Americans favored Villa,[11] who, moreover, they believed would emerge the winner of Mexico's civil war.

The Americans, however, began to question whether they were backing the right man when Obregón did the impossible, defeating Villa at the battle of Celaya in April 1915. Also, in late 1914 Villa had begun to tax property owned by U.S. citizens because of the depletion of the cattle herds (a major source of revenue) and expanding war expenses; the resultant wavering of American business support created economic difficulties which further weakened Villa politically and militarily.[12] The decisive blow came in autumn of 1915 at the battle of Agua Prieta, where carrancista troops under General Calles were ill-supplied and cut off from the rest of their army. The advancing villistas seemed assured of victory. But President Woodrow Wilson, having recognized Carranza's government on the 19th of October, permitted carrancista troops and supplies to pass through U.S. territory to reinforce Agua Prieta. That reinforcement, combined with tactical and technical innovations, decimated the villistas.[13]

By that time Villa's social base was too eroded to sustain or to permit him to rebuild an army. Ironically, Villa's prosperous border trade had helped transform his ragtag "people's army" into a modern professional war machine dependent on foreign resources. His political policies were intended to protect those resources rather than to serve the common people of his region, who therefore were losing reasons to support Villa while Carranza's new reformism gave them more reason to support Carranza.[14] After his defeat at Celaya, Villa had hastened to transform his dream of a nation of happy farmers into a program of agrarian reform, but his efforts created problems with the conservative side of the villista leadership and came too late to recover lost popular support. As Villa lost territorial control, villista campesinos could not depend on him to protect them if their homes or towns fell to the carrancistas.[15] The best protection for their lives and property was to be on the winning side.

By December 1915 Villa retreated with a small contingent of men into the north-central region of Mexico. They degenerated into

brigandage but engaged in raids and skirmishes against the carrancistas, whose national strength continued to increase as villismo fell
to its lowest point.

Villa's decline disinfatuated many, but a more severe blow to his
image came from the political reversals that cast him into the role
of an "enemy of the Revolution." With Madero, the Constitutionalists, and the Convention, Villa had been at the forefront of the
insurgent masses. But as the carrancistas gained the support of the
lower classes in 1915 and 1916, Villa was excluded from the dominant course of the revolution. His glamor disappeared along with
his invincibility; only his reputation for barbarity remained, directed for the first time against the faction favored by the popular
classes.

Yet Villa's popularity survived. Worry about their safety caused
many campesinos in Villa's territory to withdraw their support from
him, apparently without nullifying his popular appeal. The *corridos*
of the era suggest that Villa's decline elicited sympathy from the
common people, who despite their awe for the irresistible Centaur
of the North, may have liked Villa more as an underdog. The *corridos* portrayed "a very human and humane Villa facing adversity
with grief but with dignity and apparently concerned more with
the well-being of his men than with the fortunes of battle."[16]

The fact that Villa's popularity did not dissolve with his strength
contradicts the stereotype of Latin American people blindly following whatever strongman comes along, as does the fact that Carranza inspired no popular enthusiasm even when he had the most
power. It seems possible that middle-class fascination with Villa
was the most fatuous, the most dependent on his indefatigability,
while among the campesinos his popularity stemmed from their
identification with him. To them he was not exotic, not an atavistic
curiosity, but one of their own.

Whatever its class variations, Villa's popularity revived nation-
ally when he attacked Columbus, New Mexico, on March 9, 1916.
Five hundred villistas sacked the town, killing seventeen *yanquis*.
That the U.S. Army killed over one hundred villistas did not di-
minish the thrill of nationalistic vengeance experienced by many
Mexicans of all classes.[17]

There is still no conclusive explanation of Villa's motive for the
raid.[18] But his relations with the United States had deteriorated in

the previous year, and border incidents had increased in the previous months; villistas, if not Villa, had made forays into U.S.
territory and had killed several North Americans in Mexico.[19] The
U.S. government criticized Carranza's inability to guarantee the
safety of foreigners or to stop the troublesome villistas. With the
Columbus raid, the United States decided to take direct action.
Under the command of General John J. Pershing, the Punitive Expedition, which eventually included ten thousand soldiers, marched
into Mexico in vain pursuit of Villa.

Carranza demanded the withdrawal of the expedition—but only
belatedly. At first he suggested reactivating an 1880s pact that gave
Mexico and the United States the mutual right to pursue bandits
and Apaches across the border, and agreed that the United States
could pursue Villa in Mexico should any further incidents occur.
President Wilson proceeded as if Carranza had approved of the
Pershing incursion.[20]

It is likely that only the *políticos* argued about the exact wording
or proper interpretation of international laws and the communiqués
passing between Washington and Mexico City. Carranza wanted to
defeat Villa, and it was suspected that he was not adverse to letting
Yankee soldiers do the work for him. Although Mexican reaction
to the Columbus raid ranged from unabashed gloating to condemnation of the irresponsible provocation of a dangerous neighbor,
patriotic outrage overwhelmed the issue of whether the raid was
right or wrong once the U.S. Army crossed into Mexico. If the
U.S. Army was against Villa, that was for many Mexicans reason
enough to be for him. Opposition to the United States became
support for Villa, who grew more popular every day that he eluded
Pershing's grasp.

The recklessness of the attack on Columbus and the ineffective-
ness of the Punitive Expedition created the image of a clever Villa
making fools of the Americans. Villa was now seen as the executor
of the true, if forbidden, desire to avenge the many humiliations
Mexico had suffered from the United States. His "uniquely successful mockery of North American military might" inspired many
songs, including "one of the most famous *corridos* of all time, *La
Persecución de Villa*, which as recently as 1950 was still being sold in
Mexican markets."[21] The song greatly exaggerated the size of the

Punitive Expedition the better to show off Villa's skill at besting the American soldiers.

The Columbus affair made Villa a symbol of Mexican nationalism and compromised Carranza's nationalist reputation. The band of renegade villistas swelled to an army of ten thousand by the end of 1916, and Villa was able to "maintain it as a decisive force in Chihuahua State until 1919."[22] His soaring prestige affected even the carrancista troops—Obregón ordered that any soldier shouting "Viva Villa!" should be shot immediately.[23]

The carrancista leadership remained inalterably opposed to Villa, who officially became an outlaw when a constitutional government was instituted in 1917. But unlike those other outlaws, the zapatistas, the villistas did not become respectable when Obregón overthrew Carranza in 1920 because the animosity between Villa and Obregón exceeded that between Obregón and Zapata. Obregón did not know Zapata personally, as he did Villa, nor had he fought him directly. In addition, Carranza and Pablo González, who had been most personally involved in crushing Zapata, were by 1920 Obregón's main rivals for power; shared dislike for those two men had facilitated an alliance between Obregón and the zapatistas. Furthermore, with Zapata's death the zapatistas had no other practical alternative to an alliance with Obregón, who undoubtedly found the ghost of Zapata more tractable than the living man would have been.

Villa, however, was alive and kicking. The government could not bring the villistas into its fold without dealing with Villa personally. And because Villa lacked a definite program, villismo could not be incorporated or co-opted programatically as zapatismo was. His men's loyalty was to him rather than to an articulated principle, therefore the man himself had to be won over, and that Obregón could not do.

Nevertheless, Villa recognized the new government in the summer of 1920 after lengthy negotiations with Interim President Adolfo de la Huerta, who granted him a hacienda ("Canutillo"), a pension, and the funds to maintain an armed guard of fifty men. In exchange, Villa swore loyalty to the regime.[24] Some saw the settlement as a sign of Villa's weakness ("he had to surrender") or his corruptibility ("he sold out"). Others saw it as a sign of the government's weakness for bargaining with a criminal it was unable to control. Most people were probably relieved that another step had been taken toward national peace. In keeping with the war-weary mood, the press now pictured Villa as an old soldier—calmer, more mature, desirous of the domestic pleasures long denied him by battle and hardship.[25]

Given that Villa appeared to have truly "retired" at Canutillo, Obregón apparently judged it best to leave him alone, although he had opposed de la Huerta's decision to pardon him.[26] During Obregón's presidency, the press regaled the public with photographs and stories about the new Villa plowing, shoeing horses, building schools for orphans, holding his children, and growing fat. It was a benevolent Villa, full of candor and homespun wisdom. There were occasionally reports that he was becoming a ruthless capitalist or exploitative landlord, but they did not disturb the predominantly bucolic image of Villa.

On July 20, 1923, Villa was shot to death along with several close friends as he drove into Parral, Chihuahua, supposedly to visit his mistress.[27] The murder fully dominated the news for a week and occupied the better part of it for a month longer—an amount of publicity far in excess of that given to the assassinations of Madero, Zapata, or Carranza. In addition to the minutiae of the murder, anecdotes from Villa's life, resurrected rumors, and "I was there" stories, opinion columns poured forth with favorable assessments of him. The outpouring was all the more remarkable in comparison to press reaction to the deaths of Carranza and Zapata. Villa was hailed as a diamond in the rough who could have been president or as great as Napoleon, if only he had been educated. There were also stories meant to belie his reputation as a brute with women: a reporter who had interviewed Villa at Canutillo emphasized his delicate gallantry toward the reporter's female companion.[28]

The press celebrated Villa's Mexicanness—an approach that indulged his faults as part of the national character and by the same token glamorized ordinary Mexicans:

[Villa's] three great vices denounce our typical . . . psychology: good horses, fine cocks, pretty women. It is very much ours . . . that symbol of the *charro* who lives with the beast—revolutionary centaur . . . who falls in love like a passionate ingenue, more mestizo or Indian than creole.[29]

The racial reference illustrated the trend to identify the mestizo as "the Mexican," and the trend to identify Mexicanness with masculinity was evident in the description of a fondness for pretty women (something common among heterosexual men everywhere) as a national trait. But Villa was not merely of the people, he was for the people as well: "Proverbial . . . is the enormous love and affection of the people for their paladin. Because Villa was that: the plebian champion *por excelencia*."[30] Another article, "Who Francisco Villa Really Was," suggested that

for the Humble who Moaned under the Lash of the Foreman, Villa was the Avenger; for those who suffered the Exploitations of the Boss, Villa was justice; for those who Burn with Fury at the Territorial Theft of '47, Villa was the Mexican Soul Confronting Pershing: for the Speculators in Land and Blood, Villa was a Bandit and Monster.[31]

A few of Villa's eulogizers even ventured to criticize the contemporary situation, depicting him as superior to the politicians squabbling for political power:

When everyone was fighting among themselves for the apple, Francisco Villa . . . withdrew from the fray of base passions. He, . . . the most controversial and perhaps the most transcendental figure of the Revolution, was working the land when he fell.[32]

This writer denied that Villa had political ambitions, showing him—again—as a decent, hardworking man with the grace and wisdom to settle down when his day of glory had ended. He implied that Villa had not been defeated, but had retired voluntarily—a view expressed in the *corridos* as well, one of which said that he simply "got tired of fighting."[33]

In general, however, journalists presented Villa's positive and negative qualities as exaggerated opposites. Describing him as a man of irreconcilable and incomprehensible contradictions made Villa more exciting and mysterious, yet it also indicated journalists' lack of empathy for him.

In contrast, the campesinos in the north apparently were not concerned with Pancho Villa's personality per se; they accepted and identified with him.[34] Most writers, who were usually middle-class, lacked this intuitive class-based empathy for Villa. Even when they thought they liked him, they referred to him (as they had to Zapata) as an enigma or paradox, while Madero and Carranza, whose ways were so similar to their own, struck them as neither enigmatic nor paradoxical regardless of whether they liked them or not.

Writers, therefore, often were unable to integrate Villa's "contradictory" qualities in order to assess his role in the revolution. Instead they listed the contradictions, disclaimed intention to judge him, and settled for a politically noncommittal stress on his importance:

Francisco Villa, whatever the value that posterity bestow upon him, was a man who in certain moments concentrated a formidable nucleus of popular strength and sympathy. . . . Common bandit, or enlightened warrior . . . , sanguine and unconscious vandal, or a man representative of the race, despite all his defects, . . . Villa has had universal notoriety.[35]

We do not pretend to make an . . . erudite study, nor a definitive critical judgment, . . . of one of the most controversial and eminent figures of the liberating movements initiated in 1910.[36]

The nonjudgmental approach resulted from more than journalistic indecision or attempted objectivity. In mid-1923, as the intra-elite struggle over the coming presidential election grew heated, and journalists needed to know which way the political winds would blow before taking a stand for or against Villa. Furthermore, it was widely believed that men high in the government were responsible for Villa's murder.

According to Alfonso Taracena, Villa had "signed his own death sentence" when he had publicly bragged, "I CAN MOBILIZE FORTY THOUSAND MEN in forty minutes. . . . Let them bring me one of those little flash-in-the-pan generals (*generalitos de petate*) to see if he can mobilize forty thousand men in forty minutes. Not even in two days, sir!"[37]

Villa added that he had eighteen hundred "partners" with new arms and ammunition. He spoke unfavorably of Plutarco Elías Calles,

Obregón's presidential choice, while praising the passed-over presidential hopeful, Adolfo de la Huerta.[38]

Many people basically agreed with Taracena's explanation of Villa's downfall. Congressional investigators of the assassination reported that "the man on the street" suspected that Obregón or Calles had ordered Villa's murder out of fear that he would support de la Huerta as an opposition candidate. Others suspected that Calles' enemies killed Villa in order to discredit Calles.[39] In either case, such suspicions indicated that Villa still had great political influence and was perceived as a threat to Obregón's power.

In August 1923, Senator Jesús Salas Barraza unexpectedly announced that he had killed Villa for his atrocious crimes and boasted that he had done Mexico a great service by ridding it of a "hyena."[40] His confession gave the press the occasion to print gruesome stories about Villa, and Salas received considerable publicity as the man "man enough" to kill the fearsome Villa. Salas was convicted of the murder, but not everyone was convinced that Salas had acted from personal motives alone or even that he was truly Villa's murderer. One reporter claimed that "no one in the street believes that Salas killed Villa," because "no one gives credence to what the Government says."[41] That incredulity seemed justified when Obregón, who had denounced Villa's murder as "treason," had Salas released from prison after serving only a few months of his twenty-year sentence.[42]

Once the furor over Villa's death had subsided, the government formally ignored him. The Mexico City press reported no commemoration of his death in 1924, or in the next five years—an absence made more conspicuous by the commemorations of the deaths of so many other men in the month of July: Hidalgo, Juárez, even the Emperor Iturbide, with President Álvaro Obregón and pioneer aviator Emilio Carranza added to the list in 1929.

In 1929 and 1930, the government campaigned vigorously for national unity, in the spirit of which it was proclaimed:

It is criminal to try to elevate one of the personalities of the Revolution at the expense of another. . . . We should love and esteem our Chiefs as they are, with their defects and with their virtues. Our leaders are not infallible in the style of the Pope . . . , they are humans, they work among us . . . and we should always be in solidarity with their actions, because it is the only way of consolidating in men the unity of the Revolution.[43]

Pancho Villa was the only major revolutionary figure who did not benefit from the unity campaign. There were still no reports of any commemorations of his death in Mexico City in 1929 or in the 1930s, although the Cárdenas administration softened toward Villa as it turned against Obregón and Calles in 1935. At that time, Villa's widow, Luz Corral, and other relatives began to attend the Madero memorial events, but no events were held in the capital specifically in Villa's honor.[44]

Villa's official oblivion was not fully attributable to his losing position at the end of the revolution. Carranza had also lost, and lost more immediately and dramatically to Obregón. Yet instead of the formal silence which the government maintained toward Villa, it had openly vilified Carranza, then elevated him to official hero status. It may have been inevitable that Carranza, Father of the 1917 Constitution, would become an official hero as the regime sought institutional stability, while Villa's image defied ready ideological incorporation. Nevertheless, the crucial difference in the two men's official treatment lay with Villa's popularity.

That popularity—which carried in it reminders of the power of the popular classes when mobilized—irritated the obregonistas and symbolically undermined their hegemony just as the living Villa's popularity had undermined the carrancistas back in 1914. The regime could do little to counteract the public's enthusiasm for Villa because any direct attack on his image could provoke popular protest or even enhance his popularity, which was fueled by notoriety. The government's silence, therefore, with its implicit denial of Villa's importance, may have been the only means to counteract his fame. To treat the Centaur of the North—the "cyclone made flesh"[45]—as unworthy of notice, also constituted the greatest insult that could be meted out to his memory.

Government silence, however, did no good. It merely left Villa's image to be shaped more by popular tastes, fiction writers, and journalists than by official propagandists.[46] Because Villa was not part of the increasingly "institutional" Revolution, his image retained a more rebellious quality and had more latitude and inconsistencies in its development. As a result, Villa's public image mirrored the politics of the successive presidencies less closely than those of Madero, Zapata, and Carranza; yet because most writers and journalists were middle-class and, relative to Villa, had only

minor political grievances or social differences with the regime and
its leadership, their treatment of Villa was broadly compatible with
the regime's ideology and the dominant culture.

Martín Luis Guzmán provides excellent examples of the bourgeois view of Villa in his account of the Convention of Aguascalientes in 1914; the account was serialized in 1926, 1927, and 1928
in *La Prensa*, *La Opinión*, and *El Universal*, then published in book
form as *El Águila y la Serpiente*. Guzmán despised both Carranza
and Obregón, who, he believed, were leading the revolution to "the
most unbridled and unrestrained absolutism." He therefore supported Villa, whom he regarded as "too irresponsible and instinc-
tive even to know how to be ambitious."[47] Guzmán apparently
found it hard to regard Villa as a person:

> His attitude, his gestures, the movement of his restless eyes, gave him a
> resemblance to a wild animal in its lair. . . .
> Pancho Villa . . . had more of the jaguar about him than a man. A
> jaguar tamed, for the moment, for our work, or for what we believed was
> our work; a jaguar whose back we stroked with trembling hand, fearful
> that at any moment a paw might strike us.[48]

The maderista Federico González Garza gave a similar account
of his decision to support Villa, who was again described in nonhuman terms. Villa

> was a troglodyte, a beast . . . a destructive force difficult to control. But
> just as a man does not feel humiliated when confronted by the blind and
> irresponsible forces of nature, like the hurricane or earthquake . . . whose
> dangers the human . . . must either flee or accept; so we preferred to
> constantly risk our lives, but without humiliation, as was the case at Villa's
> side, rather than to lead a life of comfort and feasting at the side of the
> *Primer Jefe*, but always feeling humiliated.[49]

In addition to a nonhuman characterization, Villa was frequently
portrayed as the embodiment of the masses—in González Garcia's
words, "an extraordinary example . . . of the power and bravery
of the Hispanic-American race, moved more by his native blood
than by [his] remote Spanish heritage."[50] The prominent carrancista Juan Barragan wrote that

according to the simple criteria of the people who suffered . . . during the
. . . [*porfiriato*], Villa WAS THE AVENGING ANGEL AND THE HOPE OF RESTI-
TUTION. . . . . He was the rebellion out of control, the cry of protest that
refuses to be a stifled murmur, but instead transforms itself into action,
whatever that may be. . . . .[51]

Such remarks were probably intended to be positive; yet the notion that Villa represented the common man in conjunction with
the notion that Villa was not quite human suggests that the middle
class had difficulty comprehending the common people in general.
The class sense that the masses were a bestial force underlay the
political elite's authoritarian approach to government.

Throughout the 1920s and 1930s, Villa was often the subject of
the detailed descriptions of the battles and controversies of the revolution which appeared in Mexico City's periodicals. The authors
often had had prominent positions in the revolution and hoped to
prove some point by revealing information previously known to
only a few people or to themselves alone.

By the late 1920s, ordinary people were weary of the historical
disputes that still provoked the political elite and intellectuals, and
they were increasingly cynical about the Revolution. Following the
war years, many people migrated to Mexico City, where peace and
an improved educational system expanded the market for periodical
literature, particularly for that aimed at the new urban masses.
Among the new tabloids and sensationalist magazines which spe-
cialized in blood, guts, sex, and romance, Pancho Villa was one of
the favorite topics.

Sensationalism had always been present in the literature about
Villa. After his death, it became more sentimentalized, focusing on
his supposed emotions as much as his actions. The sentimentalism
related to the "discovery" that Villa had numerous wives—a fact
not widely publicized until they began to fight to inherit his estate
or for pensions for the children he had fathered.[52] Each of the
women, whose claim to fame or escape from poverty depended on
their relationship to Villa, stressed her romance with him while
denigrating his involvement with other women. Wife Luz Corral,
for example, claimed that Villa used to confide to friends that "Luz
is the coach and these other [women] . . . are mules."[53] She said
that "reactionaries" had fabricated stories of Villa's polygamy to

make him appear to be a man "without feelings." Unable to deny his many sexual encounters, she argued that the women were responsible for them because "women always seek out important men."[54]

Corral and Austreberta Rentería, whom Corral included among the "mules," were the most contentious of Villa's widows. During Calles' fall from power, renewed press interest in Villa extended to these two women, who were anxious to tell their tales. Rentería complained about her poverty and the consequent ill health of one of her children. She denounced the injustice of treating Villa's family so poorly while "all" of Obregón's "mistresses" and "bastards" received comfortable pensions and privileges from the government. She too absolved Villa for his philandering, claiming that unscrupulous panderers who "exploited" Villa "in every sense" used to bring women to him. Villa's virility would then make it impossible for him to resist the offered pleasure.[55]

Villa's virility itself was a topic of great interest. Among magazine stories about Hollywood stars, soccer players, and photographs of blonde bathing beauties, there appeared articles like "Love and F. Villa" and "How Pancho Villa Made Love."[56] At times they contained interviews with Corral or Rentería, in which cases the sexual suggestiveness ended with the articles' titles. Instead the reader was regaled with anecdotes about Villa's husbandly responsibility or his genuine affection for his mother-in-law. Historical facts were revealed in unbearable detail: Rentería flatly denied to one reporter that Villa went to bed with two guns strapped to the small of his back, because, she explained, she would not let him— "Pancho, I used to say, you'll ruin your kidneys if you keep wearing those pistols."[57]

Fictionalized biographical vignettes about Villa were more titillating. Often the authors concentrated on Villa's sexual feelings, projecting onto him their own notions of what a "he-man" would feel.[58] One writer re-created Villa's experience of puberty ("one day the sexual instinct awakens, vigorous") and described the subsequent abduction of a woman, who "delivers herself body and soul." The writer also described another incident in which Villa, driven by his desire for children ("that cry of the species more powerful than social conventions"), abandoned an especially beloved woman because she was infertile.[59] Another writer told of

Villa's moral struggle to resist the temptation to deflower a beautiful young girl. The girl's parents were blamed for giving him every opportunity to do just that, while Villa was sympathetically portrayed as not wanting to hurt a woman he "respected" and worrying about how long he would be able to resist the "animal imperative" ("I can't stop myself from being a man"). Fortunately for the magazine reader's pleasure, the animal imperative triumphed.[60]

One of the favorite tales about Villa was that he had become a fugitive, and then a bandit, after killing the man who raped his sister. Embellished many ways, the story provided the opportunity to write a lurid account of a rape and murder under the guise of denouncing the injustice which permitted the powerful to degrade the honor of a poor man by abusing "his" women. Writers described the sister as beautiful or described the growing urgency of the rapist's lust with physical detail, providing their readers with vicarious participation in the rape and then, to make it proper, with vicarious participation in the rage and revenge of Villa.[61]

Considered together, the sentimental tales of Villa upheld a traditional concept of a man's life: hot-blooded rebellious youth, the character-building struggle for self-control over his sexual appetites, and finally the quiescence of the appetites accompanied by acceptance of the tame comforts of hearth and home. In 1938 a journalist wrote that Villa retired from the revolution because of a "weariness . . . of the soul, the will, the imagination," and that he wanted only to be a "normal man, bourgeois, with the tastes and the pleasures of ordinary beings."[62]

That remark punctuated the middle-class and conservative character of the sentimental treatment of Villa. In the first place, calling Villa an ordinary being erased his role in the revolution, implying that his private life was his "real" life while treating political activity as transient or superficial, a "phase" that the "real" person passes through.

Second, it maintained the statistically untenable position that the bourgeois experience was the normal human experience while ignoring the inability of ordinary people to "retire" regardless of their weariness. The Revolution had not given them haciendas, sinecures, pensions, or bribes, or, in the majority of cases, even the workable plot of land promised by the agrarian reform laws.

Third, if the fiercest revolutionary of all had succumbed to the "normal" tendency to renounce the wild rebellion of his youth, then certainly lesser men could demand no more of themselves. The middle-class revolutionaries, who were some of the few people better off than they had been under Porfirio Díaz, could comfort their consciences with the thought that revolutionary ardor was a psychological condition that inevitably waned.

And finally, the quote about Villa was a corollary to the middle-class difficulty in relating to the common people. When Villa died, journalists had lamented that he could have been truly great had he been educated, which was to say, had he been bourgeois. Fifteen years later, another writer declared that Villa was indeed bourgeois, and where others had seen an animal or superhuman force leading illiterate hordes that threatened to trample civilization back into barbarism, he saw "a normal man."

The conservative, sentimental style of portraying Villa represented in part the trend toward factional conciliation in that it portrayed him in a way more acceptable to sociopolitical groups previously opposed to him.

However, in as much as Villa's growing acceptability stemmed from his transformation into a middle-class figure, it measured the co-optation of the revolutionary potential of the lower classes rather than real advances against the hegemony of the middle classes. Whitewashing Pancho Villa also obscured the class nature of the movement he had led and therefore suited the government's claim that the revolution was a "Mexican" phenomenon in which there were no fundamental or necessary class conflicts: all classes' interests could be, after a period of adjustment, subsumed under the good of the nation, represented by the government. The government, which was also the Revolution, was above all, and would arbitrate any conflicts of class interests should they arise.[63]

The Cárdenas administration continued its predecessors' policy of ignoring the anniversary of Villa's death, but it created an atmosphere which permitted more positive attention to Villa in the press. That improvement resulted from the administration's condemnation of Villa's enemies, Obregón and Calles, and from the ultra-right's adoption of Villa. One fascistic group assumed the name of Villa's special escort: *Los Dorados* (The Golden Ones).[64] A desire to prevent the right from capitalizing on Villa as a symbol may have spurred the government to co-opt his image for its own pur-

poses. The closest thing to an "official" image of Villa appeared
during the Cárdenas administration in the first movie made by the
government-run Mexican film industry—*Vámonos con Pancho Villa*
(Let's Go with Pancho Villa).[65]
The movie was based on the novel by Rafael M. Muñoz. In 1928
part of the story was serialized in *El Universal*; it later became a
play and in 1931 appeared in book form.[66] In 1935 it was adapted
for the film. The government subsidized the film and provided federal troops and military equipment for its impressive battle scenes.[67]

The movie opened with a written dedication to the loyalty that
Villa inspired in his men.[68] The viewer knew from the outset that
the film would draw upon the popular belief that the villistas, especially the *Dorados*, were fanatically devoted to Villa. The dedication provided some defense against those who might be offended
by a glorification of Villa personally. And finally, the idea that
soldiers' loyalty was in and of itself admirable complemented the
government's attempt to professionalize the army in order to dis-
courage military revolts.

In the opening scenes, the viewer meets the six good-hearted,
naive friends who call themselves the *Leones* of San Pablo. Angered
by the injustices of Huerta's government, they go off in holiday
spirit to join the great Pancho Villa. When they arrive at the villista
camp, formed around the train which served as transport and hab-
itation, they are dazzled by the scene that greets them. Dogs bark,
the camp bustles with activity. Dark women in shawls pat out tor-
tillas; ragamuffin children play among the boxcars; an Indian soldier nuzzles the woman asleep on his shoulder; an amorous drunk
makes advances at a fat, formidable *soldadera* who brooks no non-
sense; great crowds with cartridge belts doubled across their chests
and huge sombreros on their heads mill about. An omnipresent
manly chorus sings "La Adelita."[69] An ebullient and—one senses
—self-important Villa distributes corn to the grateful multitude
gathered about him.

The awestruck *Leones* meet Villa, who seems amused by their
unsoldierly aspect and gives the youngest, Miguel Angel del Toro,
the nickname *Becerrillo* (Little Calf). In the ensuing battles the *Leones*
fight bravely: no sacrifice is too great if it is for Villa. The viewers,
however, begin to doubt Villa merits such devotion, for he exhibits
no personal concern for the *Leones*. He accepts their bravery as a

matter of course, pursuing victory in a professional, efficient manner. Three of the *Leones* die heroically; Villa's regret rings hollow. He promotes the surviving *Leones* to the rank of general and makes them part of the prestigious *Dorados*, but the audience knows the honor was cheap because of the way Villa casually dispensed the general stars from an envelope full of them. The *Leones* remain oblivious to their role as cannon fodder; they adore Villa.

When only two *Leones* are left alive, one catches smallpox. Without regard for his own health, Tiburcio tenderly nurses Becerrillo in the boxcar that serves as their spartan billet. Word goes to Villa in his spotlessly outfitted modern car that the disease has appeared in camp—this on the eve of a crucial battle:

Villa [exasperated and peremptory]: Smallpox in the trains. What a fine way to greet me when we're almost in Zacatecas. We have to attack tomorrow. . . . Get those sick people out of the cars. . . . Do what you want, but don't let anyone else catch it.

Fierro: It seems that one of the afflicted is from your escort. Miguel Angel del Toro.

Villa [momentarily taken aback]: Becerrillo? Of the *Leones?* . . . [recovering his brusque manner] Ah! What a mess! OK, OK, well, it doesn't matter. We're at war and the troops come first.

[Fierro and a doctor go to Tiburcio to tell him the contagion must be stopped.]

Tiburcio [losing his temper]: Well, what do you want me to do? Leave him in the middle of the field like a dog? Isn't he a man like us, and better than many?

[The doctor repeats that the entire train is in danger. Fierro threatens to "take measures" himself if Tiburcio does not cooperate.]

Tiburcio [calmer, again the obedient soldier]: General, we are in battle. You are the commander. Order what must be done and I myself will be the first to carry it out.

Doctor: Everything must be gotten rid of: his arms, his clothes, his blankets . . . even him.

Tiburcio: Gotten rid of? I don't understand!

Doctor [businesslike]: It is necessary to cremate the body.

Tiburcio [still uncomprehending]: Cremate?

Fierro [angrily]: Burn it, man, burn it!

Tiburcio [shocked]: Like he is? Alive?

Fierro: Alive or dead. It makes no difference to me! But you heard me. It must be burned! Right now!

Tiburcio [horrified and enraged]: Burn him? Burn him alive? Have you two gone mad? Is this the pay for a soldier of the revolution? Is this an army of men or a pack of dogs?

Fierro [screaming]: Don't argue with me! The life of one man isn't worth anything if it is for saving the rest, and above all, I give the orders here! Did you hear! Shape up and obey the order! Right now you burn him and all his junk. I give you five minutes! If you don't do it, someone else will.

[Fierro and the doctor leave. The deeply shaken Tiburcio goes into the boxcar, tearfully says good-bye to the delirious Miguel Angel, then shoots him in the head. He begins dragging the body and things into a pyre, while the onlookers, afraid of smallpox, draw back from his approach.]

Tiburcio [muttering contemptuously]: Miserable beggars! As if you were going to live a hundred years!

[Tiburcio sits in the boxcar doorway, slowly smoking a cigaret while Becerrillo's body burns in the background. Fierro and Villa come walking toward the wagon to see if Tiburcio has followed orders. Tiburcio's face lights up when he sees Villa. He jumps to attention.]

Villa: What's been done with Becerrillo?

Tiburcio [pointing to the fire]: There he is, General.

Villa [looking around, shouting orders]: Get these cars moving. This wagon stays here.

Tiburcio [expectantly]: And me, General?

Villa: You stay here!

Tiburcio [surprised, he steps toward Villa]: Stay here? I'm not going to fight at Zacatecas?

Villa [quickly drawing back]: Don't come near me! You stay here until I send for you.

[Tiburcio stops, his face blank but his eyes really seeing Villa for the first time. He sees that Villa, like other mortals, is afraid of getting small-pox, and that Villa is discarding him.]

Tiburcio [stiffly]: Very well, General.

Villa [shouting orders to the others]: Let's go!

Tiburcio [whispering tersely to himself]: Very well, here it ends.

[Tiburcio shoulders his bedroll and walks off into the night. End of film.]

In this manner the film, which began with an ingenuous enthu-siasm for a folkloric revolution, closed with a brutal exposure of the illusion for which men gave themselves in meaningless sacri-fice—the dramatic negation of the myth of Pancho Villa.[70]
Paradoxically, the depiction of Villa as an efficient, modern, re-sponsible military man was key to this negation. His cold, imper-sonal manner nullified whatever improvement that depiction could have made over the image of him as an irrational "troglodyte." He was a marvelous military machine but personally unworthy of the men who followed him; he did not reciprocate their affection and loyalty, he exploited it, and discarded them when they were no longer useful to him. Any sense that Villa regretted sacrificing Be-cerrillo dissolved when Villa displayed fear of the disease, horror and rejection of Tiburcio, and a total lack of compassion for either Miguel Angel's or Tiburcio's plight.
The denouement of *Vámonos con Pancho Villa* could be seen as an indictment of the futile and dehumanizing nature of the revolution, a condemnation of personalism, a glorification of the common sol-dier, and a "tragic-but-just" approach to the revolution. If the film's intention had merely been to question heroes' worthiness, soldiers' motives, loyalty, or the ironies of the revolution, any generic *cau-dillo* would have sufficed as a vehicle. But to take up Villa and then present him so negatively could only have been done to defame his popular image. Consideration of what the film did not excerpt from the novel further reveals its anti-Villa character.[71]
In the novel, Villa had nothing to do with the order to burn Miguel Angel, although he was afraid of smallpox and left Tiburcio behind. Tiburcio's departure from the villista camp was barely the halfway point of the story. He then returned home, farmed, and

yearned for the day that Villa would come for him, as he had promised to do.

Years pass and Villa becomes a renegade with a motley crew of men as fearful of their paranoid leader as of the soldiers who pursue them. The public turns against Villa, but Tiburcio remains a villista in his heart and teaches his son to be one also. By chance Villa rides by Tiburcio's *ranchito* one day; when Villa recognizes him, he tells Tiburcio to get his gear and come along. Tiburcio is elated. His joy passes, however, when he remembers that he must stay to care for his wife and daughter. Villa shoots the wife and daughter, telling Tiburcio that he no longer has any reason to stay at his farm. Tiburcio stands with his gun in his hand but is incapable of killing his *jefe* Villa. He marches away with the villistas, bringing his son with him.

This is Villa the Evil, the ruthless sociopath who mesmerizes his men. The men are loyal out of fear and what is, for the novel's readers, an irrational bond. Yet in the novel, this extremely negative image of Villa is overwhelmed by the villistas' assault on Columbus, portrayed as the redemption of national honor, and justified by the United States' designs on Mexico: "The United States wants to swallow Mexico," says Villa. "Let's see if this little bone sticks in its throat."[72] The raid restores his glory:

Villa was once again . . . the powerful master of men, captivator of multitudes, as he was . . . when he reached the zenith of his splendor in the bloody struggles . . . in which the Constitutionalists went to the sacrifice with their blood boiling and their throats vibrating in an identical battle cry that was at once mad enthusiasm for their cause and fervent homage to their invincible *jefe*.[73]

Villa, pursued by the Punitive Expedition, is wounded and takes refuge in a cave, accompanied by a few men, including Tiburcio, who swear never to let him fall, dead or alive, into the hands of American soldiers. On a foray for food, Tiburcio is captured by the gringos. When tortured by their Apache guides, Tiburcio admits that he is a villista and knows where Villa is. But, he taunts the soldiers, he will never tell them where he is. The soldiers stop the torture and attempt to cajole information from him. They bind his flayed feet, take him to an American field hospital, clean him,

feed him, and promise him wealth and protection if he will tell
them where Villa is. Tiburcio refuses. He tells the soldiers that
Villa killed his wife and daughter, a revelation that stupefies them.
They offer Tiburcio the opportunity to take vengeance on Villa.
Tiburcio refuses.

The sergeant sat with his mouth open, unable to comprehend.

"Pancho Villa killed them? You follow Villa?"
"Yes."
"You obey Villa? You defend him?"
"Yes."
"You're crazy."
"Crazy . . . Yes . . . "
"Oh! I don't believe you, you have a fever again. Me, if a man killed
my wife, I'd kill that man. I wouldn't defend him."
"I do."

. . . "I do." His moral triumph was in those two words. Incurable
. . . a prisoner, old, hearing his grave being dug, he was certain of his
superiority to the sergeant, doctors, nurses, the hundreds of soldiers, . . .
to the entire army.[74]

In contrast to the movie, in which Tiburcio's painful recognition
of Villa's "true" character seems to definitively dispel his devotion,
the novel shows Tiburcio to be fully conscious of Villa's character:

Tiburcio had only one way to take vengeance: man to man. He would
have said to him: "Pancho Villa, you are the worst bandit I know; you
have killed my wife and daughter. You have a gun and so do I: let's see
who shoots first." But he never would have killed him from the back, nor
would he have taken advantage of him when wounded. . . . He would
never inform on him so that ten thousand men, with cannons, with machine guns, with airplanes, could lay siege to a cave where there were only
three men hidden, determined not to be taken alive.[75]

Tiburcio's loyalty to Villa is purposeful and devoid of illusions.
He chooses to live by the values of patriotism and loyalty, regardless of the worthiness of the object. That this choice leads to his
death heightens the sense of Tiburcio's spiritual triumph. Tiburcio
is a sophisticated, existential version of the stereotypical Mexican
macho revolutionary who disdains to avoid death, greeting it head

on with a defiant cry of "Viva Mexico!" or "Viva Villa!" But he is
also the macho described by Carlos Monsiváis: the man who charges
to his death bravely because life leaves him no other choice.[76] In
the willful assumption of the inevitable there is psychological mas-
tery of material conditions, but no change in those conditions. It is
the ambiguous triumph of the fatalistic and the doomed.

The novel redeems Villa by making him a symbol of Mexican
national honor and by making Tiburcio a highly sympathetic character. At the end of the story, the carrancistas, who kill Tiburcio
because he is a villista, are as bad as the gringos or worse, for in
the context of the novel it is treasonous for a Mexican to oppose
Villa.

Rather than detracting from Villa's image, the novel strengthens
it by removing it from the realm of the rational. There is nothing
particularly romantic about rational loyalty; it may even be tainted
by suspicions that it is self-serving. Tiburcio's suffering reveals the
depth of his allegiance to Villa; he is elevated by his martyrdom.
This villismo is not prompted by anything commonly regarded as
self-interest or political belief; therefore it cannot be controlled by
appeals to those interests, it cannot be co-opted. Therein, for those
who would institutionalize the revolution, lay its dangerousness.[77]

But the villismo of the novel *Vámonos con Pancho Villa* was not
the same as that of the film. And whereas the novel (taking into
account all its published forms) enjoyed great success, the movie
was a commercial failure despite its many excellent qualities.[78] It
was cohesive, emotional, dramatic; it contained popular stereotypes
of the revolution as well as some battle scenes which are even today
cinematically breathtaking. The most plausible explanation of the
movie's box office failure is that it did not give the public the Villa
that had proven so popular in the literary versions of Muñoz' story.

Apparently the anti-Villa propaganda had backfired. The government had kept Villa outside the bounds of official acceptability
as a revolutionary hero, and there his image had flourished and
multiplied. Most versions of Villa were projections of one sort or
another of middle-class prejudices about the lower classes, and while
they therefore obscured the class aspects of the factional struggles
of the revolution, they did not become directly supportive of the
Revolutionary government. By the time the cultural apparatus of
the government began to attempt to shape Villa's image for its own

purposes, rather than allowing it to be shaped by popular tastes and psychological needs, it was too late. Popular tastes wanted Villa to be thrilling, not respectable. They were enamored of Villa the daring Robin Hood, the satyr and monster, the unpredictable deviant, the grimy *guerrillero* and outlaw with uncanny power over men. The public rejected the movie which showed a well-groomed, impersonal Villa who looked and acted like a professional officer from the National Military Academy.

The other important revolutionary figures had been sanitized, homogenized, and made into symbols of the regime. Their names were evoked to harness people's fervent hopes and emotions about the struggle of 1910–1917 to the regime's program of demobilization of the masses, stabilization, and authoritarian centralization. The official heroes suffered a parallel loss as symbols of rebellion as their images were put into service for the "law and order"of the regime.

Who then could serve as a symbol of opposition? Who could provide vicarious defiance of the new order which concentrated wealth and power once again in the hands of the few while failing to meet the needs of the many? Who but Pancho Villa?

The weakness of his political program, the amorphous nature of his struggle—which caused many to denounce him as "just a bandit," a power-seeker rather than a revolutionary—paradoxically worked in Villa's favor. He had not been incorporated into the official roster of heroes and was in a sense unincorporable because there was no law or reform to promulgate which would allow the government to say, "Here, we have fulfilled the goals of villismo."

The trend to obscure the socioeconomic character of the factional struggles in the revolution also worked to enhance Villa's popularity. By deemphasizing the class significance of Villa, his rebellion was left with little specific content. This meant, given that Villa was still represented as a rebel, that Villa became the rebel without a cause. Thus he became a symbol of rebellion, even of rebelliousness per se, who could express equally the desire to strike back against the insults and injustices suffered at the hands of the Yankees and the desire to break society's sexual taboos.

It was Villa—not Madero, Carranza, or even Zapata—who inspired the most songs, stories, and movies, he who was the most popular. Only in the 1960s did the Mexican government finally acknowledge this most genuinely popular revolutionary hero, making him an official national hero in 1965 and reentombing his remains in a monument in the heart of the capital. But although these honors came more than four decades after his assassination, many people opposed them.[79] The Centaur of the North still aroused controversy, as he does even today.

CHAPTER 6

Mystification and the Consolidation of the Mexican State

> What the world supplies to myth is historical reality, defined, even if this goes back quite a while, by the way in which men have produced or used it; and what myth gives in return is a *natural* image of this reality. And just as bourgeois ideology is defined by the abandonment of the name "bourgeois," myth is constituted by the loss of the historical quality of things.
>
> Roland Barthes, *Mythologies*

The preceding chapters traced the evolution of the posthumous public images of four leaders of the Mexican revolution as part of the post-revolutionary government's struggle to consolidate a war-torn, divided nation. The men's real personalities and actions were only the raw material out of which their heroic images were fashioned. Although the journalists and propagandists may have preferred one political tendency to another, as a whole they were males belonging to the middle classes, from which the government and the chief opposition groups of the 1920s and 1930s were formed. In addition to conscious attempts to shape the heroes to suit their own factional preferences, they inevitably imbued them with the values and character of the dominant culture. The public images of Carranza, Madero, Zapata, and, with qualifications, Villa, became vehicles for reinforcing that culture.

The propaganda surrounding these four heroes had a number of common traits: the claim that the government was revolutionary; the promotion of nationalism; the obfuscation of history; the denigration of politics; Christian imagery and the promotion of Catholic values; and patriarchal values and the "masculinization" of the heroes' images. These characteristics form the internal ideology and psychology of the myth of the Mexican Revolution. Each is fraught with contradictions that feed circularly into the others. The myth of the Revolution might collapse were it to rest on any one of them, but it does not—it shifts back and forth, moving between contradictions, eluding confrontation with them.

The common traits of the Revolutionary myth are separable only as poles of a dynamic, not as autonomous components, but for analytic purposes they will here be addressed separately. We will consider the most immediate, practical reasons for the genesis of each trait as well as its underlying source and its depoliticizing effect on public consciousness.

THE CLAIM THAT THE GOVERNMENT WAS REVOLUTIONARY

In the 1920s and 1930s the Mexican government's claim that it was revolutionary was justified historically in that virtually its entire leadership, including that of the military and the official political party, had participated in Madero's "revolution" against Porfirio Díaz and/or in the movement to oust Victoriano Huerta. The claim was also politically necessary, for the people—from the discontented segments of the bourgeoisie to the masses of impoverished campesinos—had made it clear that they would fight against a return to a dictatorial, Díaz-like regime. They wanted a government that at the very least would realize Madero's promise of democracy. Those who wished to restore the old order ceased to be a viable national political force when the revolutionaries defeated Huerta in mid-1914. By 1920 it was to be expected that Obregón would call his government revolutionary, just as any other major political leader, with equal historical justification, would have done.

The more important issue was the kind of revolutionary regime Obregón claimed to have ushered in with the Revolt of Agua Prieta.

Because there were no significant avowedly counterrevolutionary political factions in 1920, the term "revolutionary" had little value in distinguishing among the factions, whose ideologies ranged from right to left. From the outset of the revolution, Madero's "effective suffrage, no reelection" and an ill-defined desire for reform constituted the only common ideological grounds among the revolutionaries. Gradually questions of reform—what kind? how much? how soon?—brought to the fore strong differences that contributed to the bloody wars of 1914–1916.

During those wars Álvaro Obregón aligned with the most conservative faction, the carrancistas, within which he represented one of the more—but certainly not the most—leftist tendencies. He used his impressive political acumen and military skill to defeat the convencionistas, thereby assuring that Mexico would be controlled by middle-class reformists rather than by men like Villa or Zapata. In view of Obregón's role in the revolutionary wars, then, it would have seemed appropriate for him to identify his presidency with the middle classes, and himself as a middle-of-the-road moderate.

Nevertheless, when Obregón became president in 1920 he publicly identified his administration with the lower classes, presenting himself as the champion of the campesinos, whose leaders he had fought so hard to defeat a few years before. Out of the array of interpretations given the revolution at that time, Obregón chose to define it as popularly based; he gave the official Revolution the public face it has maintained to this day, the face of the peasant. Why did President Obregón adopt this radical posture?

In the first instance, his radical posture maximized his differences from the very unpopular Carranza, minimizing his previous association with him and justifying the Agua Prieta Revolt as a matter of principle rather than personal ambition. Second, and more important, it demonstrated that Obregón had learned from Carranza's mistake: the popular classes could not be ignored with impunity.

Despite the fact that the years of civil war had decapitated the lower-class leadership and that the carrancistas formed a national government in 1917, the defeat of the popular factions had not been definitive. The middle-class revolutionaries had persuaded some popular organizations to accept their rule but had not fully demobilized them or converted them to their worldview. The masses could not be counted on to remain disorganized if too aggrieved. It was necessary to appease some popular demands both to stave off rebellion from below and to prevent other middle-class rivals for national power from capitalizing on lower-class discontent. Although organizationally weak, the lower classes retained political and military weight sufficient to give the advantage to whichever of the rival middle-class factions seemed to serve their interests best.

The inadvisability of war also encouraged Obregón to make peace with the revolutionary popular classes. Economically, the government could not afford to undertake a campaign to crush the popular movements once and for all. Furthermore, in order to win diplomatic recognition for his government and to begin reconstruction of the devastated country, Obregón needed to convince foreign governments and investors that he truly controlled Mexico and that Mexico was a safe place for their capital. The quickest road to stability lay in persuading the masses that he was their friend.

It was not, however, an easy road for Obregón to travel, for the policies that might win over the popular classes might alienate the conservative support which he also needed. Social reforms could antagonize investors and alarm the U.S. government, which had been in the throes of anti-communist extremism since the Russian revolution.[1] Much of the national and international bourgeoisie opposed anything that hinted at Mexico's following the same course as the *bolcheviques*. In addition, to secure the loyalty of the ex-carrancista elite, Obregón needed to appease their desire for capitalist development and/or to permit them to grow rich at public expense, and he therefore could not vigorously pursue effective reform programs.[2]

In short, the Obregón administration needed to placate both the right and the left—a predicament shared by many—but with a crucial difference: to maintain domestic legitimacy it had to assume a "revolutionary" posture rather than a centrist one. In what could be parodied as a policy of speaking loudly and carrying a little stick, Obregón initiated the Mexican government's now standard practice of verbally championing the popular classes and the Revolution while neglecting the promised reforms and making deals with the "imperialists" it often denounced. The government's revolutionary appearance surpassed its practice.[3]

The lack of ideological clarity in the revolution helped the government to maintain the contradiction between its image and its practices. That lack of clarity was evinced in the term "revolutionary" itself, which functioned more as a historical adjective than as an ideological one and which frequently contradicted traditional connotations.

The resultant confusion was exacerbated by the government's adoption of quasi-Marxist jargon in the aftermath of the Russian revolution. The government sympathized with the Soviet regime in the early 1920s, and several important political figures, such as Rafael Ramos Pedrueza, were convinced partisans of it.[4] During Marxism's "golden age" in Mexico, 1917–1925, terms like "proletariat" and "imperialist exploitation" seeped into public propaganda, reinforcing the regime's radical image even though it had already rejected some of the basic tenets of communism, such as the abolition of private property.[5] When Obregón was seeking recognition of his government, for example, Calles (then one of his Cabinet) stated that he was not a "Bolshevist but rather a liberal satisfied with our government's recent steps to improve the lot of the peasants."[6]

Because of the public's ideological ignorance and the government's repression of criticism that might reveal its nonrevolutionary character, the government could define political terminology and concepts almost without concern for standard meanings. In effect, the government usurped the lexicon of socialist revolution. Under such discursive conditions, tautology impeded analysis of the government's claim that it was the Revolution, that therefore its actions were revolutionary, and that opposition to it was counterrevolutionary. To be understood, serious political criticism would have had to overcome the very language used in official pronouncements and the mainstream press, for that language tended to disguise the political character of the object of discussion. For example, following the attempt to assassinate President Ortiz Rubio in 1930, a general denounced the crime and wondered whether the criminals were "political also-rans, communists, or one of the Knights of Columbus? For us it is plainly and simply the Reaction."[7]

Nevertheless, the use of revolutionary rhetoric to co-opt reformist sentiment was a double-edged sword, for if it were convincing, people would be more likely to expect revolutionary improvements. The failure of such improvements to materialize might then promote the dissatisfaction that the rhetoric had been intended to prevent. The rhetoric could also make the disparity between appearances and policies loom larger in the public eye, and threaten to make the government a victim of its own revolutionary myth.

THE PROMOTION OF NATIONALISM

From the time of the Conquest foreign domination entailed cultural domination. Most colonizers believed that their customs and race were superior to those of the colonized. The Spaniards' imposition of their own culture devalued the cultures of the Indians, who gradually internalized many of the dominant standards by which they were judged to be inferior.

At first, Spaniard and Indian were distinct groups, but by the end of the nineteenth century a racially and culturally mixed group, the mestizos, had become numerically predominant and were found at every level of society. A mestizo culture had in fact developed, but because the economically and politically dominant classes were still the "whitest" and Indians still occupied the lowest rung of society, mestizo culture regarded its Indian heritage as a source of shame and its European aspects as superior. Even the upper classes, whose blood carried only a trace of Indian, often displayed a pressing need to imitate all things European and to dissociate themselves from the taint of a colonial society, betraying their alienation from their country and sense of inferiority vis-à-vis the Anglo-European.[8]

As a Mexican national identity slowly developed during the colonial period, resentment against foreign domination also developed. At the time of independence, nationalistic resentment focused mostly on the Spaniards. In the mid-1800s the resentment shifted toward the United States, which became after 1910 the most frequent target of patriotic anger because of its high-handed attempts to control the course of the revolution.[9]

In the years preceding the revolution the middle classes had become the most nationalistic. Díaz had created an economic situation highly favorable to foreign investors. Many members of the middle classes began to chafe against the limitations these policies placed on their own ambition; their desire to develop Mexico for their own benefit contributed to the outbreak of the revolution.[10] The carrancista leadership sprang from the ranks of the nationalistic middle classes. When they came to power they propounded nationalism and continually appealed to it to maintain popular support for their rule.

The Mexican Revolution was more than a reaction against colonial and neocolonial economic weakness and dependency—it also represented a healthy rejection of the accompanying cultural and racial inferiority complex. The greatest benefits of Mexican nationalism may have been psychological or cultural as it both bore witness to and stimulated a symbolic casting-off of the mental chains of colonialism.

Mexican nationalists repudiated the notion that foreign ways were superior and that Mexican ways should be judged by foreign standards. They insisted that Mexico's people were equal to any other and need not engage in the alienating task of imitating Anglo-Europeans, of trying to be what they were not. This new national self-esteem necessitated a positive reassessment of the despised other half of Mexico's heritage, the Indian, while the mestizo was hailed as the national archetype. Artists and scholars hastened to explore the archeological wonders of the pre-Columbian civilizations, to applaud and revive the esthetics of the artifacts they carefully preserved in museums, and to express in their work their identification with the Indian people. The frequent praise of Zapata's "typical" Mexican tastes and physical traits, the claim that he was the "most Mexican of revolutionaries," reflected the trend to glorify *lo mexicano*.

The government was in the forefront of the movement to inculcate pride in "the truly Mexican." The ceremonies commemorating the revolutionary heroes included music from "our beautiful folklore" and at times speeches in Nahuatl. In 1924, as part of its arts promotion campaign begun in 1921, the government commissioned radical artist Diego Rivera to adorn public buildings with his murals, which depicted a glorified native civilization brutalized by greedy Spaniards, and the brown, common people engaged in a long struggle against foreign oppressors and a corrupt *criollo* elite. "Mexican" art was also promoted through community education projects. For example, the guidelines for the PNR's *Domingos Culturales* stipulated that

foreign music whose morbid character depresses the spirit of our people must be eliminated absolutely.

We do not find sufficient reason to prefer foreign genres when we possess a unique richness in national arts, songs that have no equal and that are the direct expression of the popular soul. . . .

We will suppress . . . all types of exotic dances, giving preference to
our regional dances . . . that put all areas of the states and the country
into contact and that exalt our own esthetic sense.[11]

Nationalists sought to guard against the nefarious influences of
foreign fashions, fads, and media. Hollywood's impact on the popular psyche generated special concern because it dominated such a
large part of the film market. Beginning in the 1920s, the Mexican
government wrangled with U.S. filmmakers, threatening to ban their
movies in Mexico if they continued to portray Mexicans as "greas-
ers" and bandits.[12] Educators and political leaders pointed to the
need to use films as propaganda for the betterment of Mexican society. In the 1930s the nascent Mexican film industry attempted to
challenge U.S. domination of the Latin American market and to
provide positive images of Mexico as an antidote to U.S. films said
to be transforming Mexicans into gringos, "with grave loss to the
national spirit."[13] The secretary of public education, Carlos Trejo
y Lerdo de Tejada, denounced Yankee "cinematographic imperialism" as a "weapon of political propaganda, . . . the means by which
they accomplish the Saxon-Americanization of our people."[14]

Nevertheless, nationalistic pride in *lo mexicano* exceeded the improvements that the Revolution brought to the lives of ordinary
people. The Indians, the campesinos, the majority of "typical"
Mexicans continued to live in poverty and were made to bear the
burden of a reconstruction that mostly served the Revolutionary
elite. In the 1920s and 1930s the army may have been a greater
scourge to the common people, especially in the countryside, than
had been Porfirio Díaz' army and his dreaded rural police force.[15]

In short, the new racial pride materially benefitted few Indians
and did not end racism in Mexico. The white man's dominant status showed in the low regard for the Indian on the street, in the
persecution of the Chinese in the northern states, and in the exclu-
sion of black immigrants.[16] The government tried in the 1920s to
attract colonists to the sparsely populated areas of the country but,
in the words of Secretary of State Calles, "consider[ed] the immigration of colored people to be prejudicial to the country, because
instead of bettering our race, it weakens it, thereby complicating
our ethnic problem, serious in itself." The secretary of agriculture
assured the public that the government would continue to permit
the immigration of white people only.[17]

There were more subtle forms of prejudice. The use of the phrase "our ethnic problem" to refer to Indians in a mostly Indian population illustrated the European-identified solipsism that saw the white or Europeanized minority as the social norm. The characterization of Zapata and Villa as exotic exemplified this perspective. Numerically, there was more justification in calling the whiter Mexicans "ethnics" in order to distinguish them from the racial norm, yet because the middle and upper classes ruled the country, they also defined the dominant social attitudes.

Similarly unconcious caste bias appeared in educational projects designed to help Indians, such as the *Casa del Estudiante Indígena* in Mexico City. Education meant facilitating the Indians' or campesinos' ability to function in Mexico's capitalistic Europeanized society; it was not suggested that that society learn to adapt to the Indians', nor that the two coexist as equals. Unlike the old-fashioned racists who believed the Indians incapable of progress, the middle-class reformers of the 1920s and 1930s believed they could be saved by being trained in modern ways, that is, by being "de-Indianized." While the reformers' belief had practical validity—for instance, Indians would have been better able to defend their rights against corrupt officials or landowners if they knew their rights or could speak, read, and write Spanish—it was valid because non-Indian society was racist. The benevolent intentions of the reformers did not negate the ethnocentrism in the attitude "we will help the Indian by making them more like us."

The ethnocentrism of the middle-class nationalists was also evident in the patronizing character of many efforts to preserve native and popular culture. They may have helped save traditional songs, dances, and customs that might otherwise have disappeared under the commercial cultural deluge from the United States. They may also have deadened it and alienated it from the very people whose living culture it was, by transforming it into folklore—the stuff of ritualized state ceremonies and museum exhibits, the hackneyed fare of tourist attractions. The term "folklore" itself, ironically an anglicism, belied the distance and the foreignness with which the middle class viewed the "truly Mexican" culture it professed to admire.

The ambivalence, contradictions, and covert racism of the middle-class nationalists reflected the fact that they were indeed a "middle" class—below the Europeans, Yankees, and the "white"

Mexican elite; above the Indians, the campesinos, and the urban poor. When confronted with the prejudices of their traditional "betters," they felt a racial and cultural affinity with the lower castes/classes and deplored the social dominion and racism of the Anglo-Europeans. When, however, the only relations in question were those between the middle class and the lowest castes/classes, the traditional prejudiced social hierarchy bothered them much less because it gave them many advantages over the "inferior" masses.

With the revolution the middle classes were politically ascendent, but old racial attitudes were ingrained in the culture and in the revolutionaries themselves. In general, nationalists were more concerned to convince middle-class Mexicans that they were not inferior to Anglo-Europeans than to convince them that they were not superior to the Indians and common people.

The work of Diego Rivera provides an acute example of the contradictions in the Revolution's nationalism. Rivera, a leading leftist in the 1920s and 1930s, portrayed in his murals a communist interpretation of Mexico's history and its future. Why did the Mexican government, anxious to convince other governments that it was not communist, commission Rivera to put such ideological compositions on the walls of its buildings?

To return to Barthes' terminology, the murals were a primary language conveying a revolutionary vision of society. Yet as part of the metalanguage of the myth of the Revolution, they buoyed up the image of the new government as nonracist, egalitarian, and tolerant of communist views, when in practice it was not. Domestically, Rivera's murals made excellent "revolutionary" propaganda for the government. Many of Rivera's political cohorts objected to his working with the government, and the dissension within the radical opposition may have been a side benefit for the government from employing Diego Rivera. At the time of Rivera's expulsion from the Communist Party, his fellow communist and close friend Tina Modotti wrote: "We all know that these positions have been thrust upon him by the government precisely to bribe him and to be able to say: 'The reds say we are reactionaries, but look, we are letting Diego Rivera paint all the hammers and sickles he wants on public buildings.' "[18]

Many conservatives also objected to Rivera and the subject matter of his murals; his paintings of Zapata and the zapatistas in the

Ministry of Public Education provoked considerable controversy, for example.[19] Nevertheless, Rivera's work attracted international attention and helped place Mexico in the vanguard of Western art; furthermore, the murals' themes increased international awareness of Mexico's history, people, and customs. Rivera's work enhanced world opinion of Mexico, and the resultant gratification of nationalist sentiment gradually eclipsed conservative objection to its radical ideological content.

The nationalism of the middle classes had contributed to the outbreak and course of the revolution, but when the middle-class revolutionaries had wrested national control from the old regime, it ceased to be, with important exceptions, a progresssive force. It increasingly became a force to dull political criticism and to detain the advance of the laboring classes by disguising middle-class interests as national interests. The government manipulated nationalist sentiment to increase its own strength and win support for its capitalist policies.[20]

There were trivial applications of nationalism as a form of social manipulation, as when a hat manufacturers' association, laboring under the misconception that North Americans did not wear hats, ran this advertisement:

TAKE COVER *FROM SUSPICIONS*. Put on a hat. The hat identifies you—proof that *you* don't let yourself be influenced by exotic fashions—and that you don't succumb to *pochismo*.

Can you imagine a *charro* without his rich, traditional, and beautiful braid-trimmed hat? In the city we are not *charros*. But we are still Mexicans.[21]

The very pettiness of this example suggests how pervasive was the pressure to be a patriotic Mexican, and especially to not be a *pocho* (one who is Americanized and thus not a "real" Mexican). There were, however, more serious examples. To wit, anti-feminists sought to discredit the Mexican women's movement as un-Mexican in character and by virtue of the participation of several North American women.[22] In 1923 César Morales of the Ministry of Public Education drew upon the stereotype of the cold, mannish gringa to oppose feminism on the grounds that it would destroy "the ingenuousness and modesty of the Mexican woman, converting her into a virago just as is happening today to American women, who are different from ours."[23]

Other critics of the women's rights movement directly argued that it ran counter to the national good. Mexico, they said, needed to increase its population in order to prosper, and birth control (a major feminist goal) would prevent that increase. In reference to the proceedings of the 1923 Congress of the Panamerican League of Women, which took place in Mexico, *El Demócrata*'s editoral stated: "We believe that . . . patriotism is being forgotten in these discussions. Has the progress of feminism . . . really diminished the idea of *la patria* among the people?"[24]

Similarly, working people were encouraged to participate in official political activities but were discouraged from other political activities by appeals to their sense of patriotic responsibility. By the end of the first decade after the revolution it was clear that the government had failed to carry out the promised reforms. Official sources, however, blamed workers who fought for improvements on their own for the economic ills suffered by the masses. As one general said in 1930:

Each excess, each riot or act which disturbs the [public] order and which they [the troublesome workers] constantly provoke . . . only brings more poverty to the proletarians, robbing them of their children's bread, for a lack of confidence and certainty directly attacks business centers, paralyzing the activities that produce the collective well-being.[25]

In the case of a 1938 strike against a theater that exhibited Mexican-made films, a magazine editorial denounced the strikers as "obstructionists" who seemed "to redeem our masses; but ultimately they strengthen the chains that bind us to the industry of other countries."[26] People who incite workers, the editorial continued, only alienate other Mexicans, thus harming national unity and national interests.

Such remarks may seem incongruous in a regime that cultivated a revolutionary image. Yet rather than contradicting nationalism, the Revolutionary myth reinforced it through its equation of the Revolution with the government, which represented the nation. Criticisms of the government's ideological inconsistencies could be dismissed with the claim that the "uniquely Mexican" Revolution

had no need to adhere to "*doctrinas exóticas.*" One historian gave the
following description of this phenomenon:

Thus, while nationalism leaves behind its inferiority complexes in economic matters . . . , in political matters it trembles . . . before the idea
of contamination. And the fear is such that the idea of the revolution is
isolated, in the texts, from the rest of the universe, by means of an obviously ridiculous and false pretense of autogeneration, uniqueness and
originality. . . . A nationalism bordering on hysteria insists on sterilizing
the idea of the revolution.[27]

Like its revolutionary claims, nationalism posed a dilemma for
the Mexican government. While it promoted domestic unity, it also
could cause tension in Mexico's foreign relations. Cárdenas' expropriation of foreign oil, for example, is probably even now the most
popular act of any Mexican president, although it caused U.S.-
Mexican relations to deteriorate so seriously that some Americans
called for an invasion of Mexico. Conversely, Obregón's concessions to American-owned oil companies in contravention of the
constitution (the Bucareli agreement) helped win diplomatic recognition of his new government and improved Mexico's relations with
the United States, yet the Bucareli agreement was widely regarded
as a betrayal of national integrity and was one of the most criticized
acts of Obregón's presidency.

In general, however, nationalism helped build the myth of the
Revolution. Propaganda strengthened the myth further by weak-
ening the political consciousness and historical awareness needed to
make a critical examination of it.

THE OBFUSCATION OF HISTORY AND THE
DENIGRATION OF POLITICS

As Roland Barthes said in his *Mythologies*,

The world enters language as a dialectical relation between activities, between human actions; it comes out of myth as a harmonious display of
essences. A conjuring trick has taken place; it has . . . emptied [reality] of
history and has filled it with nature, it has removed from things their
human meaning so as to make them signify a human insignificance. . . .
[In bourgeois society] *myth is depoliticized speech.*[28]

The Mexican regime's use of the revolution as a symbol to unify the nation contradicted one of the most obvious characteristics of the revolution—its disunity. In 1914 the revolutionaries split roughly along class lines, leading to the wars from which the middle-class factions emerged victorious over the campesinos and radicals. The subsequent struggles among the middle-class revolutionaries were largely personalistic, but still murderous.

The factionalism, treachery, and venality of so many revolutionaries caused considerable cynicism and disillusionment even in the early years of the revolution, as illustrated by Mariano Azuela's *Los de Abajo*. This classic novel of the revolution, written in 1915, dealt with the reaction of idealistic constitucionalistas when confronted with the barbarity and criminality of their companions-in-arms. Referring to their struggle against Huerta, one character commented: "What a terrible disappointment it would be, my friend, if those of us who are putting into this all our enthusiasm, our hopes, and our very lives to overthrow a bandit who is a murderer should turn out to fashion a monstrous pedestal for a hundred or two hundred scoundrels."[29]

Carranza's administration convinced many people that the scoundrels had indeed taken over the revolution; in 1920 the aguaprietistas claimed that they had delivered the revolution out of the hands of the scoundrels in order to make it once again worthy of popular support. Obregón had used the notion of restoring the revolution to justify his revolt against Carranza, but there was no one, true revolution to restore. Differences had emerged before Madero became president and had grown more severe with time; some spoke of different revolutions, such as the 1910 revolution, the 1913 revolution, the agrarian revolution, and at one point the aguaprietistas' insurrection was called "our latest revolution."

Obregón's administration did not say which of the revolutions it would restore. It denounced Carranza and proclaimed itself agrarianist even though it had more in common with the carrancistas. The "revolution" of its propaganda was appropriately vague, with decreasing historical references to factional struggles that could raise questions about the political genesis of the new government or disturb the image of *the* Revolution.

The trend to mute past differences continued as the Mexican government struggled for hegemony in the 1920s and 1930s. A misrepresentation of Carranza's political position, for example, accompanied his gradual official acceptance, as when the land reform decrees he issued from Veracruz in early 1915 were cited as evidence of his radical outlook rather than as an expedient measure to break popular support for Zapata and Villa.

After the 1929 campaign to bring all political forces under the umbrella of the PNR, less emphasis was put on Carranza's role in Zapata's assassination. In 1930, the government distributed a calendar that featured Zapata's picture for the month of April. The picture's caption merely stated that he had been "treacherously assassinated in moments of blind political passion."[30] A memorial pamphlet honoring Carranza that year mentioned neither the factional nature of, nor the names of those responsible for, his assassination, stating only that the Plan of Agua Prieta had disavowed Carranza as president and that he died—rather than saying that he had been assassinated—on May 21, 1920.[31]

A "homogenization" of the official revolutionary heroes also contributed to the image of a unified Revolution. Propagandists diverted attention away from the factional differences among the heroes and toward their supposed personal characteristics. Because a major goal of the propaganda about Madero, Zapata, and Carranza was to make them national heroes, propagandists attributed traditional heroic characteristics to them: courage, strength, integrity, perseverance, manliness. To those qualities they added the nationalistic virtues of Mexicanness and dedication to the Mexican people. During the revolution, these three leaders clearly represented different political movements, but in the 1920s and 1930s their images grew more similar as they were portrayed chiefly as brave Mexican men, heroes of an undifferentiated national revolution. Zapata could still be hailed as the champion of the campesinos, but his specific class significance blurred because the Revolution had appropriated the campesino as its own symbol. Carranza was hailed as a great revolutionary, but never as the champion of the middle class. ("Bourgeois ideology is defined by the abandonment of the name 'bourgeois' . . . ," wrote Barthes.)[32]

The homogenization of the heroes implicitly denied that the pursuit of often hostile class interests had been an important force in the revolution. It created the impression that the revolution had been a unified rising-up of a people whose common Mexicanness was their most salient and determinant characteristic. The revolutionaries' internal conflicts were explained away as "personal" ambitions or "political passions" which were "blind" and therefore irrational.

The propagandists' tendency to invert cause and effect further mystified the history of the revolution. Rather than depicting the revolution as the product of human actions, they frequently treated it as the historical actor, using phrases such as "principles conquered by the Revolution," or "one of the most interesting men the Revolution has given."

Such phrases may have been only a convenient way of speaking, but it was a way of speaking that reinforced the reification of the revolution. The capitalization of the word "Revolution" and the popular phrase "the Revolution is the Revolution" were both part of the tendency to treat the revolution as a thing in itself requiring no further definition, a force apart from people and beyond their responsibility. For example, one of the most famous passages in *Los de Abajo* said, " . . . the revolution is a hurricane, and any man who is swept up in it is a wretched helpless dry leaf."[33] Two decades later, in the midst of the Cárdenas administration, a journalist made a similar comparison, saying: "The causes of revolutions are as obscure as those of earthquakes. A revolution erupts in the same way that rocks appear and springs flow forth after a geological process of thousands of years."[34]

The regime's propaganda also denigrated politics. The various admonitions to keep "politics" out of the commemorative ceremonies showed that the revolution was "above politics"—a desirable place to be, given that national leaders' machinations frequently gave people reason to regard politics as the crass, dirty business of unscrupulous men.

Treating the revolution as "above politics" helped protect the government from criticism and fostered the illusion that the government's critics were the only ones to capitalize on the heroes to promote their own interests. Shielded by their Revolutionary title, government politicians could denounce a rival or cohort who had become a liability. By pointing to politicians' faults, especially those who did wrong in the name of the revolution, the government as a whole could be protected from critical scrutiny—a ploy Barthes calls the acknowledgement of "the accidental evil of a class-bound institution the better to conceal its principal evil."[35] At the 1924 Zapata memorial, for example, a speaker introduced presidential candidate Calles with a diatribe against politicians that applied equally well to Calles even though the speaker implied that Calles was not a politician. "Campesinos," he cried,

> do not let yourselves be tricked. . . . Before coming to you politicians generally go to anterooms of the landowners in order to fabricate disgusting lies . . . , fooling the landowners as well as all of you. Fortunately we have here a man who will follow the road initiated by the martyr Zapata: General Calles. He is clean. . . . [36]

Despite the denigration of politics, interest in the revolution remained unabated. It was one of the major themes of periodical literature, although at times the authors took special measures to assure readers that their stories were apolitical. One Leopoldo Zamora Plowes prefaced his story about Villa with the claim that "this is not a political novel. Nor does it have political tendencies. . . . It is a historical novel, without didactic pretensions and without the passions of sectarianism."[37]

Free from the taint of "politics," the revolution became a fountain of new folklore and stereotypes that would become national symbols: the "Adelita"—the tough, self-sacrificing soldier woman and camp follower; the "Juan"—the humble, anonymous Indian soldier in an ill-fitting uniform; the guerrilla/bandit—the steely-eyed, fearless man with cartridge belts doubled across his chest. The revolutionary wars, like many wars, generated innumerable tales of heroism, the soldier's loyalty to his companions, ill-fated love affairs, and so forth. Those images and tales, however, did not simply belong to a past war, they belonged as well to the ongoing Revolutionary regime and were treated as a part of the national identity, as an attribute of *lo mexicano*. *Revista de Revistas*, one of the longest-running magazines in Mexico, conducted a short-story contest in 1928, announcing it to its readers with the proviso that "the theme of all the works that are included in this contest will be absolutely MEXICAN, without treating political or religious subjects, although this condition in no way excludes revolutionary topics."[38]

CHRISTIAN IMAGERY AND THE PROMOTION
OF CATHOLIC VALUES

Because the Catholic Church exercised vast temporal as well as religious power in Mexico for hundred of years, it thoroughly permeated the culture. Even nonbelievers were familiar with basic Christian tenets, and the church provided most of the formal education for the population, especially the rural poor. For many it was the sole educator.

On the simplest level, government propagandists' frequent recourse to Christian language and analogies helped make their pronouncements about the Revolution comprehensible to the common people. The familiarity of the Christian rhetoric made government propaganda more acceptable and more accessible than Marxist or other overtly political rhetoric did. It also countered the conservative complaint that the government's supposedly materialist, socialist philosophy made it insensitive to the spiritual nature of the human being.

At the same time, the propaganda's Christian rhetoric functioned as the symbolic adjunct to government efforts to restrict the church to narrowly defined religious matters while increasing government power in an enlarged sphere of secular concerns. The propagandists appropriated Christian language and analogies. By replacing their religious content with Revolutionary content, they secularized them and put their psychological force in service to the government.

The secularization of Christian symbols could have indicated a radical reconception of human capacity in relation to God. In the repeated comparisons of the revolutionary heroes to Christ lay the germ of the idea that humans are their own salvation, that God is or is in the human. The comparisons to Christ could have reflected the argument that the qualities attributed to God are projected human qualities and the reification of those projections is God. According to this argument, such reification diminishes people's collective ability to determine their social existence; when people recognize these things they will reclaim their godly qualities and God will cease to exist.

The use of Christian language in Revolutionary rhetoric, however, was not an attempt to negate a reified view of the world.

Most revolutionaries—despite the opposition of many to the Catholic Church—were neither Marxists nor atheists, and the radical potential of their appropriated Christian symbolism remained undeveloped. Instead the regime's propaganda perpetuated a religious, particularly Roman Catholic, mentality, with the reified Revolution as the new "religion."

The transference of religious feeling to the Revolution was also encouraged by the "sanctification" of the revolution's "martyrs." Their sanctification—promoted by treating the (Christian) virtuousness of their supposedly immaculate character as more important than their political roles—was completed with the ritualistic commemoration of their martyrdoms and the development of a full iconography around each of the official heroes. The insistence that the cults were above politics fortified their religious aura.

The religious approach to the revolution helped the government consolidate by reproducing in civic culture the hierarchical, patriarchal, authoritarian social order then characteristic of Catholic culture. Catholicism traditionally encouraged fatalism, discouraged freedom of conscience, and insisted on obedience to the church. It declared that the men in its hierarchy were the only people capable of interpreting the true religion, for via the popes they had inherited Christ's ordination of Saint Peter as Keeper of the Faith. All decisions in matters of faith were to be left to the church hierarchy; popular participation was not desired, nor was popular understanding of the hierarchy's decisions. The only requirement was that people do as their religious leaders instructed.

During the revolution the Catholic Church suffered legal attacks on its doctrine and institutional existence as well as physical attacks on its property and priests. Such attacks had occurred during the previous century, although less frequently, and were to continue in the decades following the revolution. The greater break from the traditional order was the irruption of the masses as a determinant force into the political life of the nation.

In radical departure from the political passivity taught by the church, the masses had come to believe that society should serve their welfare rather than only the elite's, and for nearly a decade they experienced their own power to shape events. Their collective understanding of what would actually improve their welfare was limited and their comprehension of their experience was inchoate,

which made it easier for the middle class to preserve their dominion over them. Nevertheless, the masses could no longer be used
with impunity. The dominant classes could still exploit them, but
only if they maintained the pretense that the "people's" welfare was
being served. This was something of a hollow victory for the masses,
yet it sufficed to create problems for the government by compelling
it to work within the parameters of a "revolutionary" public image.
The government's difficulty in maintaining mass support could be
lessened inasmuch as the population could be convinced to revert
to the passive acceptance of authority from which it had departed
at the beginning of the revolution.

Despite its continued struggle against Catholicism as a religion
and as a rival institution, the Revolutionary government did not
struggle to eliminate the patriarchal, authoritarian sociopolitical
mentality traditionally part of Catholic cultures. It merely sought
to supplant the church as the supreme institution and so continued
to promote those "Catholic" virtues that encouraged unquestioning
popular faith in its doctrines, reverence for its leaders, and loyalty
to its institutions.

The Madero, Zapata, and Carranza cults became vehicles for ap-
plauding humility, endurance of suffering, and sacrifice for the
Revolution. The presidents were endowed with a pope-like authority by presenting them as the heirs of the revolutionary Christs,
Madero and Zapata. In an atmosphere in which it was claimed that
Madero had triumphed because of the "justice of his ideal" rather
than the "support of the armed masses," and in which the official
party assured campesinos that they could "count on someone to
look out for you," the comparisons of the revolutionary heroes to
Christ did not imply that ordinary people were capable of heroism.
Instead it retained the Christian meaning of an extraordinary being
ordained from above come to save them; it discouraged democratic,
active engagement in political self-determination and encouraged
people to wait for leaders, to accept their authority. The leaders
and the authority, of course, were those of the government.

The last common trait of the Revolutionary propaganda, the promotion of patriarchal values and the masculinization of the public
images of the heroes, will be taken up in the following chapter.

CHAPTER 7

The Stabilized State and the Rise of Machismo

The [villistas] could not stop talking about what they had been a part of [in Columbus], they were intoxicated by the indelible memory of those three hours when they had the pride of a previously unviolated and supposedly inviolable nation under their feet. It was a sexual satisfaction they had experienced since they crossed that imaginary line that seemed to vibrate like an arm that wanted to stop them . . . ; the blood completed the illusion of a violent coupling [*himeneo violento*].

Rafael Muñoz, *Vámonos con Pancho Villa*

Women actively participated in the 1910 Revolution and in leftist, rightist, and feminist groups from 1920 to 1940.[1] The demands and dislocations of the war forced many women out of their traditional roles, which were further liberalized by the currents of social permissiveness and experimentation that also affected Europe and the United States during the 1920s. Women's legal status improved under the post-revolutionary government but did not reach parity with that of men. Mexican society remained profoundly sexist.

Sexism suffused the thinking and language of the day and was therefore amply reflected in the contemporary literature and the regime's propaganda. It was evident in the equation of strength and political power with sexual potency and masculinity (a corollary to the argument that women would lose their femininity if they acquired political power, equal rights, or suffrage), and in the fact that "virile" was the favored positive adjective for men, while a lack of virility was commonly attributed to ideas or men one did not like, as when one speaker ridiculed his opponents as castrated men. The higher value placed on male friendship also testified to the patriarchal quality of Mexican culture. For example, in a magazine story, two men, strangers to one another, engage in a machete duel for a "provocative fifteen-year-old girl" whom the one man wishes to take from the other; each is an excellent fighter who has never been beaten. As each realizes that he cannot beat the other, he is overcome with admiration for the other's skill and strength; they call off the fight and agree to share the girl (whose wishes in the matter are not mentioned) as a token of their mutual respect.[2] One of the most startling examples of the primacy of male relationships occurred in the novel *Vámonos con Pancho Villa*. Tiburcio's profoundest attachment was to Villa; his wife and children were only impediments. Villa also saw them as impediments, and so he killed them. But he killed only Tiburcio's girl child; he spared the boy because he too could become a villista.

If man-to-man bonds were valued, those of soldiers in battle—perhaps the quintessentially "masculine" activity—were especially glorious.

And to the comrade, oh! The comrade! . . . to him is owed a sacred place in the heart, . . . to love him as a brother, . . . to unite your emotions, your pleasures, and your sufferings and thus you will be a single soul that feels, . . . a single intelligence that thinks, a strong potent whole, capable of carrying out actions that transcend glory. . . .[3]

The relationship between the soldier and his female companion was idealized in a markedly different fashion. The following poem by the popular orator Baltasar Dromundo was included among those that the PNR's *Domingos Culturales* recommended for inspirational readings at civic ceremonies:

La Soldadera

You have deadened your feet
on the stones of the road;
Your belly is rent
by a barbarous tenderness,
multiplier of births;
on the rags over your teats

have been hung
those crucified in this agrarianist hour;
with your blood full of bacteria
you have filled with Nazarene sons,
as if with seeds,
the furrows of the Revolution;
and your sanctified brown flesh
opened at the command of Emiliano Zapata.
Because you gave birth to our children in the streets
or in prison;
because the victors possessed you
and we lost you in the pillage of all the disasters
when you were carrying our children in your flesh;
because they filled you with excretions
and hanged you from the trees,
because many like you stayed behind rotting
in the middle of the road . . .
And because you
like us,
have gambled your life . . .
                                        Sister *soldadera*,
          Blessed are thou![4]

In contrast to the fraternal ideal of the bond between male soldiers, the poem depicted an unequal relation between male and
female soldiers or camp followers characterized by the women's
service and sacrifice for the men. Dromundo glorified that inequality, praising the *soldadera* for allowing the men to use her body, for
enduring the abuse of the enemy troops, for suffering her body to
be "rent" to give sons to the Revolution. The carnality of this *soldadera* differed sharply from the ethereal motherhood commonly
depicted at the time and contradicted the notion that chastity was
the supreme female virtue. Similarly, the *soldadera*'s sanctification
through the sexual embrace of the revolutionary, symbolized by
Zapata, contrasted with the Virgin Mary's asexual conception of
Jesus.

These contrasts, with their studied grittiness, may have offended
conservative standards of propriety. Yet glorifying female sacrifice,
especially through motherhood, fit within general patriarchal and
Catholic concepts of a woman's role. Dromundo's *soldadera* was the
"revolutionary" rendition of the whore-with-a-heart-of-gold, a ste-

reotypical figure generated by the dichotomous image of women as virgins/whores. His *soldadera* fought for the Revolution through her men, and although he praised her, he saw the men, the "Nazarene sons," as the earthly and earthy saviors of Mexico.[5]

Given Mexico's deeply sexist culture, the glorification of the revolutionaries' manliness, especially that of lower-class men, represented an advance over pre-revolutionary social consciousness. The caste hierarchy of the *porfiriato* had deprived lower-class men of their manhood, or personhood, in that it brutalized their physical existence and denied them sociopolitical equality with upper-class men. It also deprived them of their manhood in the patriarchal sense: their class position made it difficult to provide adequately for their families or to exercise their patriarchal privileges of exclusive sexual control over "their" women. Class privileges of the upper-class men permitted them to meet their economic obligations to their families, to protect their sexual privileges (from lower-class men, although not necessarily from their equals), and to violate the patriarchal privileges of lower-class men, whose women they could seduce or abuse with virtual impunity.

The tales told about the revolution and life during the *porfiriato* often involved the sexual manifestations of class: a campesina commits suicide after being seduced and abandoned by the *hacendado*'s son; a young man runs off to join the revolution when his sweetheart is raped by the landowner; an Indian girl gives herself to the *hacendado* to protect her lover from punishment. The story about Villa's revenge for the rape of his sister was part of this same current. It is important to note that while such tales were actually tales of class abuse (men of the same class must fear retaliation for offending a man's honor), they were frequently portrayed as the usurpation of a man's patriarchal rights. A class conflict received a patriarchal, sexual expression.

In the language of sexist ideology, it may be said that racist class oppression emasculated lower-class men, who recovered their manhood during the revolution by assaulting the socioeconomic structures that had oppressed them. They then took their places, at least in theory, as equals in the post-revolutionary society. As they conceived it, equal manhood included the prerogatives of the patriarch. That entailed the continued oppression of women as women, although women shared in the improved status of their classes.

Patriarchal values were a crucial part of the ideological struggle between the church and the Mexican government, with each side appealing to those values in an attempt to discredit the other. Conservative Catholics regarded the legalization of divorce, civil marriage, coeducation, birth control, and women's working for wages as a socialist campaign to undermine Christian morality and the Christian family, which they believed to be dependent upon female subjugation to the male. They painted lurid pictures of the corruption of children exposed too soon to "the facts of life," of women seduced and abandoned when there were no laws to bind their husbands to them permanently.

The advocates of the liberalization of sex-related laws claimed that education and freedom in sexual matters would ennoble relations between men and women by making them a matter of informed choice rather than ignorance and superstition. Nevertheless, these sexual liberals were not always free of patriarchal attitudes, for in arguing their case they often appealed to patriarchal concepts of family honor, just as the Catholics did, and exploited men's fears about their control over their wives. They differed from the Catholics in that they accused the priests themselves of being the greatest danger to women's purity and the sanctity of the family, and of abusing women's sexual ignorance. "Fathers of families, husbands, brothers, and men in general," were warned that "the confessional has always been a school of prostitution," where priests seduced not only their female relatives but also their sons, for "sodomy is a common practice . . . among priests."[6] Husbands were also cautioned that

from the moment of confession their wives have lost all modesty, and are obligated by the priests to conduct themselves in their conjugal life according to his judgement, whence the dissatisfaction in the marriage, the constancy toward the Church and the preference for the priest instead of the husband.[7]

El Eco Revolucionario, a newspaper published to support Cárdenas' presidential campaign, ran an article that suggested the "very respectable *DAMAS CATÓLICAS*," a conservative women's organization, already knew about the lascivious appetites of the clergy. The article went on to discredit them in a common sexist fashion—

by impugning their sexual morality. The *Damas Católicas*, said the article, knew what priests did with women, and "perhaps for that reason they are such assiduous visitors to the confessional."[8]

Existing patriarchal attitudes were exploited in other politically convenient ways as well. For example, the patriarchal ideal of manhood included the duty to provide for one's family—a useful notion during the "constructive" period of the Revolution, when it was necessary to tend to the needs of the war-ravaged population, whose most immediate problems of survival were often related to the breakdown of the traditional family structure. Hunger and disease had left their mark, and innumerable women and children who had been left without husbands, fathers, or families were ill-prepared to provide for themselves.[9] The dislocated peasants who came to the cities were ill-prepared to make the transition from farming or the chaotic libertinage of war to life as a wage laborer in the harsh independence and anonymity of city life.

The government attempted to resolve some of the resultant problems by campaigning against prostitution, venereal disease, and alcoholism, exhorting men to shoulder the responsibility for their families' health. One purpose of the many civic centers the government opened in Mexico City around 1930 was to draw "workers away from vice, forming in them a clear consciousness of responsibility."[10] Strengthening the family also provided a quick way to restore the population's physical and "moral" health, to make the most efficient use of their meager economic resources, and to create responsible workers for the rebuilding of the economy. Patriarchal values complemented the anti-vice campaign by providing an image of a "real man" as one who conscientiously supported his family rather than one who caroused and dissipated his health and earnings. One writer offered this description of Zapata:

We see him affirm with deeds his criterion of responsible manhood. . . . suffering a father's anguish to be with and to care for his children. We see him prefer his family's every call over the lure of the fiesta, the rodeo, the cockfight. . . . Thus we see him . . . a perfect model of a man responding in every economic circumstance to the needs of the woman he loved.[11]

Patriarchy influenced collective social organization as well as individual gender roles. The modeling of all relations between social superiors and inferiors on the father-child relationship ran deep in Mexico. It was evident in the relations between the landowner and the peasants in the hacienda system, for example, and in those between the clergy and the faithful. The widespread existence of *caudillos* (regional strongmen who ruled in patron-client systems) well into the 1930s provides a more obviously political example of the patriarchal organization of Mexican society. And yet another sign of the association between the father and the leader or boss is the practice of calling one's father *mi jefe*, while the popular sense of the father's superiority is evinced (negatively) by the use of the term "your father" as an insult. Referring to the song "La Cucaracha," in which Villa is called Carranza's father, Rutherford wrote " 'su padre' is a particularly insulting way of referring to one man's utter superiority over another. . . . [The] basic Mexican meaning is 'I enjoy absolute dominance over you.' "[12]

The propagandists presented the father's or *jefe*'s dominance over the son or "inferior" as a positive, mutually advantageous relationship. "The basis of Moral Instruction," intoned an article about the army, "is discipline, adherence to the *Jefe* and the comrade." With mutual responsibilities rigorously fulfilled, "there will be between the superior and the inferior a more intimate relation, greater communion of ideas, . . . and the latter will be more attached to his *Jefe*, coming to see him as a family member whom he loves and respects."[13]

Ideally the father or leader loved and protected his dependents or inferiors in return for their subordination. This ideal was reflected in the fact that the belief that Villa cared intensely about his *muchachos* (his boys, as he called them) was one of the most positive elements in his image. In the movie *Vámonos con Pancho Villa*, the *Leones*' loyalty to one another and to Villa was their greatest virtue, while Villa's failure to reciprocate constituted his greatest flaw.

In sum, the propagandists frequently praised the heroes for their manliness, attributed all the virtues of the ideal patriarch to them (wisdom, strength, courage, perseverance, self-control, dignified reserve, protection of the weak, punishment of wrongdoing), and set them up as father figures. Zapata was called Father of the Agrarianists, Carranza became the Great Father of the Fatherland, and so on.[14] This masculinization of the heroes of the regime encouraged a transference of the feelings they inspired to the government itself, which thereby symbolically claimed the role of the supreme patriarch. It facilitated the regime's exploitation of patriarchal attitudes for political purposes, appealing to the personalist mentality still important in Mexican politics while harnessing it to government institutions. The masculinization of the hero cults also reduced the need to confront personalism ideologically even as the government sought to eliminate it in practice by gradually subordinating the *caudillos* to the national state.

But the relation between the myth and patriarchy was a two-way street. Because patriarchal attitudes had autonomous currency in the culture, there were limits to how much the propagandists could manipulate them in the promotion of the hero cults. At some point the propaganda had to conform to patriarchy's standards in order to be successful, and this not all the cults did equally well. Inasmuch as the cults treated masculinity as the most important quality in a hero and weakened the political and historical understanding needed to judge the heroes by other criteria, Zapata and especially Villa were bound to eclipse Madero and Carranza, who, despite the propagandists' efforts to masculinize them, simply could not meet the prevailing standards of machismo. Zapata's and Villa's class, their reputation as womanizers and as blood-and-guts fighters, automatically gave them more macho appeal than the stolid Carranza and mild Madero could ever achieve.

It seems likely that additional factors—such as the internal tensions of patriarchy itself and the growing conservatism of the postrevolutionary regime—compounded popular preference for the macho figure over the father figure (two variants of the manly ideal) and further fused the revolutionary's image to that of the macho. These factors contributed to the institutionalization of machismo that is today a *fait accompli*.

To pursue this hypothesis, it first must be understood that patriarchy necessarily entails some repression of the "son" and the negation of his "manhood." Ideally the son accepts his inferior role because the "father" provides for him and because it is only a temporary role: the son is destined to become a father himself, with full social recognition of his manhood and power over a family of his own.

However, many things may hamper the realization of the pa-

triarchal ideal. The father, for example, may not provide adequately for the family, or the son may feel that the father is trying
to keep him in an inferior role permanently even though he feels
he deserves to be treated as an adult man. In such cases the son
may rebel against his subordination. The rebellion could include
the rejection of the entire patriarchal system, but machismo does
not. It rejects only the restraints and responsibilities that are im-
posed as the price of manhood and instead demands all manhood's
privileges by force. The macho is the male perpetual adolescent,
the swaggering bully forever proving his manhood by bravado, by
besting other men, by dominating women.

In addition to the difficulties of the father–son relationship, racism may deny a man economic opportunity, legal equality, and the
respect of others; poverty may force him to tolerate menial work
and subservience to his "betters," to be their "boy," and may prevent him from providing for his family. Social conditions may, in
short, prevent him from meeting the obligations and exercising the
rights which society tells him are the requisites of true manhood.
Under such conditions, the man's reaction against society (or the
"system," the boss, authority, etc.) is analogous to the son's reaction against the father who imposes impossible standards that must
be met before the son will be acknowledged as a "real" man. Machismo is a way of demanding that acknowledgement; it offers relief from the burdens of an inferior social status and the responsibilities a man cannot meet because of that status. The macho who
rabidly controls every aspect of his woman's life, who impresses
the men at the bar with his disdain for the consequences of drinking up his entire paycheck, who is quick to attack any man who
wittingly or unwittingly bruises his vulnerable ego, enjoys an illu-
sory sense of power as he defies the people and the conventions
that confine, repress, and impoverish his existence. His machismo,
however, does nothing to change the socioeconomic structure that
denies him his manhood in the first place.

It has already been shown that in the 1920s and 1930s the Mexican government assumed a paternal posture vis-à-vis the citizenry,
in whom a filial identification with the government was encouraged. The fulfillment of patriarchal obligations was portrayed as a
patriotic obligation as well, and the new revolutionary society
promised equality and full manhood for men of all classes and races.

But the new government did not fulfill its revolutionary promise: sociopolitical equality did not materialize and the vast majority of men continued to live under conditions that denied them the possibility of realizing the patriarchal ideal.

These circumstances, theoretically, made the relation between the Revolution and the citizenry analogous to that of the father who fails to adequately provide for his son yet demands his obedience, while the son gradually comes to realize that he will never achieve the promised manhood. In the 1920s and 1930s the government seemed to be trying to carry out reforms that would benefit the masses, and it was unreasonable to expect that it could quickly construct a prosperous and egalitarian society in the wake of a decade of revolutionary warfare and political chaos. While the regime was still forming, it was possible (although skepticism was rife from the beginning) for the popular classes to think that the Revolution would keep its promises. They could endure the difficulties of the moment because the future promised a more just society and material improvements for all.

But doubt grew over the years, and after 1940 when the institutionalization of the regime was successfully completed, it was evident that the shortcomings of the Revolution were not temporary— they were the new status quo. The "sons' " incentive to tolerate their social limitations decreased accordingly, but collective political and/or armed rebellion had been made very difficult by the expansion of the official party system, by two decades of repression of the political opposition, and by the weight of the propaganda that worked against such actions—that is, by the same forces that worked in favor of the institutionalization of the government. Rebellious feelings therefore were manifested as alienation from politics and rejection of the father-figure model of the revolutionary hero, who symbolized an impossible ideal as well as the forces that made that ideal impossible. The macho, the rebel against the father and a model of a kind of manhood within the reach of most men, became the favored image of Mexican men. This image, which had been around for some time, developed into the national stereotype in the 1940s when the Revolution abandoned its socialistic pretenses and took a distinctly conservative turn.

The mythical macho revolutionary is in essence the same creature as the patriarch revolutionary of the 1920s and 1930s (who still has not completely disappeared), but the more rebellious version of masculinity represented by the macho makes him a more appropriate symbol of revolution. And because the macho represents sexual license and aggression, the macho revolutionary expresses sexual as well as political frustration.

The greater identification with the macho strengthened the hero cults of Villa and Zapata and weakened those of Madero and Carranza. This presented little problem for the regime's propagandists, for it coincided with a decline in the need to use propaganda to sell the Revolution to the middle class and conservatives. Also, the flagging popularity of the Revolution made it desirable for the regime to strengthen its claim to Zapata and to stake a claim to Villa, men whose class identity and macho image made them more credible revolutionary symbols, more appealing to the popular classes, and therefore more useful propaganda tools.

The macho element of Zapata's image has developed over the years—witness the 1970 movie *Zapata* by Felipe Cazals in which Zapata, still in his *cananas* and spurs, beds his beautiful blond wife. It has distorted zapatismo by treating it as a personalist movement, the result of one man's charisma, rather than as a collective movement, but it has not divorced Zapata from his political roots. Nor has it generalized his popularity, for the relative lack of novels or movies about him suggests that the Mexican middle class never embraced Zapata fully. Zapata continues to symbolize the campesinos' struggle for justice because his articulate perseverance in that cause cannot easily be erased and because the Mexican government needs to preserve his political identity as evidence of its own revolutionary politics.

Villa also appealed to campesinos, but the vagueness of his politics broadened his cross-class popularity, and his lack of official recognition made him a more ready symbol of opposition to the government. To the degree that the revolution was successfully mystified, Villa's struggle was emptied of political content. Villa became a symbol of rebellion per se, through whom all manner of people could vicariously rebel against whatever injustice or social limitation they wished. And because Villa was always seen as the arch-macho, his image, more than that of any other cult figure, fused and confused sexual and political rebellion.

In the 1960s the Mexican government finally inducted Villa into the official pantheon of Revolutionary heroes. As Mexico gained international prestige, the government probably deemed it unseemly that the most famous Mexican in the world should continue to stand outside and in contradiction of the official Revolution. Additionally, when popular protest against the uneven distribution of the fruits of the "Mexican miracle" (the rapid economic growth of the 1950s and 1960s) met repression and massacre while the 1968 Olympics were in progress in Mexico City, the government faced international embarrassment and a crisis of legitimacy. The construction in 1969 of a huge statue of Villa on the avenue named for his *División del Norte* may have been part of the government's effort to restore its revolutionary image in the wake of the crisis of 1968.

And what of the efficacy of the official hero cults? In the long run the government adopted the one hero it had studiously ignored for decades, while the only one of the official heroes to survive much beyond the 1930s was the one who had been the most appropriate symbol of the campesino revolution in the first place. The cults did not significantly alter the public images that the various leaders had had during the revolutionary war.

Yet the masculinization of the heroes has contributed to the mystification of the revolution. Villa's incorporation, for example, may have been possible because his macho image so effectively obscured his political significance. Even today leftists tend to believe that Villa was basically a bandit and not a worthy hero, and to idolize the "purer" Zapata, just as the government would have them do. And scholars have only recently tried to demystify Villa's role in the revolution.[15]

Ironically, it is the myth of Villa and Zapata that keeps the public aware of them and increases the likelihood that the truth of their lives will be rescued from the myths. Because Villa and Zapata were basically class heroes who represented still unresolved grievances against the propertied classes, their images carry within history lessons that belie the myth of the Revolution. The incorporation of Villa and Zapata has at its core a contradiction: it keeps alive the threat it is supposed to subvert. The same propaganda that dazzles the public with their machismo perpetuates the possibility that the examples of their struggles may undermine the ideology of the present regime.

The final meaning of the cults remains indeterminate. The macho blends into the revolutionary and back again; the myth of the Revolution cannot be completely defined and therefore cannot be definitively rejected. This ambiguity, this continually re-created potential, gives the myth resilience and vitality. Its continued existence attests to its viability in Mexican culture. However, the fact that opposition to the government also continues indicates that the myth of the Revolution is not entirely successful: politicizing as well as depoliticizing forces are at work in Mexico. The longevity of the myth, like that of the regime it supports, stems not from the defeat of all opposition but from its capacity to co-opt opposition.

The greatest politicizing force in Mexico has been and continues to be the injustice, inequality, and poverty of Mexican society. Throughout the evolution of the myth of the Revolution, patriarchal ideology has vitiated political consciousness. The glorification of machismo is an especially effective deterrent to political consciousness because it functions as a safety valve, giving politically innocuous (though personally destructive) expression to what are, in the final analysis, political discontents caused by domestic and international socioeconomic inequities. The legitimation of machismo leaves intact the system that engenders the need for its compensatory mechanisms and even protects that system by co-opting the revolutionary potential of hostility toward the "father" and the dominant order. Whether people will see the true reason for Mexico's social ills depends upon whether they are able to see the falseness of the Revolutionary myth and ultimately the falseness of the patriarchal system that upholds it.

APPENDIX

A Discussion of Sources and Methodology

This study of the myth of the Revolution has focused on the public commemorations of four leading revolutionaries who became integral parts of the myth, for it was on such occasions that official and quasi-official pronouncements about the heroes' historical significance occurred with the greatest abundance. The memorial acts provided a way to trace the mystification process systematically and in relation to the varying political concerns of the successive presidential administrations.

Although the memorial acts were usually official affairs conducted under the auspices of the *Ayuntamiento* of Mexico City, which became a part of the *Departamento del Distrito Federal* in the 1920s, I was unable to find official records of them. The annual reports of the *Ayuntamiento* and the DDF, their *Memorias*, were kept in the *Archivos Históricos del Ayuntamiento* in the central office of the DDF in Mexico City. In consulting the *Memorias*, however, I found little information about the memorial acts. They usually stated that the office in charge of the celebrations had carried out its duties, but did not say what days were commemorated, in what way, or why.

According to the 1979 head of *Acción Civil* (the division of the DDF now in charge of civic ceremonies), there are no set policies that his office follows, no records of their plans, no formal directives from above, and no collections of their publications. He suggested that the previous offices had been operated in the same way. Tradition, he said, and the question of whether the president would attend a ceremony, determines the nature and the size of any particular commemoration. Each president has his favorite heroes. For lesser occasions, political discretion on the part of the planners of the ceremonies is the main guide. If Congressman X is in favor this year, his favorite local patriot will appear in the civic calendar; if Congressman X then alienates the powers that be, his local hero quietly disappears from the civic calendar. It is a matter of bureaucratic sensitivity and self-preservation, not carefully designed directives from above, that shapes the memorial events.

If this was also the case in the 1920s and 1930s, then there was no direct documentation of the government's plans for promoting patriotism and civic virtues. But while the *Memorias* of that period seem to corroborate the idea that somehow "everyone knew" what celebrations were carried out, tradition could not have been as strong a factor then, only a few years after the deaths of the revolutionary heroes, as it is now. Especially in the 1920s, official memorial acts must have been in part an attempt to create a civic tradition.

In the Basave Collection at the Biblioteca de Mexico, the Revolution Collection at the Biblioteca Nacional, and in miscellaneous filings at the Hemeroteca Nacional, there are various leaflets and pamphlets which were apparently distributed by government offices at the commemorations of the deaths of the Revolutionary heroes. Some of the pamphlets indicate that they are part of a series, but there seems to be no way to determine the full content of the series. Unfortunately, these items are often insufficiently identified to know their source or their purpose or are miscatalogued.

The principal source for this study has therefore been the periodicals of Mexico City. They may be the only source that permits a systematic study of the public hero cults, and happily they are a very good source. Newspapers reported the official ceremonies, included excerpts from speeches, commented on relevant political gossip, and offered the reader additional essays and editorial comment on the hero of the day. Although the illiteracy rate was high in Mexico, periodicals had a broader and less elite readership than books and novels, relative to which they had greater influence upon and were a closer reflection of public opinion.

By the strictest standards of interpretation, Mexico City newspapers only speak for Mexico City. However, Mexico City was the historical hub of the nation, the seat of government, and increasingly an indicator of national trends as regionalism eroded throughout this century. From 1917 to 1940 the press there, with few exceptions, purveyed official and quasi-official attitudes about conditions in Mexico. Carranza largely controlled the press by buying it out or buying off reporters, a practice continued by his successors. Journalists that antagonized powerful people could well find their presses smashed or find themselves in jail. Criticism of the government was possible, but only by the grace of its leaders, despite the legal right to freedom of the press.

In 1934 a more bureaucratic way to keep the press in line came with the formation of PIPSA (*Productora e Importadora de Papel*, S.A.). PIPSA nominally encouraged freedom of the press by subsidizing the production of

paper in order to make it financially feasible for more periodicals to pub-
lish. However, almost from its formation, charges were made that paper
shipments were bungled or stopped altogether for periodicals that had annoyed the government. Paper was usually given on credit, which PIPSA
could suddenly call in if it wished—a legal move, but one that effectively
stopped the offending periodical from publishing. This practice too continues today.

It is difficult to gauge the extent of the restrictions on the press in the
1920s and 1930s. The problem in reconstructing unofficial censorship is
that the effectively silenced voice could not bear witness to its silencing.
Violence against the press stimulated self-censorship and "discretion." A
satirical columnist wrote in *Uno Mas Uno* in 1979 that "what can bring you
problems with the censor is mentioning the existence of censorship. In
Mexico there is no censorship, there is only the voice of prudence that
cries out from the interstices of the heart."

The bibliography lists the majority, but not all, of the periodicals consulted. There were many sporadic publications that yielded no information
relevant to this study and were not included. From the 1920–1940 period
the assassination dates were examined in at least four periodicals, with
variations according to how early relevant articles began or how long they
continued. In cases of nondaily periodicals or missing issues, the nearest
dates were consulted. *El Universal* was the only daily newspaper that published throughout those two decades; along with the other important dailies of the period—*Excelsior*, *El Nacional*, and *El Demócrata*—it provided a
stable, mainstream view of the major events in Mexico. The other periodicals listed were of a diverse nature socially and politically and helped
to round out the impression created by the big daily newspapers.

Notes

CHAPTER 1

1. "Today . . . the Mexican Revolution remains a vital force in Mexican life. Everything and everyone Mexican—even the anti-revolutionary who most loudly rails against . . . the events of half a century—exists in an atmosphere permeated with its spirit. Every major topic is approached, considered, accepted, or rejected in terms of what the Revolution is supposed to stand for, and no serious proponent of just about anything would dream of forgetting to claim legitimacy for his . . . point of view by labeling it the authentic voice, perhaps the only authentic voice, of the Revolution. Nor would a newspaper . . . seem complete without its memoir of a hero of those hectic days during which the Revolution was being formed, or its editorial exhorting Mexico to live up to the ideals for which such men fought." Robert E. Scott, *Mexican Government in Transition* (Urbana: University of Illinois Press, 1959), p. 96.

2. The phrase "the Revolution is the Revolution" (also occasionally spelled with lower case *r*s) apparently evolved from the phrase "the Revolution is revolution," which John D. Rutherford, *Mexican Society During the Revolution: A Literary Approach* (Oxford: Clarendon Press, 1971), p. 120, says was first attributed to Luis Cabrera on 20 June 1911 in the Mexico City papers *El País* and *El Diario del Hogar*. Cabrera was reminding people that the Revolution was a difficult and violent event, not a "garden party"— a remark in the spirit of "You can't make an omelette without breaking eggs," and one more sensible than its subsequent renditions.

3. This study does not enter the debate over whether the Mexican Revolution was a "true" revolution and, if so, what kind. For an overview of the debate, see Stanley R. Ross, *Is the Mexican Revolution Dead?* (New

York: Knopf, 1966); Donald Hodges and Ross Gandy, *Mexico 1910–1976: Reform or Revolution?* (London: Zed Press, 1979); for an analysis of the ideologies of the revolutionary factions, see Arnaldo Córdova, *La Ideología de la Revolución Mexicana: La Formación del Nuevo Régimen* (Mexico: Ediciones Era, 1973).

4. Roland Barthes, *Mythologies*, selected and translated by Annette Lavers (New York: Hill and Wang, 1972), p. 109.

5. Ibid., p. 143.

6. The ceremony described is a composite of ceremonies the author attended in Chinameca and Cuautla on 10 April 1979, and in Cuautla and Anenecuilco on 8 August 1979.

7. A campesino (from *campo*, meaning field or countryside) is a person, usually poor, from the country. The word encompasses peasants who own their own land and agricultural laborers who work someone else's land.

8. Barthes, p. 122.

9. Samuel Ramos, *El Perfil del Hombre y la Cultura en México* (Mexico: Imprenta Mundial, 1934), translated by Peter G. Earle as *Profile of Man and Culture in Mexico* (Austin: University of Texas Press, 1962); Octavio Paz [Jr.], *El Laberinto de la Soledad* (Mexico: Fondo de Cultura Económica, 1959), translated by Lysander Kemp as *The Labyrinth of Solitude* (New York: Grove Press, 1961).

10. Díaz came to power in 1876. Around 1900 a lively, persecuted opposition developed, a disproportionate part of which came from northern Mexico. For a study of the opposition, see James D. Cockcroft, *Intellectual Precursors of the Mexican Revolution, 1900–1913* (Austin: University of Texas Press, 1968). For a study of the most radical opposition, see David Poole, ed., *Land and Liberty: Anarchist Influences in the Mexican Revolution: Ricardo Flores Magón* (Montreal: Black Rose Books, 1977).

11. Ambassador Henry Lane Wilson supported the anti-Madero conspirators, permitted them to use the U.S. Embassy, and applauded Huerta's assumption of the presidency. Ernest Gruening, *Mexico and Its Heritage* (New York: Century, 1928), pp. 570–72; Stanley R. Ross, *Francisco I. Madero, Apostle of Mexican Democracy* (New York: Columbia University Press, 1955), pp. 293–311.

12. When Woodrow Wilson became president in 1913, he opposed Huerta's undemocratic procedures and was concerned that his pro-British attitude might undermine the United States' influence in Mexico. See Robert E. Quirk, *An Affair of Honor: Woodrow Wilson and the Occupation of Veracruz* (Lexington: University of Kentucky Press, 1962).

13. From the stenographic record of the preliminary interview of Villa and Zapata in Xochimilco on 4 December 1914, reprinted in a pamphlet

by the *Dirección General de Acción Social y Cultural* in honor of the hundredth anniversary of Zapata's birth (1979). This and all translations are mine.

14. The animosity between Carranza and Villa had become pronounced prior to the Aguascalientes Convention. Adolfo Gilly, *La Revolución Interrumpida: México, 1910–1920: Una Guerra Campesina por la Tierra y el Poder* (Mexico: Ediciones "El Caballito," 1971), pp. 87–138; Robert E. Quirk, *The Mexican Revolution, 1914–1915: The Convention of Aguascalientes* (Bloomington: Indiana University Press, 1960); Linda B. Hall, *Álvaro Obregón: Power and Revolution in Mexico, 1911–1920* (College Station: Texas A&M University Press, 1981), pp. 59–94.

15. Hall, ibid., pp. 95–119, attributes the Constitutionalists' recovery largely to Obregón's populist policies in Mexico City, and sees those policies as part of Obregón's cultivation of a power base independent of Carranza.

16. Friedrich Katz, *The Secret War in Mexico: Europe, the United States, and the Mexican Revolution*, with portions translated by Loren Goldner (Chicago: University of Chicago Press, 1981), pp. 307–8; Merle Simmons, *The Mexican CORRIDO as a Source for Interpretive Study of Modern Mexico (1870–1950)* (Bloomington: Indiana University Press, 1957), p. 262.

17. Katz, *The Secret War*, pp. 146, 318, and Hall, p. 115, say Carranza annoyed Obregón by exempting some businessmen from some of the taxes Obregón levied during the 1915 occupation of Mexico City.

18. Gruening, pp. 318–31, 393–493, lists many examples of the corruption and political violence in fourteen different states between 1921 and 1927; Córdova, *La Ideología*, pp. 376–79, lists the fortunes made by the revolutionary elite. Jesús Silva Herzog, *Una Vida en la Vida de México* (Mexico: Siglo Veintiuno Editores, 1972), pp. 101-9, lists political assassinations and concludes that "assassination, corruption and the PNR initially formed the triangle of Mexico's political stability."

19. Córdova, *La Ideología*, pp. 486–90. For a brief discussion of the Bucareli conferences, see John W. F. Dulles, *Yesterday in Mexico: A Chronicle of the Revolution, 1919–1936* (Austin: University of Texas Press, 1961), pp. 145–76, 188–96; Lorenzo Meyer, *México y los Estados Unidos en el Conflicto Petrolero (1917–1942)* (Mexico City: El Colegio de México, 1968), pp. 81–103. For criticism of the conferences by one who joined the De la Huerta Revolt, see Vito Alessio Robles, *Los Tratados de Bucareli* (Mexico: n.p., 1937).

20. Dulles, pp. 271–79; Gruening, pp. 357–90.

21. Tension between church and state had existed since the colonial period. The Catholic Church's immense wealth and temporal power irritated the government when it wished to have greater control or a larger

income. The liberal constitution of 1857 disincorporated indigenous communities and the church, whose vast lands were sold. Although the strong anti-clericalism of that period was ameliorated by Díaz' benign neglect of the church, it did not disappear. The clergy had a long history of dissipation that, especially in conjunction with their political conservatism, earned them many progressive people's dislike. This old antagonism reopened during the revolution and burst into war when church leaders denounced Calles' policies and the 1917 constitution. Dulles, pp. 296–315. Because the church opposed agrarian reform and other progressive legislation, the *cristeros* are often regarded as ignorant dupes or reactionaries. Jean A. Meyer, *The Cristero Rebellion: The Mexican People Between Church and State, 1926–1929*, translated by Richard Southern (Cambridge: Cambridge University Press, 1976), regards them as opposing the encroachment of an authoritarian state.

22. Despite resistance from some callistas, in late 1926 the constitution was amended to permit a nonconsecutive presidential reelection. Dulles, pp. 332–54, describes Obregón's election campaign and the Serrano and Gómez revolts. Their revolts and assassinations are described in Vito Alessio Robles, *Desfile Sangriento* (Mexico: n.p., 1936), pp. 223–44, and in Alfonso Taracena, *La Verdadera Revolución Mexicana*, vol. 12, *Decimasegunda Etapa* (Mexico: Editorial Jus, 1963), pp. 89–140. Both also discuss other crimes attributed to Obregón and Calles.

23. Obregón's assassin, Leon Toral, became a hero to Catholics; in leftist and pro-government circles he represented the backward fanaticism of religion. For an account of the assassination and the sensational trial of Toral and his spiritual mentor, the "holy woman" Madre Conchita, see Dulles, pp. 362–78, 396–403.

24. Dulles, pp. 379–95; Emilio Portes Gil, *Quince Años de Política Mexicana*, 2nd ed. (Mexico: Ediciones Botas, 1941), pp. 13–21. Although Calles was not thoroughly pleased that Obregón would become the next president, most historians do not attribute responsibility for Obregón's death to him.

25. *Memoria del H. Ayuntamiento de la Ciudad de México, 1925.* "Conmemoraciones Patrias," p. 251.

26. Partido Nacional Revolucionario, *Domingos Culturales*, Circular no. 5, 8 July 1930.

27. Ibid., p. 4.

28. Edwin Lieuwin, *Mexican Militarism: The Political Rise and Fall of the Revolutionary Army, 1910–1940* (Albuquerque: University of New Mexico Press, 1968), pp. 103–4; Dulles, pp. 436–58; Portes Gil, pp. 247–81.

29. Alfonso Taracena, *La Verdadera Revolución Mexicana*, vol. 16; *Decimasexta Etapa* (Mexico: Editorial Jus, 1965), pp. 29–52, details events leading up to the massacre and reaction to it in Mexico City. He claims that

Notes   155

the PNR's *El Nacional* began its campaign against yellow journalism at this
time in order to stifle news about the disappearances and murders, which
occurred between 9 February and 9 March 1930.

30. Relations between Mexico and the Soviet Union, established in 1924,
began to deteriorate in 1928 as Mexico's relations with the United States
improved, causing the Soviets to denounce Mexico as an instrument of
American imperialism. Mexico accused the Soviet Union of promoting es-
pionage and subversion in Mexcio and anti-Mexican demonstrations in foreign countries. See Portes Gil, pp. 373–89. At the time of the break in
relations, many leftists were detained or deported, but harassment of the
left was not new. In early 1929 a Cuban communist exile, Antonio Mella,
was shot in Mexico City, and rumor had it that the Mexican government
had permitted agents of the Cuban dictator Machado to kill him. Mella's
murder provoked anti-government demonstrations, while the inquiry into
his death provoked sensational anti-communist publicity, much of which
defamed Mella's lover, Tina Modotti. Modotti, an actress, photographer,
and dedicated communist, was exiled in 1930. Mildred Constantine, *Tina
Modotti: A Fragile Life* (New York: Paddington Press, 1975), pp. 129–72.
For background on the Communist Party in Mexico, see Harry Bernstein,
"Marxismo en México, 1917–1925," *Historia Mexicana* 4 (April–June
1958):497–516.

31. Dulles, pp. 634–49, 659–73. For the wider significance of Calles'
exile, see Lorenzo Meyer, "El Primer Tramo del Camino," in *Historia General de México*, vol. 4 (Mexico: El Colegio de México, 1977), pp. 158–64.

32. Under Cárdenas, 811,157 people received an average of 22.1 hectares of land each. Under Calles, 297,428 people received an average of
10.6 hectares each. Under Carranza, 46,398 people received an average of
3.6 hectares each. James W. Wilkie, *The Mexican Revolution: Federal Expenditure and Social Change Since 1910*, 2nd ed., revised (Berkeley: University
of California Press, 1970), p. 194.

33. Lorenzo Meyer, "El Primer Tramo," pp. 187–99; Albert L. Michaels, "The Crisis of Cardenismo," *Journal of Latin American Studies* 2 (May
1970):51–79.

34. Albert L. Michaels, "Las Elecciones de 1940," *Historia Mexicana* 21
(July–September 1971):80–134; Lieuwen, pp. 129–38. For a general analysis
of Cárdenas' administration, see Arnaldo Córdova, *La Política de Masas del
Cardenismo* (Mexico: Ediciones Era, Serie Popular, 1974).

CHAPTER 2

1. *El Imparcial*, 27, 28, 31 May 1910; 21 February 1911. For a description of attitudes toward Madero during the revolt against Díaz, see Ruth-

erford, pp. 134–41. For biographical information, see Ross, *Madero*, pp. 3–33.

2. *El Imparcial*, 16, 26 May, 8 June 1910; 26 January, 2 April 1911.

3. *El Imparcial*, 27, 28 May 1910.

4. *El Imparcial*, 21 July, 1, 5, 28, 30 August, 24, 26 October 1911; 2, 5 February 1912. Rutherford, pp. 144–47, and Ross, *Madero*, pp. 231–35.

5. Rutherford, pp. 142–43.

6. *El Imparcial*, 21 July, 15 September, 12, 24 October 1911; 13, 26 January 1912.

7. Michael C. Meyer, *Huerta: A Political Portrait* (Lincoln: University of Nebraska Press, 1972), p. 65; Ross, *Madero*, pp. 312, 333.

8. Ross, *Madero*, p. 287.

9. Rutherford, p. 145.

10. This cynicism was seldom directed at Madero, but rather at those who joined the revolution for less than idealistic reasons. Particularly in the novels of Mariano Azuela, people are portrayed as swept up in the revolution without knowing why, or as jumping on the revolutionary bandwagon for the purpose of self-enrichment. Skepticism about people who suddenly join the revolution is also evident in Gregorio López y Fuentes' novel about zapatismo, *Tierra* (Mexico: Espasa-Calpe, 1933) and in the movie *El Compadre Mendoza* (1933).

11. *El Heraldo de México*, 18–24 February 1920.

12. *Excelsior*, 23 February 1921; *El Demócrata*, 23 February 1921; *El Universal*, 24 February 1921.

13. Ibid.

14. *El Universal*, 22 November 1921.

15. A *velada* was an evening program, usually a "refined" affair with musical and literary recitations, held in a theater or other auditorium.

16. *El Heraldo de México*, 21, 23 February 1922; *Excelsior*, 22, 23 February 1922; *La Raza*, 23 February 1922.

17. *El Demócrata*, 23 February 1923.

18. He had also been a member of the *Ateneo de la Juventud*, founded in 1901 to vivify intellectual and artistic life in Mexico. Other members included Martín Luis Guzmán, José Vasconcelos, and Diego Rivera.

19. *El Universal*, 21 December 1921.

20. *Excelsior*, 22 February 1923.

21. *El Mundo*, 22 February 1923.

22. Lorenzo Meyer, "El Primer Tramo," pp. 116–17.

23. *Excelsior*, 23 February 1924.

24. *Diputado* Luis L. Leon, quoted in *La Raza*, 23 February 1922. Leon held many political positions and was very close to Calles.

25. *Rumbos Nuevos*, February 1926. Speaker unidentified.

26. For the debates over the formulation of the anti-clerical articles of the constitution, see Robert E. Quirk, *The Mexican Revolution and the Catholic Church, 1910–1929* (Bloomington: Indiana University Press, 1973), pp. 79–112.

27. For an overview of the church during the revolution and clerical response to land reform, see Gruening, pp. 211–22.

28. David C. Bailey, *Viva Cristo Rey! The Cristero Rebellion and the Church-State Conflict in Mexico* (Austin: University of Texas Press, 1974), pp. 50–53; Dulles, p. 300; Quirk, *The Mexican Revolution and the Catholic Church*, pp. 139–41.

29. *Excelsior*, 23 February 1925.

30. In 1918 CROM had 7,000 members; in 1924, 1,200,000; and in 1927, 2,500,000. President Carranza opposed CROM, Obregón tolerated it, and Calles promoted it. Gruening, pp. 338–39. An industry-by-industry account of CROM activities and a description of Morones' lifestyle is given in Gruening, pp. 343–90.

31. *El Globo*, 23 February 1925.

32. *El Universal*, 23 February 1925.

33. Excerpts from a Secretary of Public Education memorandum to public schools, quoted in *El Demócrata*, 18 February 1926.

34. *El Universal*, 23 February 1927.

35. *Excelsior*, 23 February 1927.

36. *El Universal*, 23 February 1928; *Excelsior*, 23 February 1928.

37. Lieuwin, pp. 103–4; Dulles, pp. 436–38; Portes Gil, pp. 247–81; L. Ethan Ellis, "Dwight Morrow and the Church-State Controversy in Mexico," *Hispanic American Historical Review* [henceforth, *HAHR*] 38 (November 1958):506–28.

38. Alfonso Taracena, *La Verdadera Revolución Mexicana*, vol. 16, *Decimasexta Etapa*, pp. 29–52; Portes Gil, pp. 373–89.

39. *Excelsior*, 23 February 1929; *El Universal*, 23 February 1929; *La Prensa*, 23 February 1929.

40. *El Universal*, 23 February 1930. Other reports of the memorial events appeared in *Excelsior*, 21, 22, 23 February 1930; *La Prensa*, 23 February 1930.

41. *El Universal*, 23 February 1930.

42. Lorenzo Meyer, "El Primer Tramo," pp. 140, 156–7; Eyler N. Simpson, *The Ejido, Mexico's Way Out*, with a foreword by Ramón Beteta (Chapel Hill: University of North Carolina Press, 1937), pp. 117–18. For a discussion of fascist elements during Cárdenas' administration, see Nathaniel Weyl and Sylvia Weyl, *The Reconquest of Mexico: The Years of Lázaro Cárdenas* (London: Oxford University Press, 1939), pp. 341–69.

43. Francie F. Chassen de López, *Lombardo Toledano y el Movimiento Ob-*

158

rero Mexicano (1917–1940) (Mexico City: Editorial Extemporaneos, 1977); Robert Paul Millon, *Mexican Marxist: Vicente Lombardo Toledano* (Chapel Hill: University of North Carolina Press, 1966).
44. *El Universal*, 23 February 1935.
45. *Excelsior*, 22 February 1935; the ARM is described as "fascist-like" by Dulles, p. 628.
46. *El Nacional Revolucionario* [henceforth, *El Nacional*], 22 February 1935.
47. Dulles, pp. 636–46.
48. Lorenzo Meyer, "El Primer Tramo," pp. 158–64; Lieuwen, pp. 113–21; Dulles, pp. 634–49, 659–73.
49. *El Universal*, 23 February 1937.
50. Ibid.; *El Nacional*, 23 February 1937.
51. *Novedades*, 23 February 1938. The ceremonies commemorating Obregón's death had been larger and more publicized than those of Madero, Carranza, and Zapata until Calles' exile, after which they rapidly became insignificant.
52. *Excelsior*, 23 February 1938; *El Universal*, 23 February 1938.
53. George W. Grayson, *The Politics of Mexican Oil* (Pittsburgh: University of Pittsburgh Press, 1980), pp. 15–16; Weyl and Weyl, pp. 298–99, 303.
54. The PRM was a reorganization of the PNR. One of the major changes was the addition of sectors representing the campesinos and government employees to the party structure. The PRM continued to be the official government party. See Arnaldo Córdova, "La Transformación del PNR en PRM: El Triunfo del Corporativismo en México," in James W. Wilkie, Michael C. Meyer, and Edna Monzón de Wilkie, eds., *Contemporary Mexico: Papers of the IV International Congress of Mexican History*, Latin American Studies Series, vol. 29 (Berkeley: University of California Press, 1976), pp. 211–27.
55. Lorenzo Meyer, "El Primer Tramo," pp. 193–95.
56. Grayson, pp. 15–18; Weyl and Weyl, pp. 243–44. Also see Joe C. Ashby, *Organized Labor and the Mexican Revolution Under Lázaro Cárdenas* (Chapel Hill: University of North Carolina Press, 1963).
57. Cedillo, Juan Andreu Almazán, Joaquín Amaro, and Cárdenas had been the leading generals and had worked closely with the government since the 1929 Escobar Rebellion. Cárdenas removed Amaro from a cabinet position in 1935 because of his close ties to Calles but appointed Cedillo secretary of agriculture that same year. The loss of Cedillo's support, following the loss of Amaro's support, was a sign that Cárdenas did not have a strong military backing.
58. Cedillo apparently had the sympathy of Almazán, Amaro, Abelardo Rodríguez, and other key leaders. Lorenzo Meyer, "El Primer Tramo,"

p. 165. For a brief description of Cárdenas' handling of Cedillo's revolt, see William Cameron Townsend, *Lázaro Cárdenas, Mexican Democrat* (Ann Arbor, Mich.: George Wahr, 1952), pp. 208–9, 275–79.

59. Lorenzo Meyer, "El Primer Tramo," pp. 166–67.

60. *El Universal*, 23 February 1939; *El Nacional*, 23 February 1939.

61. Lorenzo Meyer, "El Primer Tramo," p. 166. Diego Rivera, who claimed that the real fascists were in the PRM, was one of the most famous leftists who supported PRUN. See Michaels, "Las Elecciones de 1940," pp. 22–23. For the viewpoint of the fascistic *Partido Nacional de Salvación Pública* (PNSP), see the book by one of its founders, Bernardino Mena Brito, *El P.R.U.N., Almazán, y el Desastre Final* (Mexico: Ediciones Botas, 1941).

62. *El Popular*, 23 February 1940; Alberto Morales Jiménez, "Madero y Pino Suárez," *El Nacional*, 22 February 1940.

63. *El Nacional*, 23 February 1940.

CHAPTER 3

1. Jesús Sotelo Inclán, *Raíz y Razón de Zapata* (Mexico: Editorial Etnos, 1943), gives the history of Anenecuilco, fixing Zapata firmly in the position of a traditional village elder. John Womack, Jr., takes a similar approach to Zapata and uses Sotelo Inclán's work in his *Zapata and the Mexican Revolution* (New York: Knopf, 1969; Random House, 1970). See also Gildardo Magaña, *Emiliano Zapata y el Agrarismo en México*, 5 vols. (Mexico: Editorial Ruta, 1951–1952), and John McNelly, "Origins of the Zapata Revolt in Morelos," *HAHR* 46 (May 1966):153–69.

2. Article 27 of the constitution of 1857 prohibited corporate bodies, including Indian communities, from owning property. The Indians were ill-prepared to assume private ownership of individual parcels and were rapidly dispossessed by the entrepreneurial elite. Liberal ideology and the period of reform ushered in with the 1857 constitution are discussed in Wilfred Hardy Callcott, *Liberalism in Mexico 1857–1929* (Stanford: Stanford University Press, 1931; reprint ed., Hamden, Connecticut: Archon, 1965), pp. 1–102.

3. As part of his modernization effort, Díaz welcomed foreign investors and squelched all protest against his policies. Friedrich Katz discusses campesinos' situations in various parts of Mexico during the *porfiriato* in "Labor Conditions on Haciendas," *HAHR* 54 (February 1974):1–47. Also see Francois Chevalier, "Un Factor Decisivo de la Revolución Agraria de México: 'El Levantamiento de Zapata' (1911–1919)," *Cuadernos Americanos* 113 (November–December 1960):165–87.

4. Zapata had at least nine children, but apparently only had contact

with the eldest, Nícolas. Womack, pp. 107, 242, 325. The Sra. Leonor Álfaro Vda. de Mejía, in an interview by Ximena Sepúlveda and María Isabel Souza in Cuautla, Mexico, on 31 August 1973 (Instituto Nacional de Antropología e Historia, Oral History series, PHO/1/100), described Zapata as sexually abusive. In *Excelsior*, 9 June 1970, Doña Petra Portillo, one of Zapata's wives, said that she was abducted by him, but "that was the custom then." She also said many women offered themselves to Zapata.

5. Womack, pp. 242, 288.

6. Chevalier, pp. 172–74; Womack, pp. 100–101. Conservatives had the same reaction to Madero's plebian support.

7. *Imparcial*, 23 May 1911; 15 May 1911.

8. *Imparcial*, 20 June 1911.

9. Jesús Villalpando, "Vidas Paralelas: Lozada, el 'Tigre de Alica,' y Zapata, el 'Atila del Sur,' " *Revista de Revistas*, 10 September 1911, pp. 1–3.

10. Womack, pp. 90–96, 109–12.

11. Womack, pp. 124–26.

12. The *Plan* was not widely known in Mexico City until published in *Diario del Hogar*, 15 December 1911. The background and translation of the *Plan* are given in Womack, pp. 393–404.

13. Gilly, pp. 61–66.

14. *El Universal*, 12 April 1919.

15. Ibid.; *Excelsior*, 12 April 1919.

16. "El Último Amor de Zapata," *El Universal*, 14 April 1919.

17. *Excelsior*, 12 April 1919.

18. *Uno Mas Uno*, 10 April 1979.

19. "Land and Liberty" (*Tierra y Libertad*) was the slogan of the zapatistas.

20. Félix Díaz (Porfirio's nephew) and Manuel Peláez each sought zapatista support for their revolts against Carranza. The zapatistas regarded them as too conservative and rejected both alliances before deciding to support Obregón. Womack, pp. 292–358.

21. Some of the positions held by zapatistas will be cited below. Womack, pp. 331–87, discusses the political situation in Morelos in the 1920s and 1930s.

22. "Como Murió Emiliano Zapata," *El Heraldo de México*, 10 April 1921.

23. "El Sacrificio de Emiliano Zapata No ha sido Esteril," *El Demócrata*, 10 April 1921.

24. Paul Hanna, "México en 1921," *El Universal*, 19 April 1921. The

article's preface states that it first appeared in *The Nation* but cites neither the date nor the translator.

25. From reports of the ceremony. *El Demócrata*, 12 April 1921; *El Heraldo de México*, 12 April 1921; *El Universal*, 12 April 1921. Hereafter all references not identified by the name of the article are from reports of the memorial ceremonies in the cited newspaper.

26. *El Universal*, 12 April 1921.

27. Ibid.

28. *El Heraldo de México*, 12 April 1922.

29. Rafael Ramos Pedrueza, "10 de Abril de 1919," *El Heraldo de México*, 10 April 1922.

30. Octavio Paz [Sr.], "Hoy se conmemora el Tercer Aniversario de la Muerte de Gral. Emiliano Zapata," *El Heraldo de México*, 10 April 1922.

31. Editorial, *El Demócrata*, 10 April 1921.

32. Martín Luis Guzmán, "Quienes Conquistaron La Libertad de Prensa de Que Gozan Bulnes y Moheno," *El Universal*, 27 April 1921.

33. Ramos Pedrueza, "10 de Abril de 1919."

34. Francisco Bulnes, "Juárez y Zapata," *El Universal*, 26 April 1921.

35. "Una Tirada del General Pablo González Contra el Zapatismo," *El Universal*, 16 May 1921.

36. Bulnes, "Juárez y Zapata."

37. Ramos Pedrueza, "10 de Abril de 1919."

38. *El Demócrata*, 8 April 1924.

39. For example, *El Demócrata*, 10 April 1923, subheadlined a full-page article, "How the Leader of Agrarianism in Morelos Lost His Life in the trap that the Chief of the Eastern Army Corps, of such accursed memory, artfully set for him."

40. *El Demócrata*, 11 April 1923; *El Universal*, 13 April 1923.

41. *El Demócrata*, 10 April 1923.

42. Crisófero Ibáñez, "Emiliano Zapata," *El Demócrata*, 10 April 1923.

43. *El Universal*, 11 April 1924.

44. Ibid.

45. Ibid.; *El Demócrata*, 11 April 1924; *Excelsior*, 12 April 1924.

46. *El Demócrata*, 12 April 1924.

47. Editorial, *El Universal*, 14 April 1924.

48. *El Universal*, 11 April 1924.

49. Leonor Célis Gil, "La Fuerza Física y Moral de Zapata," *El Demócrata*, 11 April 1925.

50. Editorial, *Excelsior*, 8 April 1925.

51. *El Universal*, 12 April 1925.

52. The PNA representative was Rodrigo Gómez, who was accused of

instigating the political attack on Gildardo Magaña at the rancorous memorial banquet in 1923.

53. *El Universal*, 8, 12 April 1926.

54. *Excelsior*, 13 April 1927.

55. *El Universal*, 11 April 1928.

56. *La Prensa*, 10 April 1929.

57. *Excelsior*, 13 April 1929; *La Prensa*, 13 April 1929.

58. *El Universal*, 13 April 1929.

59. *La Prensa*, 11 April 1929.

60. The *corridos* about Zapata (four-fifths of which came from Morelos) overwhelmingly depicted him as a man of ideals; only two carrancista *corridos* depicted him negatively. Zapata's death did not alter his image in popular *corridos*, although imitation *corridos* by government propagandists (notably José Muñoz Cota, Baltasar Dromundo, and Germán List Arzubide) introduced notions of his personal goodness (leniency with prisoners, compassion for the poor and wounded, etc.) that had not been present in the authentic ones. Simmons, pp. 286, 294–96, 312–18.

61. Octavio Paz [Sr.], "Sábado de Gloria," *El Universal*, 14 July 1929, Sunday Supplement.

62. Quirk, *The Mexican Revolution and the Catholic Church*, pp. 215–47; Callcott, pp. 351–83; Ross, "Dwight Morrow."

63. Paz, "Sábado de Gloria."

64. *El Nacional*, 11 April 1930; *El Universal*, 11 April 1930; *La Prensa*, 9 April 1930.

65. *El Nacional*, 11 April 1930.

66. *Excelsior*, 7–11 April 1930.

67. *El Universal*, 11 April 1930; *El Nacional*, 11 April 1930.

68. José T. Melendez, "El Apostol del Agrarismo," *El Nacional*, 10 April 1930.

69. Esperanza Velazquez Bringas, "El Aniversario del Zapata," *El Nacional*, 10 April 1930.

70. *El Gráfico*, 10 April 1931; *El Universal*, 10 April 1931; *El Nacional*, 11 April 1931; *La Prensa*, 11 April 1931.

71. *Diario de los Debates de la Cámara de Diputados*, XXXIV Legislatura, México, 27 July 1931, cited in Carlos Sierra, Jr., "Emiliano Zapata: Señor de la Tierra y Capitán de los Labriegos," Boletín Biobibliográfico de la Secretaría de Hacienda y Crédito Público 361, Supplement (15 February 1967):2–24.

72. Ibid.

73. Ibid.

74. From a speech by Diputado Guadalupe Pineda recorded in *Diario*

de los Debates de la Cámara de Diputados, XXXIV Legislatura, México, 25 August 1931, cited in Sierra, "Zapata," p. 10.

75. Sierra, "Zapata," p. 10.

76. "Emiliano Zapata," *El Nacional*, 11 April 1932.

77. *El Universal*, 11 April 1932.

78. Germán List Arzubide, *Emiliano Zapata: Exaltación* (Jalapa, Veracruz: Talleres Gráficos del Gobierno de Veracruz, 1927), p. 9; "Una Fecha de Dolor es el 10 de Abril," *El Nacional*, 8 April 1933; José Muñoz Cota, "Emiliano Zapata," *El Nacional*, 10 April 1934; Rafael Ramos Pedrueza, "Emiliano Zapata," *El Nacional*, 10 April 1932.

79. *El Nacional*, 12 April 1933.

80. Ibid., 11 April 1933.

81. Secretaría de Acción Agraria del Partido Nacional Revolucionario, *Biografía del Caudillo Suriano General Emiliano Zapata y Parte Oficial de su Muerte* (Mexico: n.p., 1934), p. 14. This pamphlet may have been distributed at the 1934 Zapata memorial in Mexico City or may have been the text of the speech given by Carlos Reyes Áviles at the Cuautla memorial that year. See *El Nacional*, 11 April 1934; *El Universal*, 11 April 1934.

82. E. Barreiro Tablada, *Zapata: XV Aniversario* (n.p., 1934), Revolution Collection, Biblioteca Nacional, Mexico City.

83. Baltasar Dromundo, "A Quince Años de Zapata," *El Nacional*, 10 April 1934. Dromundo tended to wax melodramatic in his suppositions about Zapata's personal life. In his "Homenaje a Emiliano Zapata," *El Nacional*, 10 April 1935, he painted a picture of Zapata's loneliness: "From victory to victory, defeat to defeat, . . . his life passes without a woman's smile. . . . Brief were the pauses, brief . . . those nights in which he could feel a woman's eyes watching over his sleep. . . . [Brief] the caress, and the next day, . . . the Revolution brought him back . . . to desolate reality."

84. Baltasar Dromundo, "Homenaje a Emiliano Zapata," *El Nacional*, 10 April 1935.

85. *El Nacional*, 12 April 1933.

86. Editorial, *El Nacional*, 10 April 1933.

87. Lorenzo Meyer, "El Primer Tramo," p. 140. Governors Lázaro Cárdenas of Michoacan, Agustín Arroyo Ch. of Guanajuato, and Adalberto Tejeda of Veracruz continued to carry out agricultural reforms in their respective states.

88. Ibid., p. 156.

89. Wilkie, p. 194.

90. Sierra, "Zapata," p. 12.

91. Comité Reinvindicador Pro-Emiliano Zapata y Unión de Revolu-

cionarios Agraristas del Sur, *XXVII Aniversario de la Proclamación del Plan de Ayala* (Mexico: n.p., 1938), Revolution Collection.

92. Baltasar Dromundo, "Homenaje a Emiliano Zapata," *El Nacional*, 10 April 1935; Barreiro Tablada, *Zapata: XV Aniversario*.

93. *El Nacional*, 9 April 1933. Ramos Pedrueza's articles were repetitious. The passage quoted here had appeared, almost verbatim, in his articles "Emiliano Zapata," *El Nacional*, 10 April 1932, and "Trayectoria de una Vida Ejemplar," *El Nacional*, 10 April 1939.

94. *El Nacional*, 11 April 1936.

95. Sierra, "Zapata," p. 12. The measure to make 10 April a day of mourning was passed by the Mexican Congress on 14 December 1937.

96. *El Popular*, 11 April 1940.

97. *El Universal*, 12 April 1939.

98. Editorial, *El Popular*, 12 April 1939.

99. *El Popular*, 11 April 1939; *El Universal*, 12 April 1939.

100. "Apuntes de Actualidad," *El Nacional*, 10 April 1940.

101. *El Nacional*, 11 April 1940.

102. Ibid.

103. Lorenzo Meyer, "El Primer Tramo," p. 167.

104. *El Nacional*, 11 April 1940.

105. Villa became the topic of numerous movies, which are listed in note 65 of Chapter 5. The two zapatista novels are *Campamento* (Madrid: Espasa-Calpe, 1931) and *Tierra* (Mexico: Editorial México, 1933), both by Gregorio López y Fuentes. Zapata eventually became the subject of a U.S.-made film, Elia Kazan's *Viva Zapata!* (1952) and a Mexican film, Felipe Cazals' *Zapata* (1970).

CHAPTER 4

1. Dirección General de Acción Educativa, Recreativa, de Reforma y Social, *Don Venustiano Carranza*, Propaganda Cívica, no. 110 (Mexico: Talleres Gráficos de la Nación, 1930), p. 3. This pamphlet was distributed on 21 May 1930 in honor of the anniversary of the death of "this great Revolutionary." The standard work on Carranza is Charles C. Cumberland, *Mexican Revolution: The Constitutionalist Years* (Austin: University of Texas Press, 1972); one of the latest works, which attempts to show him in a favorable light, is Douglas W. Richmond, *Venustiano Carranza's Nationalist Struggle, 1893–1920* (Lincoln: University of Nebraska Press, 1983).

2. From the *Plan de Guadalupe*, reprinted in Córdova, *La Ideología*, pp. 444–45. Córdova, pp. 190–98, discusses the plan, which contained no provisions for social or agrarian reforms.

3. *El Heraldo de México*, 2 August 1923. Martín Luis Guzmán in *El*

Águila y la Serpiente (Spain: n.p., 1928; reprint ed., Mexico: Compañía General de Ediciones, 1956), pp. 66–70, 180–81, describes Carranza as a pompous man who insisted on the complete sycophancy of the men under his command. John Reed in *Insurgent Mexico* (New York: n.p., 1914; reprint ed., New York: International Publishers, 1969), pp. 245–53, implies that Carranza and his coterie were arrogant, bureaucratic, and indifferent to the welfare of the campesinos.

4. Katz, *The Secret War*, pp. 134, 146, 288.

5. Ibid., pp. 254, 256–57.

6. Gilly, pp. 101–7; Katz, *The Secret War*, pp. 260–66.

7. The occupation of Veracruz angered Zapata, but he refused to divert his war efforts to ousting the Yankees. The occupation helped the zapatistas because Huerta withdrew troops from their territory and sent them to guard against further invasion. Womack, pp. 185–86. Villa enjoyed the informal support of the U.S. government and bought his supplies in the United States, and may have therefore hesitated to condemn the occupation. Clarence C. Clendenen, *The United States and Pancho Villa: A Study in Unconventional Diplomacy* (Ithaca, New York: The American Historical Association and Cornell University Press, 1961), pp. 82–92, says Villa forced the Constitutionalists to moderate their response to the occupation, thereby averting a military conflict between the two countries. Carranza agreed to the U.S. military presence in Veracruz as long as revolutionary forces were not attacked, but continued to make diplomatic demands for complete U.S. withdrawal. Katz, *The Secret War*, p. 197.

8. Clendenen, pp. 117–30; Berta Ulloa, "La Lucha Armada," *Historia General de México*, pp. 64–68.

9. From the *Ley de 6 de Enero de 1915*, reprinted in Córdova, *La Ideología*, pp. 455–57. This and Carranza's other reform decrees are discussed on pp. 199–208.

10. Callcott, p. 252; Quirk, *The Mexican Revolution and the Catholic Church*, pp. 72–76; Gilly, pp. 180–81. Particularly important were Obregón's arrangements with the radical *Casa del Obrero Mundial*, whose members usually opposed collaboration with the government but agreed (over the objections of its more radical members) to join the carrancista army in exchange for labor reforms. Ulloa, pp. 78–79; Gilly, pp. 181–86. See also John M. Hart, "The Urban Working Class and the Mexican Revolution: The Case of the Casa del Obrero Mundial," *HAHR* 58 (February 1978):1–20, and Jean Meyer, "Los Obreros en la Revolución Mexicana: Los 'Batallones Rojos,' " *Historia Mexicana* 21 (July–September 1971):1–37.

11. Córdova, *La Ideología*, pp. 214–15; Gilly, pp. 226–27.

12. Córdova, *La Ideología*, pp. 215–47, and Gilly, pp. 227–32, discuss the formulation of the 1917 constitution. Also see E. V. Niemeyer, Jr.,

The Revolution at Queretaro: The Mexican Constitutional Convention of 1916,
Latin American Monographs, no. 33 (Austin: The University of Texas
Press and the Institute of Latin American Studies, 1974).

13. Katz, *The Secret War*, pp. 310–13; Clendenen, pp. 259–95.

14. Gruening, p. 144; Katz, *The Secret War*, pp. 290, 295, 318–19, 325.

15. Gilly, pp. 210–16; Katz, *The Secret War*, p. 293.

16. Rutherford, p. 167.

17. Simmons, pp. 130–36.

18. Dulles, pp. 21–22. Lieuwen, pp. 51–52, argues that while the controversy over the 1920 elections were part of the struggle between "civil-
ianism" and "militarism," it was not a contest between civilians and military men, as all the presidential contenders had supporters of both kinds.
Also, Obregón rejected his "militarist" label, saying that he had a "civil-
ianist spirit," and had resigned his commission on 12 September 1919.

19. Alfonso Taracena, *Venustiano Carranza* (Mexico: Editorial Jus, 1963),
pp. 302–18.

20. *El Demócrata*, 22 May 1920; *El Heraldo de México*, 22 May 1920.

21. *El Demócrata*, 23 May 1920; *El Heraldo de México*, 23 May 1920.

22. *El Heraldo de México*, 23 May 1920.

23. Simmons, p. 136.

24. Rutherford, p. 165.

25. *El Heraldo de México*, 23 May 1920.

26. *Excelsior*, 22 May 1925.

27. *Excelsior*, 22 May 1925; *El Universal*, 22 May 1925, 22 May 1927;
Excelsior, 22 May 1927.

28. All quotes in this paragraph are from *El Universal*, 22 May 1927.

29. Item in the "Sociales y Personales" column, *Excelsior*, 21 May 1930;
El Nacional, 22 May 1930.

30. *La Prensa*, 23 May 1930. In the early 1920s estimates of the size of
the crowds at the Madero and Zapata ceremonies ranged from 5,000 to
20,000. By the early 1930s, there were regularly choruses of 2,000 people
participating in both the Madero and the Zapata memorial programs in
Mexico City.

31. *El Nacional*, 22 May 1930.

32. From the speech by *Diputado* Enrique Soto Peimbert, recorded in
the *Diario de los Debates de la Cámara de Diputados*, XXXIV Legislatura,
México, 25 August 1931, cited in Sierra, "Zapata," p. 10.

33. Ibid.

34. *El Universal*, 21 May 1933.

35. *El Universal*, 22 May 1934.

36. Luis Cabrera [Blas Urrea], *Veinte Años Despues*, 3rd ed. (Mexico: Ediciones Botas, 1938), p. 173.

37. Rutherford, p. 166. Contrasting with the attempt to make Carran-

za's beard a symbol of masculinity was a popular ditty that likened his beard to a woman's pubic hair.

38. Dulles, pp. 609, 646.

39. See Ross, "Dwight Morrow," and Robert Freeman Smith, "The Morrow Missions and the International Committee of Bankers on Mexico: The Interaction of Finance Diplomacy and the New Mexican Elite," *Journal of Latin American Studies* 1 (November 1969):149–66. Eyler N. Simpson, *The Ejido*, p. 581, commented, "I make no pretense to passing any final judgments on Ambassador Morrow's policies and actuations in Mexico. I simply note the fact that coincident with his presence in Mexico the life went out of the revolution."

40. *El Universal*, 18 May 1937, claimed that Obregón believed Calles to be responsible for Villa's murder and intimated that de la Huerta knew the true murderer but refused to talk about it. *El Universal*, 19 May 1937, blamed Obregón's rival, Benjamin Hill, for Carranza's murder but said that Calles was "satisfied" with the murder. *El Universal*, 20 May 1937, brought up the Huitzilac massacre, and both *La Prensa*, 17 May 1937, and *El Universal*, 20 May 1937, discussed the possibility of reinvestigating Carranza's death.

41. *La Prensa*, 22 May 1937.

42. From the speech by Marciano González. *La Prensa*, 22 May 1937.

43. *El Universal*, 22 May 1937; *El Nacional*, 22 May 1937.

44. *El Universal*, 22 May 1939.

45. *Novedades*, 22 May 1940.

46. *Novedades*, 21 May 1939. The fascistic, anti-Semitic nature of the *Partido Nacional de Salvación Pública* is evident in a book by one of its founders, Bernardino Mena Brito, *El P.R.U.N., Almazán, y el Desastre Final*.

47. *El Nacional*, 22 May 1939.

48. Editorial, *El Popular*, 23 May 1939.

49. *Novedades*, 21 May 1939; Editorial, *El Popular*, 23 May 1939.

50. *Novedades*, 21 May 1939; *El Nacional*, 22 May 1939; *El Popular*, 22 May 1939.

51. Antonio Islas Bravo, "D. Venustiano Carranza," *El Universal*, 20 May 1938.

52. *El Nacional*, 22 May 1939; *El Universal*, 22 May 1939; *Novedades*, 22 May 1940.

53. *El Nacional*, 22 May 1940; *Excelsior*, 22 May 1940.

54. Islas Bravo, "D. Venustiano Carranza."

CHAPTER 5

1. Katz, *The Secret War*, p. 38.

2. Rutherford, pp. 152–53.

168   Notes

3. Villa gave interviews freely, and films of his battles in Chihuahua,
Juarez, and Torreon were shown commercially in the United States in
1914. There were rumors (still unsubstantiated) that Mutual Films Cor-
poration paid Villa $25,000 for the exclusive right to film his campaigns
and that Villa had agreed to attack only during daylight to facilitate the
filming. Clendenen, pp. 75–76; Carlos Monsiváis, "Notas Sobre la Cultura
Mexicana en el Siglo XX," *Historia General de México*, p. 438.

4. Many North Americans gathered along the border to watch troop
movements and battles on the Mexican side. The onlookers were sometimes so close that they were hit by stray bullets. Clendenen, p. 210. For
photographic evidence, see Gustavo Casasola, ed., *Historia Gráfica
de la Revolución 1900–1940*, vol. 1 (Mexico: Editorial Gustavo Casasola,
n.d.).

5. Villa was born in 1878 in Rio Grande, Durango. There are several
popular biographies of Villa by people who knew him, such as Elías Torres,
Vida y Hazañas de Pancho Villa (Mexico: n.p., 1975) and Luz Corral Vda.
de Villa, *Pancho Villa en la Intimidad*, with a prologue by José Vasconcelos
(Mexico, n.p., 1948), but the authors seem to want to capitalize on their
relation to Villa or to perpetuate his legendary quality. Most accounts of
Villa's popularity succumb to the tautological explanation that he was very
charismatic. More historical explanations of villismo have appeared, the
most thorough of which, Katz's *The Secret War*, supercedes all others and
is used extensively here.

6. Monsiváis, "Notas Sobre la Cultura," p. 438.

7. Reed, p. 252; Federico González Garza, " 'Si Carranza Me Lo Or-
denara, Yo Pararía el Sol . . . ,' " *El Universal*, 15 July 1930.

8. Gilly, pp. 101–6; Katz, *The Secret War*, pp. 265–66.

9. Clendenen, pp. 93–96; Katz, *The Secret War*, pp. 265–66.

10. Gilly, pp. 106–8.

11. Katz, *The Secret War*, pp. 146–52.

12. Ibid., pp. 152, 285–86.

13. Clendenen, pp. 208–14.

14. Katz, *The Secret War*, pp. 270–73, 281–86, 300.

15. Ibid., pp. 282–85.

16. Simmons, p. 261.

17. Katz, *The Secret War*, pp. 303, 308–9; Rutherford, p. 163. For a
detailed military account, see Haldeen Braddy, "Pancho Villa at Columbus: The Raid of 1916," Monograph no. 9, *Southwestern Studies* 3 (Spring
1965).

18. Katz, *The Secret War*, pp. 303–7, 334–44; James Sandos, "German
Involvement in Northern Mexico, 1915–1916: A New Look at the Columbus Raid," *HAHR* 50 (February 1970):70–88. Both authors agree that Villa

contemplated a raid on the United States before Wilson recognized Carranza as head of the Mexican government.

19. The most important incident, the Santa Isabel Massacre, occurred when villistas killed 17 Americans who worked at the U.S.-owned La Cusi Mining Company. Border incidents continued after the Columbus raid. Braddy, pp. 6–9; Gruening, p. 588; Katz, *The Secret War*, pp. 339–40; Clendenen, pp. 1–6.

20. Clendenen, pp. 249–58; Katz, *The Secret War*, pp. 308, 310.

21. Simmons, p. 446.

22. Rutherford, p. 164.

23. Katz, *The Secret War*, p. 308.

24. Dulles, pp. 66–70, suggests that Calles rejected a tentative offer by Villa to join the Aqua Prieta Revolt. In any case, Carranza's death cleared the way for Villa's reconciliation with the government. Earlier negotiations for a settlement failed because Villa, apparently correctly, suspected that the chief negotiator, Ignacio C. Enríquez, wanted to trap him. Villa then approached de la Huerta, who agreed to Villa's terms of surrender.

25. Simmons, p. 265, drew a similar conclusion about Villa's popular image. But Villa also received negative publicity prior to his "retirement" when Ignacio Enríquez, whose earlier truce negotiations with Villa had failed, reported that Villa was psychotic, a coward, and a monster, ridiculing his claim that he always fought for the good of his "brothers." *El Demócrata*, 26, 27, 29 June 1920.

26. Dulles, p. 68.

27. *Excelsior*, 21 July 1923.

28. Editorial, *Excelsior*, 21 July 1923; "Lo Que No Dije Cuando Entrevisté a Pancho Villa," *El Universal*, 21 July 1923; "Villa, Con Alguna Cultura, Hubiera Sido un Napoleón," *El Universal*, 22 July 1923; "Un Villa Educado Habría Sido Presidente de la República," *El Universal*, 24 July 1923.

29. "Francisco Villa," *El Demócrata*, 21 July 1923.

30. Ibid.

31. "Quien Era en Realidad Francisco Villa," *El Demócrata*, 23 July 1923.

32. "Francisco Villa," *El Demócrata*, 21 July 1923.

33. From the *corrido* "Las Esperanzas de la Patria por la Rendición de Villa," in Simmons, p. 265.

34. Simmons, pp. 264–65.

35. Editorial, *El Universal*, 22 July 1923.

36. "Francisco Villa," *El Demócrata*, 21 July 1923.

37. Alfonso Taracena, *La Historia Extraoficial de la Revolución Mexicana, Desde las Postrimerías del Porfirismo Hasta Sucesos de Nuestros Días* (Mexico: Editorial Jus, 1972), pp. 321–22.

38. Ibid.

39. "Informe que Concreta el Punto de las Investigaciones de los Diputados que Fueron a Parral, a Canutillo y sus Contornos," *El Universal*, 2 August 1923.

40. "Yo Maté a Villa, Dice el Dip. Jesús Salas," *El Universal*, 10 August 1923.

41. *El Universal*, 12 August 1923.

42. Dulles, p. 180.

43. "Discurso Pronunciado en la Recepción Hecho al Candidato Nacional en Córdoba por Gen. Manuel Pérez Treviño," *El Nacional*, 2 July 1929.

44. *El Nacional*, 23 February 1937; *El Universal*, 23 February 1937. Calles' and Obregón's fall from grace revived interest in the possibility that they had been responsible for Villa's death. See, for example, "Salas Barraza Es Hombre de Paja en la Muerte de Villa," *El Gráfico*, 12 May 1937, and "Obregón y Calles Interesados En Que Desapareciera F. Villa," *La Prensa*, 25 May 1937.

45. "Francisco Villa y la Leyenda," *El Demócrata*, 24 July 1923.

46. Rutherford, p. 164.

47. Guzmán, *The Eagle and the Serpent*, pp. 177–78.

48. Ibid., pp. 43–44.

49. Federico González Garza, "Carranza y Villa," *El Universal*, 22 July 1930.

50. Federico González Garza, "Don Venustiano vs. Generales Obregón y Villa," *El Universal*, 19 July 1930.

51. Quoted in González Garza, "Don Venustiano."

52. *El Demócrata*, 28 July 1923.

53. "La Primera Esposa del Guerrillero Francisco Villa, Dice que Tiene Fe en que el Gobierno Hará Justicia y Castigue a los Asesinos de su Esposo," *El Heraldo de México*, 16 August 1923.

54. *Imparcial*, 5 July 1926.

55. Luis F. Bustamante, "Villa No Robaba Mujeres: Las Compraba," *Todo*, 26 March 1935, pp. 12–13; Vito Alessio Robles, "Las Memorias Dictados Por El Gral. Francisco Villa," *Todo*, 28 July 1936, pp. 10–11.

56. Enrique Pérez Rul, "El Amor y F. Villa," *Mujeres y Deportes*, 1 May 1937, p. 33; Gilberto Torres, "Como Hacía el Amor Pancho Villa," *Mujeres y Deportes*, 27 July 1935, p. 6.

57. Gilberto Torres, p. 31.

58. Rutherford, p. 153; Elías Torres, prologue to *Vida y Hazañas de Pancho Villa*.

59. Ramón Puente, "La Verdadera Historia de Pancho Villa," *Excelsior*, 19 April 1931.

60. Pérez Rul, p. 37.

61. Most versions of this story portrayed the sister as uninterested in the man who raped her, but in one version she liked the attention given her by a wealthy young dandy. She does not give in to him, however, for fear of Villa's wrath and for fear that the suitor would only use her, then abandon her because she was of such a humble class. The suitor, seeing that his wooing is coming to naught, rapes her. Luis Santa Maria, *Un Aspecto Ignorado de Francisco Villa: Relato Verídico de Algo Emocionante de la Vida del Celebre Guerrillero, de Lo Que Nadie Se Ha Ocupado Todavia* (Mexico: Laboratorios Picot, 1930(?). The author also included several tales demonstrating how tenderly romantic and unselfish Villa was.

62. Rámon Puente, "Villa en Pie," *Mujeres y Deportes*, 23 July 1938.

63. Córdova, *La Ideología*, pp. 268–76, 320–21; Córdova, *La Política de Masas del Cardenismo*, pp. 177–97.

64. *Los Dorados* was a nickname for *Acción Revolucionario Mexicana*, which was headed by a former villista general, Nícolas Rodríguez. They had several violent confrontations with leftist groups in 1935. The worst occurred on 20 November 1935 at the commemoration of the twenty-fifth anniversary of Madero's revolution in the Plaza de la Constitución. The *Dorados* appeared on horseback and leftist speakers urged the crowd to resist them. Three people died and forty-six were wounded. Dulles, pp. 628–29, 646–48.

65. The movie *Vámonos con Pancho Villa* was produced by Cinematográfica Latino Americana (CLASA) in 1935 and directed by Fernando de Fuentes. It was first exhibited in Mexico City on 31 December 1936. CLASA was founded in 1935 with government backing for the purpose of promoting a national film industry of high artistic and technical calibre. Emilio García Riera, *Historia Documental del Cine Mexicano*, vol. 1: *Época Sonora 1926–1940* (México: Ediciones Era, 1969), p. 90. Other movies about Villa include *La Sombra de Pancho Villa* (1932), *Con los Dorados de Pancho Villa* (1939), *El Secreto de Pancho Villa* (1954), *Cuando ¡Viva Villa! es la Muerte* (1958), *Pancho Villa y la Valentina* (1958), *La Guerrillera de Villa* (1967), and *Reed, México Insurgente*, (1970).

66. From the interview with Rafael F. Muñoz, by Alicia O. de Bonfil and Eugenia Meyer in Mexico City, 15 July 1970. PHO/1/25. Muñoz played the role of Martín Espinosa, one of the six *Leones de San Pablo* in the movie. Muñoz' novel *Vámonos con Pancho Villa*, was first published in Madrid by Espasa-Calpe in 1931.

67. García Riera, p. 90.

68. My thanks to Sr. Fernando del Moral of the Cineteca Nacional in Mexico City, who arranged for me to see *Vámonos con Pancho Villa* in August 1979. He also provided me with the dialogue from the film. The translations of the film's dialogue in the subsequent pages are mine.

69. This was one of the most popular songs of the revolution. The "real"

Adelita was said to have been in love with Villa. According to the tale, Villa had responded to her, unaware that she was the sweetheart of one of his soldiers, Portillo. Portillo, who always sacrificed his personal wishes for the well-being of his *jefe*, tolerated the flirtation as long as he could, then shot himself in front of Villa and Adelita. Villa was appalled that Adelita had not told him that Portillo was her *novio*, and violently rejected her. He was also moved by Portillo's loyalty, which had overcome the code of honor that permitted a man to kill any man that approached his *novia*. Months later, in a ferocious battle, an unknown soldier bravely charged through the enemy line, opening the way for a villista victory. The soldier, killed in the charge, was discovered to be Adelita, who had disguised herself as a man in order to be near Villa. Villa then built a mausoleum for these two hapless souls who, in very different ways, gave their lives for love. "El Origen de la 'Adelita,' " *Revista de Revistas*, 16 July 1933, p. 45.

70. Carl J. Mora, in *Mexican Cinema: Reflections of a Society, 1896–1980* (Berkeley: University of California Press, 1982), pp. 44–45, suggests that this film attests to the Mexican government's tolerance of free expression in film. He seems to take at face value the government's revolutionary claims and to assume that *Vámonos con Pancho Villa*, which he believes presents a negative image of the revolution, contradicted the government ideology. But the movie did not give a negative image of the revolution (the evils of the Huerta regime are mentioned, for example, and all the *Leones* are likeable or admirable characters), only a negative image of Villa. There is no evidence that movies were exempt from the government's efforts to promote its own interests through the arts, especially given that it invested one million pesos in *Vámonos con Pancho Villa*. Furthermore, there had been substantial criticism of U.S. films that portrayed Mexicans or Mexico in an unflattering fashion, as well as a stated need to produce patriotic and morally edifying movies. *Vámonos con Pancho Villa* should be regarded as at least consonant with the Mexican government's desired image of the revolution and of Villa. See García Riera, p. 90.

71. The movie included only eight of the twenty chapters of the novel: *El Puente, Becerrillo, Dínamita en la Noche, Parlamento, Así Eran Ellos, El Círculo de la Muerte, Una Hoguera*, and *El Vagón 7121*.

72. Muñoz, p. 176.

73. Ibid., p. 180.

74. Ibid., pp. 269–70.

75. Ibid., pp. 270–71.

76. Carlos Monsiváis, "El Machismo Como Impostación," *Excelsior*, 4 August 1974.

77. The original version of *Vámonos con Pancho Villa* was longer than its distributed version. The so-called missing reel takes up with Tiburcio

farming and waiting for the day he will ride again with Villa. It concludes with Villa killing his wife and daughter, and Tiburcio marching away with Villa, his son in tow.

This reel fully restores the myth of Villa's power that the released version of the film had eroded by showing Tiburcio to be disillusioned with Villa. It gives the myth a more compelling quality because it ends abruptly with the stunningly cold-blooded murder juxtaposed with Tiburcio's inability to turn against Villa. As he leaves with Villa, Tiburcio is basically glad, however distraught. Nothing blurs the drama of the scene. No further incidents, as in the novel, offer existential and patriotic justification for such loyalty. The only message is that loyalty to Villa is Tiburcio's strongest emotion. As Tiburcio and son walk down the road with the villistas, destination unknown, it seems that villismo is a phenomenon not yet ended.

The script of the missing reel is included in Federico Serrano, "¡Vámonos con Pancho Villa!" *Cine* (Mexico), December 1978, pp. 57–64, who suggests that the reel may have been excluded because it was too violent or because the movie was too long. While there is no evidence of direct censorshp, there is evidence that the political climate encouraged self-censorship. In an interview, Emilio Gómez Muriel, who worked in the film industry in the 1930s, said that the film's director, Fernando de Fuentes, had "treated the Revolution in a very interesting manner" in his earlier film, *El Compadre Mendoza*, but by the time he made the Villa film he "no longer treated the themes with such liberty." Eugenia Meyer, ed., *Cuadernos de la Cineteca Nacional*, vol. 3 (Mexico: n.p., 1976), p. 83. Given the radically different images of Villa in the two versions of the film, and that Villa still was a politically important figure, it is unlikely that artistic or economic considerations alone were behind the decision to drop the final reel. (As this book was going to press I was shown a version of the "missing reel" in which Tiburcio, pointing his rifle at Villa [who just killed Tiburcio's wife and daughter], is shot by one of Villa's escorts. Villa screams at the man that Tiburcio never would have pulled the trigger, and takes Tiburcio's son, who quits crying and smiles enthusiastically when Villa asks him if he'd like to go with him. This is a much weaker closing than the one described in Serrano's article, as it sidesteps the question of whether Tiburcio would have shot Villa, but its implication—that villismo will survive—remains substantially the same.)

78. García Riera, p. 94; interview with Salvador Elizondo, in Eugenia Meyer, ed., *Cuadernos de la Cineteca Nacional*, vol. 1 (Mexico: n.p., 1975), p. 82.

79. During the period of new positive official attention to Villa in the 1960s, Celia Herrera, a relative of one of the men accused of killing Villa,

republished her *Francisco Villa Ante la Historia* (Mexico: n.p., 1964); this vicious tirade against Villa had first appeared in 1939. More interesting, however, was Roberto Blanco Moheno's *¡Pancho Villa Que Es Su Padre!* (Mexico: Editorial Diana, 1969), which he dedicated to the students of Mexico who admired Che Guevara in order to teach them "what a true guerrilla is."

CHAPTER 6

1. For an excellent study of anti-communism in the United States in the decade following the Russian revolution, see William Preston, Jr., *Aliens and Dissenters: Federal Suppression of Radicals, 1903–1933*, with a foreword by Oscar Handlin (New York: Harper & Row, 1966), pp. 181–237.

2. Gruening, pp. 319–22.

3. José María Calderón, *Génesis del Presidencialismo en México* (Mexico: Ediciones "El Caballito," 1972), p. 244: "From the moment in which the popular classes . . . were not the ones that took power, we cannot speak of a popular revolution. On the contrary, Mexican populism is designed to prevent the popular masses from acquiring class consciousness and, so, to proceed with the original plan for capitalistic growth the revolutionary 'middle classes' had formulated."

4. Bernstein, p. 500.

5. Moises González Navarro, "La Ideología de la Revolución Mexicana," *Historia Mexicana* 10 (April–June 1961):625.

6. Alfonso Taracena, *La Verdadera Revolución Mexicana*, vol. 8, *Octava Etapa*, 21. He says the interview took place on 7 November 1921.

7. *Revista del Ejército y de la Marina*, February 1930, p. 93.

8. For an analysis of the psychological dynamics of colonialism, see Albert Memmi, *The Colonizer and the Colonized*, translated by Howard Greenfied (New York: Orion Press, 1965). See Eric Wolf, *Sons of the Shaking Earth* (Chicago: University of Chicago Press, 1959), pp. 202–56, for a description of the Indian's place in Mexican colonial society and the rise of the mestizo.

9. Mexican resentment against the United States is usually attributed to the Mexican American War of 1847. See Jorge Carrión, "Efectos Psicológicos de la Guerra de '47 en el Hombre de México," *Cuadernos Americanos* 37 (January–February 1948):127–31; Samuel Guy Inman, *Intervention in Mexico* (New York: Doran, 1919), p. 140; Frederick C. Turner, "Anti-Americanism in Mexico, 1910–1913," *HAHR* 47 (February 1967):502–18.

10. Cockcroft, p. 20.

11. PNR, *Domingos Culturales*, p. 6.

12. Allen L. Woll, "Latin Images in American Films, 1929–1939," *Jour-*

nal of Mexican American History 4 (1974):28–40; Idem, "Hollywood's Good Neighbor Policy: The Latin Image in American Film, 1939–1946," *Journal of Popular Film* 3 (Fall 1974):278.
13. Editorial, *Hoy*, 1 October 1938.
14. "En la Garras de los Lobos de Cine," *Excelsior*, 22 May 1930. The subheadline read, "The Trusts of the Movie Production Companies Are Absorbing Our Civilization."
15. Tobler, p. 52; Gruening, pp. 324–31.
16. See Charles C. Cumberland, "The Sonora Chinese and the Mexican Revolution," *HAHR* 40 (May 1960):191–211.
17. *El Universal*, 20 May 1922.
18. Constantine, pp. 165–66.
19. Jean Franco, *The Modern Culture of Latin America: Society and the Artist* (London: Pall Mall Press, 1967), pp. 74–78. For a study of Mexico's muralists, see Jean Charlot, *The Mexican Mural Renaissance: 1920–1925* (New Haven: Yale University Press, 1963).
20. According to Córdova, *La Política de Masas*, p. 80, the idea that the working class's welfare will improve as production increases is "the soul of *capitalist* counter-insurgency; in fact, it was the soul, the nucleus, the essence of that gigantic counter-insurgency movement that is the Mexican Revolution, and Cárdenas has been to date its most consummate practitioner and, at the same time, its most inspired prophet."

For general studies of Mexican nationalism, see Albert L. Michaels, "El Nacionalismo Conservador Mexicano: Desde la Revolución Hasta 1940," *Historia Mexicana* 16 (October–December 1966):213–38; Frederick C. Turner, *The Dynamic of Mexican Nationalism* (Chapel Hill: University of North Carolina Press, 1968).
21. *El Universal*, 22 February 1938.
22. In 1922 conservatives were especially concerned about the efforts of the North American "concubine" of Yucatan's governor Felipe Carrillo Puerto, Nelly Aznar, to distribute Margaret Sanger's birth control pamphlets in Mexico. *La Raza*, 19, 21 July 1922. For the history of the feminist movement in Mexico, see Anna Macías, *Against All Odds: The Feminist Movement in Mexico to 1940* (Westport, Conn.: Greenwood press, 1982); Ward M. Morton, *Woman Suffrage in Mexico* (Gainesville: University of Florida Press, 1962).
23. *Excelsior*, 23 May 1923.
24. *El Demócrata*, 23 May 1923.
25. *Revista del Ejército y de la Marina*, February 1930.
26. Editorial, *Hoy*, 1 October 1938.
27. Palacios, p. 273.
28. Barthes, pp. 142–43.

176 Notes

29. Mariano Azuela, *The Underdogs*, translated by Stanley L. Robe, in *Azuela and the Mexican Underdogs*, Stanley L. Robe (Berkeley: University of California Press, 1979), p. 197.
30. Departamento del Distrito Federal, "Calendario Cívico Mexicano 1930," Basave Collection.
31. Dirección General de Acción Educativa, Recreativa, de Reforma y Social, *Don Venustiano Carranza*, Propaganda Cívica, no. 110 (Mexico: Talleres Gráficos de la Nación, 1930), p. 4.
32. Barthes, p. 142.
33. Azuela, p. 193.
34. *El Universal*, 20 May 1938.
35. Barthes, p. 150.
36. *El Universal*, 11 April 1924.
37. *Continental*, June 1927.
38. *Revista de Revistas*, 12 February 1928.

CHAPTER 7

1. See Frederick C. Turner, "Los Efectos de la Participación Feminina en la Revolución de 1910," *Historia Mexicana* 16 (April–June 1967):603–20; Macías, *Against All Odds*; Morton, *Woman Suffrage in Mexico*. For a fascinating biography of a *soldadera*, see Elena Poniatowska, *Hasta No Verte Jesús Mío* (Mexico: Ediciones Era, 1969).
2. Desiderio Borja, "Dos Valientes," *El Nacional*, 21 February 1932.
3. *El Popular*, 20 February 1939.
4. Baltasar Dromundo, "La Soldadera," in *Domingos Culturales*, circular no. 5, pp. 53–54. Partido Nacional Revolucionario, 8 July 1930. Biblioteca de Mexico.
5. The army of the post-revolutionary regime did not share Dromundo's appreciation of the *soldaderas*, whom it banned from all military activities in the early 1920s on the grounds that they spread disease and rivalry among the troops, provided drugs and alcohol to the troops, and caused soldiers to waste their pay. *El Universal*, 14 April 1921.
6. "La Mujer y el Confesario," *Izquierdas*, 31 December 1934.
7. Ibid.
8. La Mujer en el Confesario," *El Eco Revolucionario*, 13 October 1934.
9. There were many stories in newspapers about the misfortunes of single women in the city. Many of course became prostitutes, but there were also news items about women turning to crime and numerous reports of women dressing like men as a means to better protect themselves at work or while living on the streets.
10. *Memoria del Departamento del Distrito Federal, 1938–1939*, p. 243.

11. *El Nacional*, 10 April 1934.
12. Rutherford, pp. 155–56.
13. *El Popular*, 20 February 1939.
14. *El Nacional*, 11 April 1937; *El Universal*, 21 May 1938.
15. I refer of course to Katz, *The Secret War*.

Bibliography

NEWSPAPERS AND MAGAZINES

The following newspapers and magazines were consulted for the listed issues at the Hemeroteca Nacional, Mexico City.

Continental. March 1925; August–December 1926; January, June 1927.

CRISOL. 1934.

CROM. 1, 15 February, 1, 15 April 1928.

La Dama Católica. July, August, September 1923; April, May, July 1924; February, July 1925.

El Demócrata. 7–20 April, 22–31 May, June 1920; 18–25 February, 7–12 April, 18–24 May 1921; 7–11 April, 18–24 May 1922; 18–24 February, 7–11 April, 18–25 May, 21–29 July 1923; 18–24 February, 7–12 April, 7–23 May, 19–23 July 1924; 18–24 February, 7–15 April, 18–22 May, 16–26 July 1925; 18–24 February, 7–13 April 1926.

El Eco Revolucionario. February, April, May, July, September, October 1934; February, May, July 1935; January 1936.

Excelsior. 21 January, 11–26 April 1919; 7–29 May 1920; 18–23 February, 7–14 April, 18–21 May 1921; 19–23 February 1922; 18–23 February, 18–23 May, 21–23 July 1923; 19–23 February, 17–18 April, 18–22 May, 18–22 July 1924; 19–23 February, 8–13 April, 19–22 May, 16–23 July 1925; 18–23 February, 8–15 April, 19–22 May, 18–25 July 1926; 18–23 February, 8–13 April, 19–22 May, 15 June, 17–24 July 1927; 12, 21–23 February, 8–11 April, 19–24 May, 18–25 July 1928; 17–23 February, 8–13 April, 19–22 May, 18–21 July 1929; 19–23 February, 7–11 April, 19–23 May 1930; 19 April 1931;

19–23 February, 19–22 May, 18–22 July 1932; 8–14 April, 19–25 May, 17–22 July 1933; 8–12 April 1934; 13, 17–23 February, 8–12 April, 4, 10, 18–22 May 1935; 19–23 February, 20–25 May 1936; 9, 16 August 1937; 19–24 February, 7–12 April 1938; 18–23 February, 7–12 April, 19–22 May 1940.

El Globo. 18–23 February, 8–11 April 1925.

El Gráfico. 1, 18–24 February, 9–15, 19, 26 April, 3, 10, 17–24 May, 5, 12, 18–26 July 1931; 31 July 1932, 12 May 1937.

El Heraldo de México. 27 April–30 June 1919; 18–25 February, 10–15 April, 20–24 May 1920; 21–23 February, 8–12 April, 21–23 May 1921; 21–23 February, 8–12 April, 19–23 May 1922; 10–12 April, 21–23 May, 1–27 August 1923.

El Hombre Libre. February–May, 1 July–15 November 1937.

Hoy. 25 February 1937; 11 July, 1 October 1938; 1 July 1939; 24 February 1940.

El Imparcial. 1909–1913.

Izquierdas. July–December 1934; April, May, July 1936; February, April, July 1937.

Jueves de Excelsior. June–December 1922; 1932; 8 April, 1937.

Mujer. February–April, June, October, November, December 1927; January–March, May 1928; May, June, September, October 1929.

Mujeres y Deportes. July–September 1934; April, May, July 1935; April, May, July, August 1936; 6 February, April, May, July, 8 September 1937; April, May, July, August 1938; April–August 1939.

El Mundo. 19–26 February, 7–12 April 1923.

El Nacional [*Revolucionario*]. 2, 16–26 July, September 1929; 7–11 April, 17–22 May, 17–27 July 1930; 19–23 February, 9–11 April, 17–24 May, 17–25 July 1931; 19–23 February, 9–12 April, 18–22 May, 17–24 July 1932; 19–25 February, 8–12 April, 18–24 May, 18–24 July 1933; 17–23 February, 7–12 April, 19–24 May, 17–25 July 1934; 10, 19–24 February, 7–12 April, 18–24 May, 17–28 July 1935; 16, 21–24 February, 7–13 April, 17–22 May, 7, 15, 16, 25–30 July 1936; 18–25 February, 6–11 April, 18–22 May, 18–24 July 1937; 18–27 February, 6–12 April, 21–24 May, 17–24 July 1938; 18–25 February, 7–13 April, 17–23 May, 16–26 July 1939; 18–23 February, 7–14 April, 19–22 May, 18–26 July 1940.

Novedades. 18–27 February, 7–10 April, 17–28 July 1938; 9, 18–25 February, 7–14 April, 17–26 July, 3, 8 October 1939; 18–22 May, 17–25 July 1940.

Ovaciones. 17, 18, 25 October, November 1926; 11, 13, 18, 20, 25, 27 February, April, May, July 1928.

La Palabra. 18–23 February, 17–25 July 1933; 19–22 May 1934.

El Popular. 19–23 February, 7–12 April, 19–23 May, 19–26 July 1939; 18–24 February, 7–11 April 1940.

La Prensa. 18–23 February, 7–13 April, 19–23 May, 19–26 July 1929; 19–24 February, 8–12 April, 15–23 May, 6, 13, 16–22 July 1930; 17–23 February, 7–12 April, 19–24 May, 19–24 July 1931; 19–23 February, 7–11 April, 19–26 May, 18–25 July 1932; 7–13 April, 19–24 May 1933; 17–24 May 1937; 1 March, 7–12 April, 17–22 May 1938.

La Raza. 18–26 February, 7–14 April, 19–23 May, 18–25 July 1922.

Revista del Ejército y de la Marina. July 1923; February–June 1924; February, April, May, July 1930; February, April, May 1936.

Revista de Revistas. 10 September, 29 October 1911; 18 August 1912; January–June 1920; February 1926; April–September 1927; February, 8 April 1928; February, 20 September 1931; 17 April, 26 June, 31 July, 7 August, 18 September, 20, 27 November 1932; 1, 22, 29 January, 5 February, 20 March, April, May, July 1933.

Rumbos Nuevos. April 1925; February, April, May, July 1926; February, March, July 1927; February, March 1928.

El Universal. April, November–December 1919; January–March, 7–28 April, 1 August–15 November 1920; 18–24 February, March–December 1921; January–May, September 1922; February, April, May, 21–31 July, August 1923; February, 10–19 April, 19–25 May, 20–26 July, 21–30 November 1924; 5–23 February, April, 19–22 May, 20–26 July 1925; 5–23 February, 8–12 April, 19–22 May, 20–25 July 1926; 22–23 February, 10–13 April, 21–22 May, 18–24 July 1927; 22–23 February, 10–12 April, 20–24 May, 13–24 July 1928; 17–23 February, 10–13 April, 21–25 May, 14, 18–21, 28 July 1929; 23 February, 9–11 April, 21–22 May, 15–22 July, December 1930; 22–23 February, 10–11 April, 21–24 May, 20–23 July 1931; 22–23 February, 10–12 April, 20–22 May, 19–23 July 1932; 10–23 February, 10–13 April, 7, 21–25 May, July 1933; 18–23 February, 9–11 April, 6, 13, 20–24 May, 19–23 July 1934; 19–23 February; 9–11, 20 April, 19–27 May, 19–25 July 1935; 16–25 February, 8–11 April, 7, 20–22 May, 18–26 July 1936; 19–23 February, 9–11 April, 20–22 May, 12, 18–25 July 1937; 24, 31 January, 6–27 February, 7–14 April, 19–22 May, 19–21 July 1938; 19–23 February, April, 20–22 May, 17–24 July 1939; 19–23 February, 7–11 April, 18–24 May, 18–25 July 1940.

SELECTED ARTICLES, BOOKS, AND TRACTS

Acevedo, Marta. "Sobre el Sexismo Mexicano." *Siempre!*, 13 September 1972, 36–41.

Alba, Victor. "The Mexican Revolution and the Cartoon." *Comparative Studies in Society and History* 4 (January 1967):121–36.

———. *The Mexicans: The Making of a Nation.* New York: Praeger, 1967.

Alcaraz, Rodolfo. "Sesenta Años de Periodismo Mexicano." *Historia y Sociedad* 6 (1966):107–25.

Alegría, Juana Armanda. *Psicología de las Mexicanas.* Mexico: Editorial Samo, 1974.

Alessio Robles, Vito. *Desfile Sangriento.* Mexico: n.p., 1936.

———. *Los Tratados de Bucareli.* Mexico: n.p., 1937.

Álfaro Vda. de Mejía, Leonor. Interviewed by Ximena Sepulveda and María Isabel Souza. Cuautla, 31 August 1973. PHO/1/100. Colección de Historia Oral. Instituto Nacional de Antropología e Historia.

Almond, Gabriel A., and Verba, Sidney. *The Civic Culture: Political Attitudes and Democracy in Five Nations.* Princeton, N.J.: Princeton University Press, 1963.

Amaya C., Luis Fernando. *La Soberana Convención Revolucionaria: 1914–1916.* Mexico: Editorial F. Trillas, 1966.

Anderson, Bo, and Cockroft, James. "Control and Cooptation in Mexican Politics." *International Journal of Comparative Sociology* 7 (March 1966):11–28.

Aragón Leiva, Agustín. "Hollywood y la Cinematografía." *CRISOL* 2 (March 1934):195–208.

Ashby, Joe C. *Organized Labor and the Mexican Revolution Under Lázaro Cárdenas.* Chapel Hill: University of North Carolina Press, 1963.

Atlas General del Distrito Federal. Mexico: Talleres Gráficos de la Nación, 1930.

Azuela, Mariano. *The Underdogs.* Translated by Stanley L. Robe. In Stanley L. Robe, *Azuela and the Mexican Underdogs*, pp. 169–223. Berkeley: University of California Press, 1979.

Bailey, David C. *Viva Cristo Rey! The Cristero Rebellion and the Church-State Conflict in Mexico.* Austin: University of Texas Press, 1974.

———. "Revisionism and the Recent Historiography of the Mexican Revolution." *Hispanic American Historical Review* 58 (February 1978):62–79.

Balan, Jorge, Browning, Harley, and Jelin, Elizabeth. *Men in a Developing Society: Mobility in Monterrey, Mexico.* Austin: University of Texas Press, 1973.

Barreiro Tablada, E. *Zapata: XV Aniversario.* n.p., 1934. Revolution Collection, Biblioteca Nacional, Mexico City.

Barthes, Roland. *Mythologies.* Translated and selected by Annette Lavers. New York: Hill and Wang, 1972.

Beals, Carleton. *Mexican Maze.* With illustrations by Diego Rivera. Philadelphia: Lippincott, 1931.

Beltrán, Enrique. "Fantasía y Realidad de Pancho Villa." *Historia Mexicana* 16 (July–September 1966):71–84.

Bermúdez, Antonio J. *The Mexican National Petroleum Industry: A Case Study in Nationalization.* Stanford, Calif.: Institute of Hispanic American and Luso-Brazilian Studies, Stanford University, 1963.

Bernstein, Harry. "Marxismo en México, 1917–1925." *Historia Mexicana* 7 (April–June 1958):497–516.

Blaisdell, Lowell L. *The Desert Revolution: Baja California, 1911.* Madison: University of Wisconsin Press, 1962.

Blanco Moheno, Roberto. *¡Pancho Villa Que Es Su Padre!* 2nd. ed. Mexico: Editorial Diana, 1969.

Braddy, Haldeen. *Cock of the Walk: The Legend of Pancho Villa.* Albuquerque: University of New Mexico Press, 1955.

———. "Pancho Villa at Columbus: The Raid of 1916." Monograph no. 9, *Southwestern Studies* 3 (Spring 1965).

Britton, John A. "Urban Education and Social Change in the Mexican Revolution, 1931–1940." *Journal of Latin American Studies* 5 (November 1973):233–45.

Cabrera, Luis [Blas Urrea]. *La Herencia de Carranza.* Mexico: Imprenta Nacional, 1920.

———. *Veinte Años Despues.* 3rd. ed. Mexico: Ediciones Botas, 1938.

Calderón, José María. *Génesis del Presidencialismo en México.* Mexico: Ediciones "El Caballito," 1972.

Callcott, Wilfred Hardy. *Liberalism in Mexico 1857–1929.* Stanford: Stanford University Press, 1931; reprint ed., Hamden, Conn.: Archon, 1965.

Calvert, Peter. "The Institutionalization of the Mexican Revolution." *Journal of Inter-American Studies* 10 (October 1969):503–17.

Cárdenas Cruz, Francisco. "El País Demanda Revolución de Hechos, Advierte Baz al PRI: La Paciencia Popular, Limitada." *Excelsior,* 29 June 1972.

Carrión, Jorge. "Efectos Psicológicos de la Guerra de '47 en el Hombre de México." *Cuadernos Americanos* 37 (January–February 1948):116–32.

———. *Mito y Magia del Mexicano y un Ensayo de Autocrítica.* 2nd. ed. Mexico: Editorial Nuestro Tiempo, 1971.

Casasola, Gustavo, ed. *Historia Gráfica de la Revolución, 1900–1940*, vol. 1. Mexico: Editorial Gustavo Casasola, n.d.

Ceniceros, José Angel. *Educación y Mexicanidad*. Mexico: Populibros "La Prensa," 1958.

Charlot, Jean. *The Mexican Mural Renaissance: 1920–1925*. New Haven: Yale University Press, 1963.

Chassen de López, Francie F. *Lombardo Toledano y el Movimiento Obrero Mexicano (1917–1940)*. Mexico: Editorial Extemporaneos, 1977.

Chellet Osante, Roberto. *Organización Administrativa y Política de la República Mexicana*. Mexico: Ediciones de la Academia de Capacitación, 1955.

Chevalier, Francois. "Un Factor Decisivo de la Revolución Agraria de México: 'El Levantamiento de Zapata' (1911–1919)." *Cuadernos Americanos* 113 (November–December 1960):165–87.

Chodorow, Nancy. *The Reproduction of Mothering: Psychoanalysis and the Sociology of Gender*. Berkeley: University of California Press, 1978.

Clenenden, Clarence C. *The United States and Pancho Villa: A Study in Unconventional Diplomacy*. Ithaca, N.Y.: American Historical Society and Cornell University Press, 1961.

Cockcroft, James D. *Intellectual Precursors of the Mexican Revolution, 1900–1913*. Austin: University of Texas Press, 1968.

Cohen, Calman J. "Beyond the Pathological Approach to Mexican Family Research: A Study of Authority Relations in Family and Policy." In *Contemporary Mexico: Papers of the IV International Congress of Mexican History*, pp. 367–88. Edited by James W. Wilkie, Michael C. Meyer, and Edna Monzón de Wilkie. Latin American Studies Series, vol. 29. Berkeley: University of California Press, 1973.

Comité Reivindicador Pro-Emiliano Zapata y Unión de Revolucionarios Agraristas del Sur. *XXVII Aniversario de la Proclamación del Plan de Ayala*. Mexico: n.p., 1938. Revolution Collection, Biblioteca Nacional, Mexico City.

Constantine, Mildred. *Tina Modotti: A Fragile Life*. New York: Paddington Press, 1975.

Córdova, Arnaldo. *La Formación del Poder Político en México*. Mexico: Ediciones Era, Serie Popular Era, 1972.

————. "Las Reformas Sociales y la Tecnocratización del Estado Mexicano." *Revista Mexicana de Ciencia Política* 8 (October–December 1972):61–92.

————. *La Ideología de la Revolución Mexicana: La Formación del Nuevo Régimen*. Mexico: Ediciones Era, 1973.

————. "La Transformación del PNR en PRM: El Triunfo del Corporativismo en México." in *Contemporary Mexico: Papers of the IV Inter-*

national Congress of Mexican History, pp. 204–27. Edited by James W. Wilkie, Michael C. Meyer, and Edna Monzón de Wilkie. Latin American Studies Series, vol. 29. Berkeley: University of California Press, 1973.

———. *La Política de Masas del Cardenismo*. Mexico: Ediciones Era, Serie Popular, 1974.

Corral Vda. de Villa, Luz. *Pancho Villa en la Intimidad*. With a prologue by José Vasconcelos. Mexico: n.p., 1948.

Corwin, Arthur. *Contemporary Mexican Attitudes Toward Population, Poverty, and Public Opinion*. Inter-American Studies series, no. 25. Gainesville: University of Florida Press, 1963.

Cumberland, Charles C. "The Sonora Chinese and the Mexican Revolution." *Hispanic American Historical Review* 40 (May 1960):191–211.

———. *Mexican Revolution: The Constitutionalist Years*. Austin: University of Texas Press, 1972.

De la Colina, José. "Adventuras y Tribulaciones del Eros en el Cine Mexicano." *Revista de Revistas*, 25 July 1973.

del Rio Reynaga, Julio. "Anotaciones Sobre los Medios de Información en México." *Revista Mexicana de Ciencia Política* 8 (July–September 1972):5–46.

de María y Campos, Armando. *El Teatro del Género Chico en la Revolución Mexicana*. Mexico: Biblioteca del Instituto Nacional de Estudios Históricos de la Revolución Mexicana, 1956.

———. *El Teatro del Género Dramático en la Revolución Mexicana*. Mexico: Biblioteca del Instituto Nacional de Estudios Históricos de la Revolución Mexicana, 1957.

de Mora, Juan Miguel. *Por la Gracia del Señor Presidente*. Mexico: Editores Asociados, 1975.

Departamento del Distrito Federal. "Calendario Cívico Mexicano 1930." Basave Collection, Biblioteca de Mexico, Mexico City.

Díaz-Guerrero, Rogelio. *Psychology of the Mexican Culture and Personality*. Austin: University of Texas Press, 1975.

Dirección General de Acción Educativa, Recreativa, de Reforma y Social. *Don Venustiano Carranza*. Propaganda Cívica, no. 110. Mexico: Talleres Gráficos de la Nación, 1930. Hemeroteca Nacional, Mexico City.

Domingo, Alberto. "Vamos a 'Echarnos' a Zapata Otra Vez!" *Siempre!*, 8 July 1964.

Dromundo, Baltasar. "La Soldadera." In *Domingos Culturales*, circular no. 5, pp. 53-54. Partido Nacional Revolucionario, 8 July 1930. Biblioteca de Mexico.

———. *Emiliano Zapata, Biografía*. Mexico: Imprenta Mundial, 1934.

Dulles, John W. F. *Yesterday in Mexico: A Chronicle of the Revolution, 1919–1936*. Austin: University of Texas Press, 1961.

Elizondo, Salvador. "Moral Sexual y Moraleja en el Cine Mexicano." *Nuevo Cine*, April 1961.

Ellis, L. Ethan. "Dwight Morrow and the Church-State Controversy in Mexico." *Hispanic American Historical Review* 38 (November 1958):482–505.

Elu du Leñero, Carmen. *¿Hacia Donde Va la Mujer Mexicana?* Mexico: Instituto Mexicano de Estudios Sociales, 1969.

Estol, Horacio. *Leyenda y Realidad de Pancho Villa*. Mexico: Editorial 'Divulgación,' n.d.

Fisher, Lillian Estelle. "The Influence of the Present Mexican Revolution upon the Status of Mexican Women." *Hispanic American Historical Review* 22 (February 1942):211–28.

Franco, Jean. *The Modern Culture of Latin America: Society and the Artist*. London: Pall Mall Press, 1967.

Fromm, Erich, and Maccoby, Michael. *Social Character in a Mexican Village: A Sociopsychoanalytic Study*. Englewood Cliffs, N.J.: Prentice-Hall, 1970.

Fuentes, Carlos. *La Región Más Transparente*. Mexico: Fondo de Cultura Económica, 1958.

———. *La Muerte de Artemio Cruz*. Mexico: Fondo de Cultura Económica, 1962.

García Riera, Emilio. *Historia Documental del Cine Mexicano*. vol. 1: *Época Sonora 1926–1940*. Mexico: Ediciones Era, 1969.

Gilly, Adolfo. *La Revolución Interrumpida: México, 1910–1920: Una Guerra Campesina por la Tierra y el Poder*. Mexico: Ediciones "El Caballito," 1971.

González Navarro, Moises. "La Ideología de la Revolución Mexicana." *Historia Mexicana* 10 (April–June 1961):628–36.

González Pineda, Francisco. *El Mexicano, Psicología de Su Destructividad*. Mexico: Fondo de Cultura Económica, 1961.

Grayson, George W. *The Politics of Mexican Oil*. Pittsburgh: University of Pittsburgh Press, 1980.

Gruening, Ernest. *Mexico and Its Heritage*. New York: Century, 1928.

Guzmán, Martín Luis. *El Águila y la Serpiente*. Spain: n.p., 1928; reprint ed., Mexico: Compañía General de Ediciones, 1956. Translated by Harriet de Onís as *The Eagle and the Serpent*. Garden City, N.Y.: Doubleday, 1965.

Hall, Linda B. *Álvaro Obregón: Power and Revolution in Mexico, 1911–1920*. College Station: Texas A&M University Press, 1981.

Hart, John M. "The Urban Working Class and the Mexican Revolution:

The Case of the Casa del Obrero Mundial." *Hispanic American Historical Review* 58 (February 1978):1–20.

Herrera, Celia. *Francisco Villa Ante la Historia*. Mexico: n.p., 1964.

Historia General de México. vol. 4. Mexico: El Colegio de México, 1976.

Hobsbawm, Eric. *Bandits*. New York: Delacorte, 1969.

———. "Man and Woman in Socialist Iconography." *History Workshop* 6 (Autumn 1978):121–38.

Hodges, Donald, and Gandy, Ross. *Mexico 1910–1976: Reform or Revolution?* London: Zed Press, 1979.

Inman, Samuel Guy. *Intervention in Mexico*. New York: Doran, 1919.

Johnson, Kenneth F. *Mexican Democracy: A Critical View*. Boston, Allyn and Bacon, 1971.

Johnson, William Weber. *Heroic Mexico*. Garden City, N.Y.: Doubleday, 1968.

Junco, Alfonso. *Carranza y los Orígenes de Su Rebelión*. 2nd. ed. Mexico: Editorial Jus, 1955.

Kahl, Joseph. *The Measurement of Modernization: A Study of Values in Brazil and Mexico*. Austin: Institute of Latin American Studies, University of Texas Press, 1968.

Katz, Friedrich. "Labor Conditions on Haciendas in Porfirian Mexico: Some Trends and Tendencies." *Hispanic American Historical Review* 54 (February 1974):1–47.

———. *The Secret War in Mexico: Europe, the United States and the Mexican Revolution*. With portions translated by Loren Goldner. Chicago: University of Chicago Press, 1981.

Kinzer, Nora Scott. "Priests, Machos and Babies." *Journal of Marriage and the Family* 3 (May 1973):300–12.

Levenstein, Harvey. "The AFL and Mexican Immigration in the 1920s: An Experiment in Labor Diplomacy." *Hispanic American Historical Review* 48 (May 1968):206–19.

Lewis, Oscar. *Five Families: Mexican Case Studies in the Culture of Poverty*. New York: Mentor Books, 1959.

———. *Tepoztlan: Village in Mexico*. Chicago: Holt, Rinehart, and Winston, 1960.

Leyzaola, Margarita. "Valentina, Valentina . . . " *Revista de Revistas*, 18 July 1973.

Lieuwen, Edwin. *Mexican Militarism: The Political Rise and Fall of the Revolutionary Army, 1910–1940*. Albuquerque: University of New Mexico Press, 1968.

List Arzubide, Germán. *Zapata: Exaltación*. Jalapa, Veracruz: Talleres Gráficos del Gobierno de Veracruz, 1927.

188   Bibliography

López de Escalera, Juan. *Diccionario Biográfico y de Historia de México.* Mexico: Editorial del Magisterio, 1964.

Loyala Díaz, Rafael. *La Crisis Obregón-Calles y el Estado Mexicano.* Mexico: Siglo Veintiuno Editores, 1980.

Lynch, James B. "Orozco's House of Tears." *Journal of Inter-American Studies* 3 (July 1961):376–77.

Macías, Anna. *Against All Odds: The Feminist Movement in Mexico to 1940.* Westport, Conn.: Greenwood Press, 1982.

McNelly, John H. "Origins of the Zapata Revolt in Morelos." *Hispanic American Historical Review* 46 (May 1966):153–69.

Magaña, Gral. Gildardo. *Emiliano Zapata y el Agrarismo En México.* 5 vols. Mexico: Editorial Ruta, 1951, 1952.

Mancisidor, José. *Historia de la Revolución Mexicana.* Mexico: LibroMex Editores, 1959.

Marcuse, Herbert. *Eros and Civilization; A Philosophical Inquiry into Freud.* Boston: Beacon Press, 1966.

Melgarejo, Antonio D. *Crímenes del Zapatismo.* n.p., 1913.

Memmi, Albert. *The Colonizer and the Colonized.* Translated by Howard Greenfield. New York: Orion Press, 1965.

Memoria del Ayuntamiento de la Ciudad de México, 1923–1927. Archivos Históricos del Ayuntamiento, Departamento del Distrito Federal, Mexico City.

Memoria del Departamento del Distrito Federal, 1932–1941. Archivos Históricos del Ayuntamiento, Departamento del Distrito Federal, Mexico City.

Mena Brito, Bernardino. *Carranza: Sus Amigos, Sus Enemigos.* Mexico: Ediciones Botas, 1935.

———. *El P.R.U.N., Almazán y el Desastre Final.* Mexico: Ediciones Botas, 1941.

México: Cincuenta Años de Revolución. 4 vols. Mexico: Fondo de Cultura Económica, 1961.

Meyer, Eugenia, ed. *Cuadernos de la Cineteca Nacional.* Mexico: n.p., 1975–1976.

Meyer, Jean A. "Los Obreros en la Revolución Mexicana: Los 'Batallones Rojos.' " *Historia Mexicana* 21 (July–September 1971):1–37.

———. *The Cristero Rebellion: The Mexican People Between Church and State, 1926–1929.* Translated by Richard Southern. Cambridge: Cambridge University Press, 1976.

Meyer, Lorenzo. *México y los Estados Unidos en el Conflicto Petrolero (1917–1942).* Mexico: El Colegio de México, 1968.

———. "El Primer Tramo del Camino." In *Historia General de México,* vol. 4, pp. 111–200. Mexico: El Colegio de México, 1976.

Meyer, Michael C. *Huerta: A Political Portrait*. Lincoln: University of Nebraska Press, 1972.

Michaels, Albert L. "El Nacionalismo Conservador Mexicano: Desde la Revolución Hasta 1940." *Historia Mexicana* 16 (October–December 1966):213–38.

———. "Las Elecciones de 1940." *Historia Mexicana* 21 (July–September 1971):80–134.

———. "The Crisis of Cardenismo." *Journal of Latin American Studies* 2 (May 1970):51–79.

Millon, Robert Paul. *Mexican Marxist: Vicente Lombardo Toledano*. Chapel Hill: University of North Carolina Press, 1966.

Mitchell, Juliet. *Psychoanalysis and Feminism: Freud, Reich, Laing and Women*. New York: Random House, 1975.

Monsiváis, Carlos. "Soñadora, Coqueta y Ardiente: Notas Sobre Sexismo en la Literatura Mexicana." *Siempre!*, 14 March 1963.

———. "La Cultura Mexicana en el Siglo XX." In *Contemporary Mexico: Papers of the IV International Congress of Mexican History*, 624–70. Edited by James W. Wilkie, Michael C. Meyer, and Edna Monzón de Wilkie. Latin American Studies Series, vol. 29. Berkeley: University of California Press, 1973.

———. "Machismo Como Impostación." *Excelsior*, 4 August 1974.

———. "Notas Sobre la Cultura Mexicana en el Siglo XX." In *Historia General de México*, vol. 4, pp. 303–476. Mexico: El Colegio de México, 1976.

Mora, Carlos J. *Mexican Cinema: Reflections of a Society, 1896–1980*. Berkeley: University of California Press, 1982.

Morton, Ward M. *Woman Suffrage in Mexico*. Gainesville: University of Florida Press, 1962.

Mullins, Willard A. "On the Concept of Ideology in Political Science." *American Political Science Review* 66 (June 1972):498–510.

Muñoz, Ignacio. *Verdad y Mito de la Revolución Mexicana (Relatada por un Protagonista)*. 2 vols. Mexico: Ediciones Populares, 1960.

Muñoz, Rafael F. *Vámonos con Pancho Villa*. Madrid: Espasa-Calpe, 1931.

———. Interviewed by Alicia O. de Bonfil y Eugenia Meyer. Mexico City, 15 July 1970. PHO/1/25. Programa de Historia Oral. Instituto Nacional de Antropología e Historia.

Murray, Robert Hammond, ed. *Mexico Before the World: Public Documents and Addresses of Plutarco Elías Calles*. Translated by the author. New York: Academy Press, 1927.

Needler, Martin C. "Politics and National Character." *American Anthropologist* 73 (June 1971):757–61.

————. *An Introduction to Latin American Politics: The Structure of Conflict.* Englewood Cliffs, N.J.: Prentice-Hall, 1977.

Nelson, Cynthia. "The Waiting Village: Social Change in a Mexican Peasant Community." Ph.D. dissertation, University of California at Berkeley, 1963.

Niemeyer, E. V., Jr. *The Revolution at Queretaro: The Mexican Constitutional Convention of 1916–1917.* Latin American Monographs, no. 33. Austin: University of Texas Press and the Institute of Latin American Studies, 1974.

Orozco R., Efrén. "Tierra y Libertad." Escenificación Musicada de la Revolución Suriano. Departamento del Distrito Federal Acción Cívica. 29 April 1933. Basave Collection, Biblioteca de México, Mexico City.

Palacios, Guillermo. "Calles y la Idea Oficial de la Revolución Mexicana." *Historia Mexicana* 22 (January–March 1973):320–43.

Páredes, Américo. "Estados Unidos, México y el Machismo." *Journal of Inter-American Studies* 9 (January 1967):65–84.

Partido Nacional Revolucionario. "Domingos Culturales." Circular no. 5. 8 July 1930. Revolution Collection, Biblioteca Nacional, Mexico City.

Paz, Octavio [Jr.]. *El Laberinto de la Soledad.* Mexico: Fondo de Cultura Económica, 1959. Translated by Lysander Kemp as *The Labyrinth of Solitude.* New York: Grove Press, 1961.

Peraza Landero, Rocio. "Imágenes y Anti-imágenes de la Mujer Mexicana." *La Cultura en Mexico,* supplement to *Siempre!,* 18 October 1972.

Peristany, Jean G., ed. *Honor and Shame: The Values of Mediterranean Society.* Chicago: University of Chicago Press, 1966.

Pescatello, Ann, ed. *Female and Male in Latin America: Essays.* Pittsburgh: University of Pittsburgh Press, 1973.

Phelan, John Leddy. "Mexico y Lo Mexicano." *Hispanic American Historical Review* 36 (August 1956):309–18.

Pinchon, Edgcumb. *Viva Villa! A Recovery of the Real Pancho Villa: Peon, Bandit, Soldier, Patriot.* New York: Harcourt, Brace, 1933.

Poniatowska, Elena. *Hasta no Verte Jesús Mio.* Mexico: Ediciones Era, 1969.

Poole, David, ed. *Land and Liberty: Anarchist Influences in the Mexican Revolution: Ricardo Flores Magón.* Montreal: Black Rose Books, 1977.

Portes Gil, Emilio. *Quince Años de Política Mexicana.* 2nd ed. Mexico: Ediciones Botas, 1941.

Preston, William, Jr. *Aliens and Dissenters: Federal Suppression of Radicals, 1903–1933.* Foreword by Oscar Handlin. New York: Harper & Row, 1966.

Prieto Laurens, Jorge. *Cincuenta Años de Política Mexicana: Memorias Políticas.* Mexico: Editora Mexicana de Periódicos, Libros y Revistas, 1968.

Puente, Ramón. *La Dictadura, la Revolución y Sus Hombres*. Mexico: Bocetos, 1938.

Quevedo y Zubieta, Salvador. *Mexico Marimacho: Novela Histórica Revolucionaria (Psicología Social)*. 2nd ed. Mexico: Ediciones Botas, 1933.

Quirk, Robert E. *The Mexican Revolution, 1914–1915: The Convention of Aguascalientes*. Bloomington: Indiana University Press, 1960.

———. *An Affair of Honor: Woodrow Wilson and the Occupation of Veracruz*. Lexington: University of Kentucky Press, 1962.

———. *The Mexican Revolution and the Catholic Church, 1910–1929*. Bloomington: Indiana University Press, 1973.

Ramírez Plancarte, Francisco. *La Ciudad de México Durante le Revolución Constitucionalista*. 2nd. ed. Mexico: Ediciones Botas, 1941.

Ramos, Samuel. *El Perfil del Hombre y la Cultura en México*. Mexico: Imprenta Mundial, 1934. Translated by Peter G. Earle as *Profile of Man and Culture in Mexico*. Austin: University of Texas Press, 1962.

———. "En Torno a las Ideas Sobre el Mexicano." *Cuadernos Americanos* 57 (May–June 1951):103–14.

Reed, John. *Insurgent Mexico*. New York: n.p., 1914; reprint ed., New York: International Publishers, 1969.

Reyes Nevares, Salvador. "El Machismo en México." *Mundo Nuevo* (Buenos Aires), April 1970.

Reyna, José Luis, and Weinert, Richard S., eds. *Authoritarianism in Mexico*. Philadelphia: Institute for the Study of Human Issues, 1977.

Richmond, Douglas W. *Venustiano Carranza's Nationalist Struggle, 1893–1920*. Lincoln: University of Nebraska Press, 1983.

Robe, Stanley L. *Azuela and the Mexican Underdogs*. Berkeley: University of California Press, 1979.

Rohrlich Leavitt, Ruby, ed. *Women Cross-Culturally: Change and Challenge*. The Hague: Mouton, 1975.

Ross, Stanley R. *Francisco I. Madero: Apostle of Mexican Democracy*. New York: Columbia University Press, 1955.

———. "Dwight Morrow and the Mexican Revolution." *Hispanic American Historical Review* 38 (November 1958):506–28.

———. *Fuentes de la Historia Contemporánea de México: Periódicos y Revistas*. 2 vols. Mexico: El Colegio de México, 1965.

———. "El Historiador y el Periodismo Mexicano." *Historia Mexicana* 14 (January–March 1965):347–82.

———., ed. *Is the Mexican Revolution Dead?* New York: Knopf, 1966.

Roura Parella, Juan. "Formación de la Conciencia Nacional." *Revista Mexicana de Sociología* 16 (January–April 1954):39–60.

Rutherford, John D. *Mexican Society During the Revolution: A Literary Approach*. Oxford: Clarendon Press, 1971.

Sánchez Azcona, Juan. *Apuntes Para la Historia de la Revolución Mexicana.* Mexico: Biblioteca del Instituto Nacional de Estudios Históricos de la Revolución Mexicana, 1961.

Sandos, James. "German Involvement in Northern Mexico, 1915–1916— A New Look at the Columbus Raid." *Hispanic American Historical Review* 50 (February 1970):70–88.

Santa María, Luis. *Un Aspecto Ignorado de Francisco Villa: Relato Verídico de Algo Muy Emocionante de la Vida del Celebre Guerrillero, de Lo Que Nadie Se Ha Ocupado Todavia.* Mexico: Laboratorios Picot, 1930(?). Basave Collection, Biblioteca de Mexico, Mexico City.

Sartori, Giovanni. "Politics, Ideology and Belief Systems." *American Political Science Review* 63 (June 1969):398–411.

Schmidt, Henry C. "Antecedents to Samuel Ramos: Mexicanist Thought in the 1920s." *Journal of Interamerican Studies and World Affairs* 18 (May 1976):179–202.

———. *The Roots of Lo Mexicano: Self and Society in Mexican Thought, 1900– 1934.* College Station: Texas A&M University Press, 1978.

Scott, Robert E. *Mexican Government in Transition.* Urbana: University of Illinois Press, 1959.

Secretaría de Acción Agraria del Partido Nacional Revolucionario. *Biografía del Caudillo Suriano General Emiliano Zapata y Parte Oficial de Su Muerte.* Mexico: n.p., 1934. Hemeroteca Nacional, Mexico City.

Secretaría de Educación Pública. *La Casa del Estudiante Indígena: 16 Meses de Labor en un Experimento Psicológico Colectivo con Indios, Febrero de 1926–Junio de 1927.* Mexico: Talleres Gráficos de la Nación, 1927.

———. *Algunos Datos y Opiniones Sobre la Educación Sexual en México.* Mexico: Talleres Gráficos de la Nación, 1934.

Sierra, Carlos, Jr. "Homenaje a la Constitución Política de 1917." *Boletín Biobibliográfico de la Secretaría de Hacienda y Crédito Público* 360 (1 February 1967):4–10.

———. "Emiliano Zapata: Señor de la Tierra y Capitán de los Labriegos." *Boletín Biobibliográfico de la Secretaría de Hacienda y Crédito Público* 361, Supplement (15 February 1967):2–24.

Silva Herzog, Jesús. *Una Vida en la Vida de México.* Mexico: Siglo Veintiuno Editores, 1972.

Simmons, Merle. *The Mexican CORRIDO as a Source for Interpretative Study of Modern Mexico, 1870–1950.* Bloomington: Indiana University Press, 1957.

Simpson, Eyler N. *The Ejido, Mexico's Way Out.* Foreword by Ramón Beteta. Chapel Hill: University of North Carolina Press, 1937.

Sinkin, Richard N. *The Mexican Reform, 1855–1876: A Study in Nation-Building.* Latin American Monographs, no. 49. Austin: University of Texas Press, 1979.

Smith, Robert Freeman. "The Morrow Mission and the International Committee of Bankers on Mexico: The Interaction of Finance Diplomacy and the New Mexican Elite." *Journal of Latin American Studies* 1 (November 1969):149–66.

Sotelo Inclán, Jesús. *Raíz y Razón de Zapata*. Mexico: Editorial Etnos, 1943.

Stabb, Martin T. "Indigenism and Racism in Mexican Thought: 1857–1911." *Journal of Inter-American Studies* 1 (1957):405–23.

Stevens, Evelyn P. *Protest and Response in Mexico*. Cambridge: MIT Press, Massachusetts Institute of Technology, 1974.

Sweetman, Jack. *The Landing at Veracruz, 1914: The First Complete Chronicle of a Strange Encounter in April, 1914, When the United States Navy Captured and Occupied the City of Veracruz, Mexico*. Annapolis, Md.: Naval Institute Press, 1968.

Taracena, Alfonso. *La Tragedia Zapatista*. Mexico: Editorial "Bolivar," 1931.

————. *La Verdadera Revolución Mexicana*. 18 vols. Mexico: Editorial Jus, 1960–1965.

————. *Venustiano Carranza*. Mexico: Editorial Jus, 1963.

————. *Historia Extraoficial de la Revolución Mexicana: Desde la Postrimerías del Porfirismo Hasta Sucesos de Nuestros Días*. Mexico: Editorial Jus, 1972.

————. *Zapata: Fantasía y Realidad: Un Libro Documentado Sobre el Caudillo del Sur*. 2nd ed., revised. Mexico: B. Costa-Amic Editor, 1974.

Thompson, Wallace. *The Mexican Mind: A Study of National Psychology*. Boston: Little, Brown, 1922.

Tobler, Hans-Werner. "Las Paradojas del Ejército Revolucionario: Su Papel Social en la Reforma Agraria Mexicana, 1920–1935." *Historia Mexicana* 21 (July–September 1971):38–79.

Torres, Elías. *Vida y Hazañas de Pancho Villa*. Mexico: n.p., 1975.

Townsend, William Cameron. *Lázaro Cárdenas, Mexican Democrat*. Ann Arbor, Mich.: George Wahr, 1952.

Turner, Frederick C. "Anti-Americanism in Mexico, 1910–1913." *Hispanic American Historical Review* 47 (February 1967):502–18.

————. "Los Efectos de la Participación Feminina en la Revolución de 1910." *Historia Mexicana* 16 (April–June 1967):603–20.

————. *The Dynamic of Mexican Nationalism*. Chapel Hill: University of North Carolina Press, 1968.

Ulloa, Berta. "La Lucha Armada." In *Historia General de México*, vol. 4, pp. 1–110. Mexico: El Colegio de México, 1976.

Urrutia, Elena, ed. *Imágen y Realidad de la Mujer*. Mexico: SepSetentas, 1975.

Valadés, José C. *El Presidente de México en 1970*. Mexico: Editores Mexicanos Unidos, 1969.

Vargas MacDonald, Antonio. "Ser Mexicano Es Ser Macho, Ser Macho

Es Tener Muchos Hijos; Muertos de Hambres? Allá Dios y Ellos
    Párenle!" *Siempre!*, 17 May 1972, 22–23.
Vasconcelos, José, ed. *La Caída de Carranza—De la Dictadura a la Libertad.*
    Mexico: n.p., 1920.
Vaughan, Mary Kay. *The State, Education and Social Class in Mexico, 1880–*
    1928. De Kalb: Northern Illinois University Press, 1982.
Vázquez de Knauth, Josefina. *Nacionalismo y Educación en México.* Mexico:
    El Colegio de México, 1970.
Vernon, Raymond. *The Dilemma of Mexico's Development.* Cambridge: Har-
    vard University Press, 1963.
Wasserman, Mark. "The Social Origins of the 1910 Revolution in Chihua-
    hua." *Latin American Research Review* 15, no. 1 (1980):15–40.
Weyl, Nathaniel, and Weyl, Sylvia. *The Reconquest of Mexico: The Years of*
    Lázaro Cárdenas. London: Oxford University Press, 1939.
Wilkie, James W. *The Mexican Revolution: Federal Expenditure and Social Change*
    Since 1910. 2nd. ed., revised. Berkeley: University of California Press,
    1970.
Wilkie, James W., Meyer, Michael C., and Monzón de Wilkie, Edna, eds.
    Contemporary Mexico: Papers of the IV International Congress of Mexican
    History. Latin American Studies Series, vol. 29. Berkeley: Univer-
    sity of California Press, 1973.
Wolf, Eric. *Sons of the Shaking Earth.* Chicago: University of Chicago Press,
    1959.
Wolf, Eric, and Hansen, Edward C. "Caudillo Politics." *Comparative Stud-*
    ies in Society and History 9 (January 1967):168–79.
Woll, Allen L. "Hollywood's Good Neighbor Policy: The Latin Image in
    American Film, 1939–1946." *Journal of Popular Film* 3 (Fall 1974):278–
    93.
————. "Latin Images in American Films, 1929–1939." *Journal of Mexican-*
    American History 4 (1974):28–40.
Womack, John, Jr. *Zapata and the Mexican Revolution.* New York: Knopf,
    1969; Random House, 1970.
Zea, Leopoldo. *México y Lo Mexicano.* 23 vols. Mexico: Porrua y Obregón,
    1952–1955.

Index

About the Author

ILENE V. O'MALLEY has been a student of the Mexican Revolution and of Mexican society for more than a decade. She has taught history at the University of California, Santa Cruz and has written several articles and analytical essays on Mexican and Latin American political history. Her work has appeared in *The Nicaragua Reader* and *The Alternative Review of Literature and Politics*.